Children's Homes and School Exclusion

Children's Homes and School Exclusion

Exclusion

Redefining the Problem

Isabelle Brodie

Jessica Kingsley Publishers
London and Philadelphia

First published in the United Kingdom in 2001 by
Jessica Kingsley Publishers Ltd,
116 Pentonville Road, London
N1 9JB, England
and
325 Chestnut Street,
Philadelphia PA 19106, USA.

www.jkp.com

Library of Congress Cataloging in Publication Data

British Library Cataloguing in Publication Data

ISBN 1 85302 943 2

Printed and Bound in Great Britain by
Athenaeum Press, Gateshead, Tyne and Wear

Contents

Acknowledgements

Exclusion from school is always a sensitive matter for all those concerned. During the time that the research for this study was undertaken, exclusion also became prominent in the public realm, with several cases of children excluded from school featured – often sensationally – in the national media. These circumstances increased the general sensitivity of the issue and place me in even greater debt to the children and adults who helped in the course of this study.

My greatest thanks must go to the 17 children and young people who gave me access to the stories of their exclusion from school. These stories were often linked to other stressful experiences in their lives, and I hope I have treated them with the sensitivity and compassion they deserve. As with all those who participated in the study, they remain anonymous for reasons of confidentiality.

I am very grateful to the many residential carers, social workers, teachers and other professionals, who agreed to be interviewed. Without their help, it would have been impossible to carry out the research. Some, despite many other commitments, gave additional help by referring cases and updating me on the later careers of young people. This was very much appreciated.

I am also grateful for the help of those who supervised the research on which this book is based: Professor David Berridge and John Paley, both at the University of Luton; and Professor Ian Sinclair, University of York. David Berridge has been especially generous with his time and good advice. Thanks are also due to other colleagues in the Department of Applied Social Studies for their encouragement and support. In addition I would like to thank Dr David Barrett, Head of Department, and David Berridge, for providing me with sufficient time to carry out the work for this book, and the University of Luton for financial support.

This study has often involved complex administration, and I have appreciated the help, at different times, of Lynne Pritchard, Pauline Rajaram, Charmaine Cummings and Lynda Milne. Librarians at the University of Luton and the National Children's Bureau have also provided considerable support.

Finally, my family, especially my parents, Jim and Elizabeth Brodie, and my sister Judith, and my friends have helped me keep research in perspective and provided constant encouragement. Jason Chuah, though extremely tired of the word 'exclusion', deserves special thanks for his remarkable patience and forbearance through all the peaks and troughs of this project.

Isabelle Brodie

List of Abbreviations

ADD	Attention Deficit Disorder
ADHD	Attention Deficit Hyperactivity Disorder
CHE	Community Home with Education
DfE	Department for Education
DfEE	Department for Education and Employment
EBD	Emotional and Behavioural Difficulties
EPS	Educational Psychology Service
EWO	Education Welfare Officer
LEA	Local Education Authority
LMS	Local Management of Schools
NACRO	National Association for the Care and Resettlement of Offenders
NAHT	National Association of Head Teachers
NERS	National Exclusions Reporting Scheme
NUT	National Union of Teachers
NASUWT	National Association of Schoolmasters and Union of Women Teachers
NVQ	National Vocational Qualification
OFSTED	Office for Standards in Education
PRU	Pupil Referral Unit
RSW	Residential Social Worker
SEN	Special Educational Needs
SENCO	Special Educational Needs Co-ordinator

Introduction

Excluding children

This book examines the exclusion from school of children looked after by local authorities ('in care'), and specifically those who live in residential accommodation. It is based on research into the experiences of a small group of young people living in children's homes in three local authorities during the mid-1990s.

At the time of writing, some 51,000 children in England are looked after by local authorities. The majority, 32,000, are looked after in foster care. A further 6500 live in residential accommodation, and the remainder are looked after under different arrangements which might include continued residence at home (DoH 1999). Children living in children's homes therefore represent only a minority of all children, and a small proportion of children excluded from school.

Nevertheless, the education of children living in children's homes is an issue which has attracted growing amounts of attention. In 1995, a joint study of the education of children looked after in both residential and foster care concluded:

> The care and education services in general are failing to promote the educational achievement of children who are looked after. The standards which children achieve are too low and often the modest progress they make in primary schools is lost as they proceed through the system. Despite the clear identification of this problem in several research studies and by committees of enquiry, little has been done in practice to boost achievement. (Social Services Inspectorate/OFSTED 1995 p.41)

Many subsequent reports and enquiries have reached similar conclusions, and growing pressure has been brought to bear on government and local authorities to act to improve the education of this group of young people. This book has also been written at a time when interest in school exclusion has increased dramatically. Since the research on which the book is based was undertaken in 1994–96, policy on school exclusion has also been transformed: exclusion and the education of children looked after have received high levels of attention from government and a range of new policies and initiatives with wide-ranging implications introduced (for example, DoH 1998a; Social Exclusion Unit 1998). Improvement in educational outcomes constitutes a key objective for children's services within the Quality Protects initiative, and local authorities are required to produce ongoing evidence of their efforts in this area. This is, therefore, an issue of major concern to professionals working with young people looked after who are, for whatever reason, out of school or experiencing difficulties with their education.

At this crossroads in policy and practice, however, the provision of new empirical evidence is essential. As Goddard (2000) rightly points out, there is a danger that, in relation to the education of children looked after, policy is moving ahead of the state of current knowledge. If practice is indeed to be 'evidence-based' then it is necessary that evidence from a range of perspectives is available. No study so far has examined in detail the way in which exclusion is experienced by children looked after, and how this is influenced by the interplay between the care and educational systems. This research has tried to begin to fill that gap. Although research evidence has accumulated suggesting that children looked after are at greater risk of exclusion from school, little is known about how this problem is played out in practice. This book takes the view that, unless we understand the nature of the problem, then it will be difficult to find appropriate solutions. A recurring theme is the fact that 'exclusion' has too often been considered as a homogenous problem, measured in relation to its statutory definition. Consequently, much of the complexity of the issue has been missed.

This book tries to capture some of the intricacies of exclusion, by contextualising the issue within the experience of young people looked after in residential accommodation, though the messages from this study may well have resonance beyond this specific group.

The research which forms the basis of this book is qualitative in approach and sought to understand the problem of the exclusion from school of children looked after in residential accommodation by considering the issue from the perspectives of the people who are directly involved. It aims first of all to investigate the sequence of events preceding and during school exclusion through the accounts of young people and relevant professionals and through written records. Second, it explores and contrasts participants' explanations for why exclusion occurred. Third, it has tried to investigate the way in which roles and responsibilities have been allocated to different agencies and professionals in relation to the exclusion. Finally, it has examined the influence of the law and policy guidance on the exclusion process.

In this first chapter, the exclusion from school of children living in children's homes will be placed in its broader context. First, it will be examined in relation to the issue of school exclusion more generally and the way in which this has become a matter of concern; second, the relationship between school exclusion and wider issues of disadvantage; and, finally, growing evidence regarding the educational disadvantage of children looked after.

The problem of school exclusion

Children have, of course, always been expelled from school and it seems likely that at the level of the individual and his or her family the implications of this have usually been serious. For example, in the 19th-century novel *The Turn of the Screw,* Henry James describes the shock with which the news of the expulsion of the young boy of the household is met. It is important, though, not to suggest that exclusion is invariably presented in a negative light. Media descriptions of famous pop stars and actors who were expelled from school can imply that this was an early indication of daring creativity (see, for example, *The Guardian* 23 April 1996). Breaking free from the control of the school is, however, usually only lauded when it has been followed by success in later life.

In the late 1980s and 1990s, however, exclusion from school has acquired a new kind of significance. While in the past it appears to have been rare and essentially a problem for the individual, exclusion has now been firmly placed in the public and political realm. Alongside other forms of educational disaffection such as truancy, exclusion is now perceived as a 'major public policy challenge' (House of Commons Education and Employment Committee 1998) which affects a growing number of pupils.

This changed perception of the problem must be considered in the context of the legal framework which surrounds exclusion. At the time of writing two types of exclusion exist in law – fixed-term, which can take place for up to 45 school days across the school year, and permanent. It is important to note, however, that statutory definitions of exclusion have changed several times since the term 'exclusion' was introduced in the Education (No. 2) Act 1986, replacing the more familiar 'suspension' or 'expulsion'.

Prior to this the power to exclude a pupil from school (then referred to as suspension) was contained in the 1944 Education Act, which stated:

> ...the power of suspending pupils from attendance for any cause which [the headteacher] considers adequate, but on suspending any pupil [the headteacher] shall forthwith report the case to the governors who shall consult the Local Education Authority. (HMSO 1944)

As Hayden (1995) points out, this power was extremely vague and there was therefore considerable scope for abuse. Policy regarding expulsion and suspension was determined by local education authorities (LEAs) and by individual schools, leaving scope for variation in practice. We may glean something of this from the work of Grunsell (1980) and Galloway *et al.* (1994) which suggests, for example, that the nature of the consultation between school and local education authority varied considerably depending on the individual LEA.

Lovey *et al.* (1993) suggest that the legislative changes introduced in the 1980s were aimed at introducing an element of 'common justice' into exclusion procedures. However, they should also be linked to an increase in the powers of governing bodies, and a clearer delineation of the powers of the different tiers of the education hierarchy. The Education (No. 2) Act 1986 replaced the terminology of expulsion and suspension with the generic language of 'exclusion', and made provision for three types of exclusion – indefinite, permanent and fixed-term. Exclusion was also placed within the broader discipline policies of the school. The 1986 Act provided that every school have an instrument known as the articles of government 'in accordance with which the school is to be conducted'. These are to be made by order of the LEA and must contain the provisions required by the Act. Under Section 22 (a) the headteacher is required to determine disciplinary measures to be taken with a view to promoting, among pupils, self-discipline and proper regard for authority, encouraging good behaviour, securing acceptable standards of behaviour and otherwise regulating pupils' conduct. In deciding policy, the emphasis appears to be on the positive development of good behaviour within the classroom.

Following the introduction of the 1986 Act, however, several areas of concern in relation to exclusion were identified. The National Exclusions Reporting System (NERS) had recorded a significant increase in the number of exclusions, and the Department for Education (DFE) Discussion Paper on exclusions, issued in 1993, stated that

> Too many children are excluded from school, either permanently or temporarily. There is evidence that some exclusions go on too long, and that the alternative educational provision made for many excluded pupils is subject to unacceptable variations in both quality and quantity. (p.5)

More specifically, indefinite exclusion had been criticised as increasing the possibility that pupils could fall through the net and remain outside education for unspecified periods of time. The Office for Standards in Education (OFSTED) response to the DfE's discussion paper included the recommendation that 'the concept of indefinite exclusion should cease' (OFSTED 1993). While the provisions of the new Act were being debated in the House of Lords, the Minister commented that:

> Widespread concern was registered by those responding to our discussion paper about the scope for abuse which the category [of indefinite exclusion] offers and the uncertain position in which it leaves both the child and the parents. In some cases, children of compulsory school age were ending up in what might best be described as an educational limbo. We cannot allow this to happen. (Hansard, HL, 547, col 173)

The Education Act 1993 sought to prevent these problems from escalating. Consequently Section 261 (1) (a) of the 1993 Act prohibited the use of exclusion on an indefinite basis, and Section (1) (b) limited fixed-term exclusions to 15 school days in any one term. A further important adjustment was provision for funding to follow the excluded pupil to their subsequent place of education (Section 262). This provision should theoretically act as a disincentive to informal exclusions, which prior to the 1993 Act held a certain attraction in that a troublesome pupil could be discouraged from attending school, while funding for the pupil was retained. In addition, detailed guidance was issued which outlined the way in which the exclusion process should operate, and emphasised that the sanction should not be used lightly (DfE 1994a). The guidance unequivocally states that exclusion should be used only in response to 'serious breaches of a school's policy' (DfE1994a). It is therefore not an appropriate response to what are described as 'minor offences', emotional and behavioural difficulties, or where a pupil is pregnant (DfE 1994a). It is also emphasised that the sanction should be applied consistently across the school population.

However, wrangling over the mechanics of the exclusion process did not end with the 1993 Act, or with the guidance that accompanied it (DfE 1994a). Most strident were calls for the reintroduction of indefinite exclusion, especially by teachers' unions (Hart 1996; NAHT press release 1994). It was argued that the rise in exclusions could be directly attributed to the lack of an indefinite option, in that headteachers were permanently excluding pupils whom they would previously have excluded on an indefinite basis. This argument is, however, somewhat questionable. First of all, the absence of survey data differentiating between the rates of different types of exclusion prior to 1993 makes it very difficult to postulate a direct link between the abolition of the category of indefinite exclusion and the rise in exclusions since that date. Second, the nature of the indefinite exclusion made monitoring of children excluded on this basis very difficult indeed. Little is known regarding the way in which the process of informal exclusion operated, and, indeed, how many indefinite exclusions were later made permanent. Theoretically, however, the implication of the unions' position has been to assert the importance of exclusions procedures against the significance of internal school processes as an explanation for the increase in exclusions taking place. A moderate victory was won subsequently in the 1996 Education Act, which extended fixed-term exclusion to 45 days across the school year.

Criticism was also directed at the degree of protection afforded children and their parents, including the legal provisions regarding the right of appeal. Under the 1993 legislation, the headteacher must immediately inform the pupil's parents, or the pupil if aged 18 or over, of the exclusion and the specific reason for it. They should also be notified that they have the right to make written and oral representations to the governing body and the LEA. The Law Commission, submitting recommendations for the 1996 Education Bill, noted some specific flaws regarding the rights of pupils excluded from schools for children with learning and emotional and behavioural difficulties ('special schools'). The Commission criticised the fact that there is no duty to inform a pupil who is over 18 of the period of his or her exclusion, or of the reason for his or her exclusion. Similarly, where the exclusion of such a pupil for a fixed period is made permanent, there is no duty to inform him or her of the decision or the reasons for it. In addition, there is no provision for a parent – or the pupil if he or she is over 18 – to be informed that they may make further representations to the governing body of the LEA where a fixed-term exclusion is made permanent (Law Commission 1996). The lack of attention to children's rights has also been criticised in relation to later legislation such as the Education Act 1997 (Castle and Parsons 1997).

Teaching unions, on the other hand, have complained that current appeal procedures afford protection to parents and pupils at the expense of the interests of teaching staff. These objections focus specifically on the power of LEAs to overrule the decision of a governing body to exclude a pupil. This problem emerged following the 1986 Act. The Elton Report noted that the strongest argument for removing the power of the LEA to direct reinstatement lay in the damage which could be done to the authority and morale of the headteacher and other members of staff, but argued that this could be an important external check on schools' practice (Department of Education and Science 1988). Nevertheless, the reinstatement of pupils continues to represent on of the most controversial aspects of exclusion procedures as they currently stand.

The scale of the problem

Underpinning the growing concerns about exclusion, therefore, was the apparent increase in the numbers of permanent exclusions taking place. The precise nature of this increase is hard to measure, in that it is only during the past decade that national statistics have been available – further contributing to a sense of exclusion as a new and disturbing phenomenon. However, it is important to recognise that many of the issues which have emerged as significant aspects of exclusion, for example differences in exclusion rates between schools, were identified in earlier research (McManus 1987; McLean 1987; Galloway et al. 1982; Grunsell 1980).

Available statistics on the number of exclusions taking place in England from 1990–91 to 1999–2000, presented in Figure 1.1, show a steep rise in the number of permanent exclusions up to 1997, followed by a reduction in the last two years.

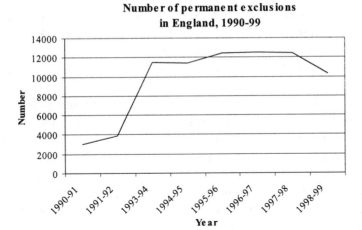

**Number of permanent exclusions
in England, 1990-99**

Figure 1.1

There are, however, certain difficulties in the interpretation of these statistics, in part due to the changes that have taken place in the methods used to collect statistics on exclusion. This process began in 1990 when NERS was set up with the purpose of monitoring the number of permanent exclusions taking place. These findings were reported in 1993, and showed an increase in the number of exclusions from 2910 in 1990–91 to 3833 in 1991–92. In 1993–94, research indicated that the number of permanent exclusions had risen to over 11,000, a dramatic threefold increase (DfE 1995). A follow-up study by the same research team and carried out for the year 1994–95 showed a further increase to 12,500 (Parsons 1996). This was significantly higher than that produced by the government's schools' census, which placed the total number of exclusions at 11,084. This difference continued into the statistics for 1995–96, when government figures stated that the number of exclusions had increased to 12, 476 (DfEE 1997), while research findings suggested that there had been 13,581 during that year (Parsons 1996). In 1997, however, DfEE data showed that the number of permanent exclusions had climbed again to 12,700 (DfEE 1998). Following the general election of 1997, the reduction of permanent school exclusion became a key factor in the policies of the new Labour administration, and a number of high-profile initiatives have been introduced to address the issue. At the time of writing these appear to be bearing fruit, and numbers of exclusions have fallen – to 12,300 in 1997–98 and still further to 10,400 in 1998–99 (DfEE 2000).

Understanding the 'rise and fall' of the exclusion problem is, however, hampered by a number of factors. First of all, the data described above relates to periods of time when different statutory definitions of exclusion were in place.

The Education (No. 2) Act 1986 made provision for three types of exclusion: permanent, indefinite and fixed-term. The NERS collected data only on permanent exclusions. However, it does not seem unlikely that indefinite exclusion could have been used in a manner which effectively constituted permanent exclusion. This may have skewed the numbers of permanent exclusions downwards.

Second, it is widely accepted that local authority recording of statistics has frequently been flawed. Hayden, Sheppard and Ward (1996) point out that data does not always distinguish between the number of exclusion incidents and the number of children to which these refer. Therefore, five fixed-term exclusions may be recorded without reference to the fact that these apply to only one child. Information regarding the number and pattern of exclusions is more complete in regard to local authority maintained schools than for independent, grant-maintained and voluntary aided schools. This variation results from the difference in regulations regarding exclusions procedures (see DfE 1994; Education Reform Act 1988.)

In addition to this, measurement of school exclusion on the basis of officially reported exclusions does not take account of those exclusions which have been described as 'unofficial' or 'informal' are hidden. This problem may also extend to officially reported exclusions; Castle and Parsons (1997) claim that in the survey of permanent exclusions carried out by OFSTED, for example, local education authorities under-reported the number of exclusions taking place.

An important question is the extent to which the introduction of a legal definition of exclusion and attempts by government to control exclusion procedures have affected the recorded rates. It is instructive to consider research carried out long before the changes to the educational system which are so frequently held responsible for the rise in exclusions. Grunsell (1980), who studied exclusions in one local authority during the late 1970s, found that a tightening up of the system of reporting exclusions had a significant effect on overall figures. In November 1976 headteachers in this authority had been instructed that the procedure for notifying suspensions was to be strictly observed. In 1977 the number of permanent suspensions rose to 63 (from 42 in 1975 and 40 in 1976) and temporary suspensions more than doubled. He concluded that there was no objective consistency in what the figures measure, and that 'at least some of the apparent increase can be explained only by more accurate reporting by schools'. Galloway et al. (1982) support this, remarking that 'The results can be virtually impossible to interpret, even if the figures themselves appear to demonstrate an obvious trend. Subtle changes in a LEA's policy on reporting exclusions may lead to major changes in head-teachers willingness to use this sanction' (p.18).

Examination of exclusions in terms of year-on-year numbers does not, however, take account of the way in which exclusions are distributed across the school population and geographically. Variations have consistently been found in exclusion rates between local authorities. This is consistent with earlier research by Galloway *et al.* (1982). The DfEE survey *(op. cit.)* found that in some LEAs the rates of permanent exclusion were ten times higher than in others, differences which could not be explained by the socio-economic characteristics of these areas. However, there were variations according to the type of LEA; the highest rates of exclusion in London LEAs were almost double those found in other areas of the country. OFSTED (1996a), examining exclusions in secondary schools, found a slight association between the level of social deprivation and the rate of exclusion in schools, but this could not in itself account for the level of difference between schools.

Exclusions are also more likely to be experienced by some groups of pupils, depending on age, gender and ethnicity. Permanent exclusions are concentrated among secondary school pupils, with the increase in exclusions by age reaching a peak in Year 10. Primary school exclusions also increased during the 1990s. Although these remain a relatively small proportion of the overall number – some 13 per cent – the complexity of the problems facing primary school pupils who are excluded should not be underestimated (Hayden 1997). A small number of young people – some 500 each year – are also excluded from special schools. This is a worrying phenomenon, especially given the lack of alternative education for these young people, but unfortunately one about which little is known.

The statistics also disguise differences between boys and girls in regard to their experience of exclusion. The majority of excluded pupils are boys, who outnumber girls at a rate of at least four to one (DfEE 1999a; Hayden, Sheppard and Ward 1996; OFSTED 1996a; DfE 1995; Galloway *et al.* 1982). In research using smaller numbers of case studies, we also find few examples of excluded girls (see, for example, Parsons *et al.* 1994). It is therefore unclear whether the pattern of exclusion between boys and girls is significantly different. However, the gender difference can be related to the fact that the most frequent reason given for exclusion is disruptive and aggressive behaviour (Hayden *et al.* 1996; OFSTED 1996a Galloway *et al.* 1982). Educational research has demonstrated that not only is this type of behaviour most likely to be perceived as troublesome by teachers, but it is also more likely to be displayed by boys (Wheldall and Merrett 1988; Merrett and Wheldall 1984).

Another important factor is ethnicity, and research has shown that African-Caribbean boys are at particular risk of exclusion. The relationship between exclusion and ethnicity has been recognised for some time; local research studies carried out during the 1980s indicated that a disproportionate number of pupils from minority ethnic groups, and specifically African-Caribbean males, experienced exclusion (Bourne, Bridges and Searle 1994). Similar findings have emerged in more recent research (Gillborn and Gipps 1996; Bourne, Bridges and Searle 1994). Determination of the way in which exclusion affects different ethnic groups is difficult as in the past local authorities frequently failed to make ethnic distinctions when collecting data on exclusions (Hayden, Sheppard and Ward 1996). However, while statistics vary, data collected during OFSTED inspections in 1993–94 show that African-Caribbean pupils were excluded almost six times the rate of white pupils (Gillborn and Gipps 1996).

What can be concluded from this discussion? Clearly exclusion statistics have been unreliable in a number of respects, and it is plausible to argue that the methodological problems with exclusions data mean that, if anything, the numbers of exclusions have been *under*estimated. The evidence also demonstrates that exclusion is a problem which must be considered in relation to factors of age, gender, ethnicity and geographical location. However, these factors do not in themselves explain how and why exclusion takes place. Exclusion is a problem which has been constructed within a particular policy context and the numbers do not, by any means, speak for themselves.

School exclusion and social exclusion

A second reason why school exclusion has attracted growing concern can be linked to the wider issue of what has been termed 'social exclusion'. This is a concept which has increasingly been adopted by government to refer to a constellation of disadvantage, including poverty, poor housing, unemployment and participation in subcultures associated with drugs and crime. The concept of social exclusion is not without its critics, not least because usage of the term has a tendency to be somewhat elastic (see Macdonald 1997) and to encompass a variety of contradictory political and social discourses. Nevertheless, it is a useful starting point for understanding some of the issues related to school exclusion. The association between social exclusion and school exclusion has also been made directly by government (Social Exclusion Unit 1998).

Certainly the experience of childhood and adolescence is structured by wider inequalities in society, including those arising from poverty, gender, ethnicity and disability. Studies show that since the mid-1970s, divisions between a prosperous majority and a depressed minority have deepened, with serious consequences for children and young people (Howarth *et al.* 1999). High unemployment and an increasing number of families with low incomes have in turn led to an increase in material and social deprivation, which has disproportionate effects on children and young people. Gregg, Harkness and Machin (1999), using data from two large-scale surveys, found that one in three children lived in households with below average income, compared to one in ten in 1968. This can be related to economic pressures such as high unemployment and changes in family structure –

specifically the increase in the number of households headed by a lone parent – but government policies during the 1980s did little to offset the effects of such factors (Bradshaw 2000; Kumar 1993).

Exclusion from school represents the most direct way in which schools can exercise their power to prevent children from participating in education. This is a serious matter, as children themselves fully realise. In one study of 3000 children in a Scottish city, over half stated that exclusion was the 'worst' punishment that could be inflicted upon them (Sanders and Hendry 1997). The school is a key agency for the socialisation of the young, and expulsion could be viewed as placing the individual outside the bounds of social control. This is no accident: as Parsons (1999) suggests, excluded pupils serve a significant social function in constituting 'markers of acceptability' within the education system. This represents a peculiarly English response to the problems of disaffection and difficult behaviour – 'exclusion', as it is currently understood within the context of the English educational system, is not evident in other European countries. Education is also an important purveyor of social and economic capital and the life-chances of those who are denied the benefits of full-time schooling are considered to be significantly reduced.

As this chapter has already discussed, the available evidence suggests that exclusion has by no means affected all members of the school population. In addition to age, gender and ethnicity, research demonstrates that most excluded pupils have troubled educational and family backgrounds. OFSTED (1996a) reported that many have experienced more than one exclusion, and that an association exists between exclusion and the lack of basic skills, especially in literacy. A significant minority of excluded children have already been assessed as having special educational needs or have had some contact with an educational psychologist. The NERS survey found that more than 12 per cent of those excluded had Statements of Special Educational Need (DfE 1993). In 1997–98 this proportion stood at 18 per cent (DfEE 1999a). These national data do not tell us how many pupils were in the process of being assessed for special educational needs at the time of exclusion. However, qualitative research into the issue indicates that this may be an important factor. In 11 case studies of pupils excluded from primary school, it was found that some assessments were out of date, in others discussions had taken place between the head teacher and the educational psychologist but statementing had not been initiated, while in yet others assessment had begun and had not been completed (Parsons *et al.* 1994). Following exclusion, children with Statements are unlikely to receive the provision to which they are entitled under the Education Act 1981 (Parsons *et al.* 1994).

Even more prominent in existing research evidence is the fact that a high proportion of children who are excluded have experienced various forms of social disadvantage, including poverty, homelessness and parental illness. The link between home background and educational attainment is of course well established in educational literature (Bird *et al.* 1980; Rutter *et al.* 1975; Douglas 1964; Tyerman 1958). However, it is difficult to escape the view that children who experience the ultimate sanction of expulsion are also those whose personal circumstances are in greatest turmoil. As OFSTED (1996a) comments, information about the home and family backgrounds of young people excluded from school reveals 'a grim catalogue of misery' (p.10). Thus, for example, Hayden, Sheppard and Ward (1996), in case studies of 65 primary school pupils excluded from school, found extensive evidence of child protection concerns, family disruption and contact with a range of external agencies.

Social disadvantage goes some way to explaining the disproportionate number of school exclusions amongst black pupils. Research evidence shows that, for example, African-Caribbeans are more likely to live in poor public housing and – in relation to black males especially – are more likely to be unemployed than their white peers (Power and Tunstill 1997). However, it would also appear that racism at the level of individual interaction is a factor. In some cases the decision to exclude has been identified as overtly discriminatory, including religious or cultural 'non-conformity', the failure to recognise the cultural elements in incidents which occur within the school and the misdiagnosis or disregard for medical or educational problems within an ethnic group (Bourne, Bridges and Searle 1994). Attention has also been drawn to the importance of pupil/teacher interaction in explaining the high level of exclusions among black pupils. Ethnographic studies have shown that black pupils experience proportionately more punishments of all types (for example, detentions and report cards) and are criticised more often than white pupils (Gillborn 1990). This has been linked to cultural styles among black pupils, and a perception by teachers that black males in particular are threatening and aggressive.

However, there also appear to be some important differences in the pattern of exclusions among black pupils. As it has been pointed out, many more boys than girls are excluded. While this holds true for black pupils, the relative over-representation of black girls (in comparison with white girls) can be at least as great as the figure for their white counterparts (Gillborn and Gipps 1996). In another research sample, the cases of most of the black children studied 'differed markedly' from those of white children. Distinguishing characteristics included their assessment by teachers as under-achieving academically, and a shorter history of disruptive behaviour (OFSTED 1996a). These differences in the pattern of exclusion suggest that much more research is required regarding the inter-relationship between ethnicity and exclusion. However, understanding of the scale of this has been hampered by the omission of many local authorities to collect data on the ethnicity of excluded pupils (Hayden, Sheppard and Ward 1996).

The relationship between school exclusion and subsequent non-participation in economic and social life can also be explained in terms of the immediate consequences of exclusion. Research suggests that children typically spend lengthy periods of time out of school as a result of an exclusion and are likely to receive only limited educational provision in the interim (Commission for Racial Equality 1996; Hayden 1997; Cohen *et al.* 1994; Parsons *et al.* 1994). A recent study (Parsons 2000) found that more than 80 per cent of permanently excluded secondary pupils spend at least one term out of school. Reintegration rates were found to vary enormously, from 23 per cent to 100 per cent at primary school level, and nine to 100 per cent amongst secondary school pupils. In regard to the education which children receive following exclusion, the 1993 Act replaced the power to provide education for excluded pupils with a duty, requiring each LEA to provide:

> ...suitable full-time or part-time education at school or otherwise than at school for those children of compulsory school age who, by reason of illness, exclusion from school or otherwise, may not for any period receive suitable education unless such arrangements are made for them. (Section 262)

The problem remained, however, that this duty could be satisfied by the provision of a few hours home tuition each week. While this was the position at the time this research was undertaken, it has since changed with government commitment to securing appropriate provision of alternative education for young people who are out of school.

'Exclusion' also has wider implications for those involved. Children experience separation from their peer groups, resulting in feelings of isolation and boredom (Pomeroy 1999; Parsons *et al.* 1997; Gersch and Nolan 1994). The consequences for the families and carers of excluded children can be equally severe. Major difficulties result simply from the fact of having a child at home throughout the day. This can have allied financial repercussions for families where a parent has to give up work in order to care for the child (Commission for Racial Equality 1996; Cohen *et al.* 1994; Parsons *et al.* 1994). Exclusion from school can therefore contribute to an ongoing cycle of social exclusion within families and communities.

Equally significant are the implications of exclusion for the wider community. Several studies, for example, have identified a link between both temporary and permanent exclusion and early offending (Hayden and Martin 1998; Audit Commission 1996; Devlin 1996; Hayden 1994; see Brodie 1997 for a summary of the evidence). This is a complex relationship, in that the reason for exclusion may in itself constitute a criminal offence. Lack of alternative education also, of course, will leave the young person with increased opportunity for association with delinquent peers, and this may exacerbated by a lack of supervision (Home Office 1995). The relationship between permanent exclusion and offending appears to be particularly strong. In one national study of young people aged 14 to 25, 5 of the 8 females and all of the 11 males who had been permanently excluded admitted offending (Home Office 1995). An Audit Commission survey also found that 42 per cent of offenders of school age who are sentenced in the youth court have been excluded from school (Audit Commission 1996). At present the evidence is limited, though further research into the nature of the causal relationship between exclusion and offending has been underway (Berridge *et al.* 2001).

The casting of excluded pupils from the school and into the community inevitably has resource implications for services. Perhaps surprisingly, attention has only gradually been focused on the extent to which other local authority agencies pick up these costs and only one study has examined this issue in detail (Commission for Racial Equality 1996). The calculation of these is complex, especially given the evidence outlined above regarding the social disadvantage experienced prior to and alongside exclusion by many of the young people concerned and their families. Also, maintaining troublesome young people in school is an expensive matter. That said, replacement education is even more costly – usually costing twice as much as standard mainstream schooling. Given that a high proportion of excluded pupils do not return quickly to school, their education costs 'cause a significant drain on the education budget' (Commission for Racial Equality 1996, p.8). In regard to the costs to other agencies, the police and criminal justice agencies assume the greatest burden, followed by social services and health.

The education of children in public care

Children looked after by local authorities and excluded from school are affected by all the factors listed above. It is important to keep in mind the fact that their experiences will be structured by age, gender, ethnicity and educational career and not only by the fact they have lived in public care. In this respect it is also essential to be aware of the fact that many children and young people will spend only a few weeks or months in a care placement, and that most will return home.

The education of children living in residential accommodation is an issue which until recently was largely neglected by researchers and policy makers. A review by Jackson, published in 1987, noted the lack of research evidence in this area, but at the same time highlighted the lack of educational attainments among this group. During the 1990s, research studies have taken greater account of educational issues, and the poor educational outcomes for those leaving the care system have continued to be highlighted (see, for example, Broad 1998;

Department of Health 1996; Biehal *et al.* 1992). Within these issues of exclusion and non-attendance have assumed a high profile. This appears to represent a significant shift in the nature of the educational problems encountered by young people looked after. In Berridge's (1985) study of 20 children's homes, for example, schooling problems were associated with frequent changes of school and of care placement rather than non-attendance. That said, there is still a serious imbalance in the research undertaken, in that the educational experiences of children living in foster care – the very much larger group – have largely been neglected (Borland *et al.* 1998; Berridge 1996; Aldgate *et al.* 1993).

Although not immediately obvious, it is possible to discern the emergence of the issue of exclusion/non-school attendance in the various reports of public enquiries into residential care published during the 1980s. Non-school attendance was noted as a problem by the Pindown Inquiry (Levy and Kahan, 1991). However, in such reports there is no mention of 'exclusion' as a discrete issue, and non-attendance is largely presented as commensurate with truancy. This corresponds with the lack of reference to 'school exclusion' in news reports of the same period. However, quite separate research being carried out at approximately the same time highlighted not only the existence but also the complexity of the issue of exclusion as it related to children looked after (Stirling 1992). Of a sample of 60 children living in 7 children's homes, 32 were not attending school. However, only two of these were *officially* excluded. On the basis of this and other evidence, Stirling argued that a policy of 'informal' or 'unofficial' exclusion was operating in some schools, and claimed that use of this option held the advantage that head teachers did not have to report the exclusion to their board of governors or to the LEA. Stirling did not consider that children living in children's homes were more likely to experience informal exclusion than other young people with behavioural difficulties; however, DfE Circular 13/94 noted, on the basis of anecdotal evidence only, that schools were more likely to informally exclude children looked after on the grounds that they had access to full-time day care. We will return to the issue of informal exclusion in greater detail in later chapters; at present it is sufficient to point out that while anecdotal evidence regarding the operation of informal exclusion in regard to children looked after, the hidden nature of this phenomenon has somewhat discouraged researchers from seeking empirical data.

As the issue of exclusion generally became more prominent, children looked after were increasingly recognised as a vulnerable group (Blyth and Milner 1996; Brodie and Berridge 1996; Social Services Inspectorate/OFSTED 1995). A joint report by the Social Services Inspectorate and OFSTED stated that it was a matter of 'grave concern' that 12 per cent of their sample of 1205 children were non-attenders or excluded. However, a subsequent report by OFSTED (1996, see also Smith 1998) noted that while most LEA had developed procedures for monitoring the rates of exclusion, few authorities recorded the numbers of pupils who are in the care of the local authority and excluded 'despite the fact that they make up a sizeable proportion of the excluded population' (p.23). The collation of such data is in many respects desirable – not least for researchers seeking accessible statistics – and this issue is now being addressed nationally and at local authority level (DfEE/DoH 1999). However, the accurate interpretation of such data also depends on an understanding of the residential context and how this relates to educational experience. Research into residential care which has taken place during the course of the 1990s has also identified problems surrounding exclusion and non-attendance. However, determining causal links between the young person's care and educational career can be difficult. More specifically, it is clear that educational difficulties are frequently a key factor in the decision to place a young person in foster or residential care. For example, Sinclair and Gibbs (1998) found that severe truancy or school exclusion was experienced occasionally by 30 per cent of their sample and persistently for 41 per cent prior to their current placement in a children's home. In a study of social work assessments of adolescents, more than two-thirds (68 per cent) of those who were of school age were reported to be persistent non-attenders, and more than a quarter had been out of school for over a year. We also know that exclusion and non-attendance continue to be significant for a significant proportion of residents currently living in children's homes. Berridge and Brodie (1998) found that of 21 adolescents of school age living in five children's homes, only three were attending school regularly. A survey in Strathclyde (Lockhart et al. 1996, cited in Borland et al. 1998) found that one in five children's home residents were not registered at any school, employment or college and almost 40 per cent were absent from school on the day of the survey.

Any explanation for the educational difficulties experienced by children looked after must, therefore, take account of the background experiences of the group. As with other young people excluded from school, poverty and other forms of disadvantage are widespread. The nature of this disadvantage was well summarised by Bebbington and Miles (1989). In their study of 2500 children admitted to care, it was found that children at greatest risk came from single parent households where the household head received income support. Other significant factors were overcrowding, mixed ethnic origin and where the household included four or more children. It was concluded that where all these factors were present, a child had a one in ten chance of entering care. If anything it would appear that the personal and social problems experienced by children looked after have increased. Berridge and Brodie (1998) compared the populations of children's homes in three local authorities in the early 1980s and the early 1990s. It was found that the extent of behavioural problems had more than doubled, and previous abuse and neglect were identified as major factors in 61 per cent of cases compared with 44 per cent in the previous study.

That said, the care system itself is frequently viewed as unhelpful in improving the educational prospects of young people, and there is considerable evidence that insufficient account has been given to the significance of education in the lives of young people looked after. This has been reflected in various aspects of their care. Unlike continental Europe, where there is a tradition of the 'social pedagogue' which combines the role of social worker and educator, the welfare and education systems have developed separately in England. Earlier research found that carers and social workers took little account of schooling, which was reflected in the environment of children's homes and the lack of educational information recorded in case files (Jackson 1987; Berridge 1985). Unfortunately, such problems continue to exist (see, for example, Francis 2000; Berridge and Brodie 1998; Borland *et al.* 1998) though there are also examples of good practice in many areas.

Care planning is another area where education is often neglected. The Children Act 1989 contains a requirement that every child should have a written care plan which should include a statement of the child's educational needs. While this has had some effect, the focus of these education plans has tended to be very narrow, often involving no more than the name of the school to be attended and with little mention of ways in which educational achievement might be promoted (Grimshaw and Sinclair 1997). Changes in placement are still frequently associated with changes of school, especially for adolescents. Sinclair, Garnett and Berridge (1995) found that over 80 per cent of their sample of adolescents in contact with social services departments had experienced a change in school during a one-year period. Similarly, in Scotland, Kendrick (1995) states that three-fifths of the school-age children in his sample changed school either at admission to the care system or during the first year of their care careers. Although continuity in schooling may have to be balanced against other aspects of a child's welfare (Borland *et al.* 1998) and such changes need not necessarily impede educational progress, too often they appear to take place in unplanned circumstances and without the provision of necessary support.

Generally, the dynamics of the relationship between exclusion from school and living in residential accommodation remain unclear. The available evidence suggests that, while we should avoid assuming a direct correlation between being looked after and educational failure (Jackson 1998), children looked after frequently experience a wide range of schooling problems. However, the significance of this for their experience within the care system and in relation to their return home has not been investigated. Existing social work research has typically examined educational factors as part of a constellation of disadvantage; equally, research into exclusion from school has treated the issue of children in care as an example of the high levels of social disadvantage experienced by excluded children. This vicious circle of cause and effect tells us little, however, regarding the way in which exclusion is experienced by the various participants in the process, or the significance of the care system for the way in which that process is experienced. A research seminar held in 1996 concluded that, in view of the high level of social services involvement with families of excluded children, evaluation of the effectiveness of social work intervention in such cases would be valuable (Brodie and Berridge 1996).

The research context

As exclusion from school has emerged as an identifiable issue, numerous explanations have emerged for both the increased use of exclusion as a sanction and, associated with this, the apparent increase in disruptive behaviour. These will be examined in detail in Chapter 2. However, it is important at this point to outline briefly the shape of the research which has emerged in response to the growing recognition of the problem.

The political demand for greater accuracy in the delineation of the scale of the problem has led to an emphasis on research which has the explicit aim of mapping the scale of exclusions and the characteristics of excluded children. This represents a significant shift from the local studies which previously characterised research into the issue (Galloway *et al.* 1982; Grunsell 1980).

Aside from surveys, the most usual approach to researching exclusion has been case studies and interviews with different individuals involved in or affected by school exclusion. Such research has typically emerged from a professional or policy agenda, and has sought to identify problems in the exclusion process, sometimes accompanied by examples of good practice. Research by voluntary organisations (Cohen *et al.* 1994; Advisory Centre for Education 1993; 1992) emphasised the lack of attention given to parental rights within the exclusion process and highlighted the confusion and stress experienced by many families following exclusion. Other research has been more closely linked to policy concerns, for example the development of more sophisticated formulae for the measurement of the costs of exclusion through detailed examination of specific cases (Parsons 1997b; Parsons *et al.* 1994).

Methodologically, then, studies of exclusion have encompassed both quantitative and qualitative approaches. However, the practice and policy emphasis of the majority of research into exclusion has tended to rule out explicit discussion of theory and methodology. In Trinder's (1996) terms, such studies are 'pragmatic' in their emphasis on producing information which is required by policy makers in both central and local government. The value of this research should not, however, be underestimated. Exclusion from school has emerged as a matter of concern within a very short period of time, and there has been an urgent need for accurate empirical data on the scale and nature of the problem.

However, there is also a need for improved qualitative information regarding exclusion. The importance of this has been indicated by a growing body of research focusing upon children's own perceptions of the experience of exclusion (Pomeroy 1999; Hayden 1997; Cullingford and Morrison 1996; de Pear and Garner 1996; John 1996; Marks 1995; Gersch and Nolan 1994). Some of these studies have been based upon a practice perspective – for example, Gersch and Nolan (1994) argue that understanding of pupils' views is crucial in developing methods for working with pupils following exclusion. Marks (1996), adopting a psychotherapeutic model, focuses on the way in which the emotional trauma of exclusion is managed by children as they seek to give an account of the experience. Exclusion has also been examined in relation to a children's rights perspective (John 1996). Generally, however, this body of research promotes a view of the child's behaviour as a rational response to their negative experiences of the educational system. It therefore runs counter to the dominant public discourse which views excluded pupils as uncontrollable and 'abnormal'. These research studies also highlight the diversity of excluded pupils as a group – some children are relieved and others resentful of exclusion. As Pomeroy (1999) comments, 'there were a range of self-perceptions and constructions with regard to learning, behaviour, and deviancy, rather than a unified and generalisable identity' (p.469). Far from being 'anti-school' most would like to return to some form of education. Such research therefore also renders exclusion a significantly more complex phenomenon; as Cullingford and Morrison (1996) point out, 'the more we explore the meaning of the term [exclusion] the more complex it becomes' (p.131), for which simple causal relationships are unlikely to prove satisfactory. However, similarly detailed analyses of the perceptions of teachers, parents, governors and others have yet to emerge.

Aims and objectives of the book

This book asserts the importance of social actors in the management and negotiation of the exclusion process. It aims to investigate the sequence of events preceding and during school exclusion through the accounts of young people and relevant professionals and through written records. In focusing upon individual stories of exclusion, it will be argued that contradictions and conflicts in the accounts given are important to an understanding of the way in which the exclusion proceeds. The study also aims, therefore, to explore and contrast participants' explanations for why an exclusion occurred. At the same time, the contextual significance of institutional and other structures is explicitly recognised, and the study will take account of the way in which law and policy relating to exclusion interact with the process.

The theoretical premise for the study is that exclusion does not represent a single event or a purely administrative procedure, but is a social process defined and negotiated by the individuals involved. The way in which individuals perceive the issue will affect their responses and actions. Unlike some other forms of qualitative research, this research has not tried to provide a detailed account of the bounded social world of a group or community (Layder 1993). Such an approach seems inappropriate given the fact that exclusion spans a range of social contexts including the school, the household and the peer group. By viewing exclusion from school as a process, account can be taken of the linkages to each of these contexts as they are perceived by significant individuals.

It is perhaps important to outline briefly why it seems reasonable to treat exclusion using this approach, and whether the resulting form of explanation adequately accounts for the phenomenon. This is perhaps especially desirable in the context of social work research, where researchers have often been too 'tardy in writing about how they arrive at their own formulations' (Little 1998, p.51), including their theoretical grounding.

This research has drawn broadly on symbolic interactionism as a theoretical approach. This is generally understood to be concerned with interactional processes and emphasises the importance of communicaton in the establishment of these. Blumer (1969) defines the approach as being based on the view that human beings act towards things – whether physical objects or people or social institutions – on the basis of the meanings these things hold for them. These meanings emerge from, and are continually modified through, interaction. Interactional processes are therefore characterised by a reciprocal exchange of meaning. In this study, therefore, the concern has been to understand the meanings which individuals attach to exclusion, and how these translate into action. A matter of particular interest has been the extent to which professionals from different backgrounds share the same understanding of exclusion, and, if interpretations are different, how this affects working relationships and the outcome for the young person.

In focusing upon individual definitions of exclusion, this research also builds upon existing knowledge. Other research has already pointed to the different ways in which exclusion might be defined, and to the ways in which it frequently represents the end point of a lengthy process of heightening tension within the school. However, relatively little attention has been given to the way in which the exclusion process interacts with other, simultaneous processes occurring in quite different social contexts – such as the care system. The way in which knowledge about these other processes is applied, and by whom such knowledge is possessed, is potentially extremely significant.

The significance of such issues has been identified in relation to other educational processes. In the area of special educational needs (SEN) for example, it has been found that processes of assessment and labelling are far from being objective and scientific and are rather 'social constructions which do not necessarily have any intrinsic meaning' (Galloway, Armstrong and Tomlinson 1994, p.106). The categories which confer a label of SEN are not, therefore, inevitable. They have emerged from a specific historical background, and their implementation is dependent on a variety of circumstances which must be negotiated by professionals, parents and children. Similarly, exclusion results from the decision, at least initially, of an individual headteacher, but is the climax of a process in which several people have been involved.

Exclusion, as we shall see, is also embedded in a complex bureaucratic and legal process (DfE 1994a; see also DfEE 1999b and DfEE/DoH 1999). For example, as noted above, exclusion should take place only in response to serious acts of misbehaviour. What constitutes a serious breach of school policy may sometimes be quite clear to those involved – for example, the case which will be examined later where a child attempted to set the school on fire – but on many other occasions is much less straightforward. This is supported by other evidence concerning the pattern of decision making in regard to exclusions. Existing research shows that, while attacks on fellow pupils and the like are frequently important reasons for exclusion, persistent disruptive behaviour is also very important. Anyone who has cast an eye over the school files of excluded pupils will be aware of the litany of problems preceding an exclusion, sometimes over several years, and typically including frequent incidents of defiance towards teachers, fights with peers, and the refusal to engage in learning. It seems important, therefore, to look beyond the behaviour of individual pupils to the wider network of relationships within which such difficulties emerge. There are, for example, different thresholds of tolerance within schools, and such factors as the amount of support which a headteacher feels the school is receiving from families or other professionals may help stay the decision to exclude for a longer or shorter period of time. Thus, while the legal definition of the process presents exclusion as an essentially bureaucratic procedure, other definitions of exclusion exist which are equally important in understanding how the problem emerges and is managed. The fact that exclusion from school is generally measured in relation to the legal definition of the term, that is in terms of official fixed-term and permanent exclusion, can also be problematic. It has increasingly been recognised that the concept of exclusion may be applied to other ways in which children are prevented from participating in the mainstream educational process, for example as a result of truancy or other informal procedures (Booth in Blyth and Milner 1996; Stirling 1992).

For children looked after, a range of individuals are potentially involved in negotiating the exclusion process. Responsibility for the welfare of this group of young people is shared between the young person's parents and by social workers on behalf of the local authority. Direct care is provided by residential social workers within the children's home. Other professionals such as educational psychologists and education welfare officers may also be involved. Young people are therefore engaged in a complex network of relationships, not even counting their personal networks of family and friends. This would imply that the number and complexity of interactional processes may be brought into relief in the experience of these children and young people, and that consequently this represents a fertile context in which to examine exclusion as a social process.

This is not to say that wider structures are unimportant. It would be naive to suppose that social actors are unconscious of the structures within which they operate (Giddens 1979). These structures provide constraints and opportunities which are recognised by individuals. It would be equally ingenuous to suppose that these same structures cannot be manipulated and managed by individuals with specific goals and intentions. Furthermore, as Blyth and Milner (1994) point out, exclusion from school cannot be seen only in terms of young people's experiences of education and schooling but 'as part of the complex relationship between individuals, families, the labour market, health and state support and surveillance services' (p.293). This perspective has become increasingly important at policy level, as the question of school exclusion has become integrated into ideas relating to social exclusion (Social Exclusion Unit 1998). Other research evidence also indicates that school processes are significant (Osler 1997; OFSTED 1996a; Galloway et al. 1982). These social and institutional structures represent the context within and upon which individuals act, and may be perceived as important explanations for these actions. The fact that we are concerned here with the exclusion from school of children living in children's homes requires consideration of a second set of policies and institutional arrangements which may also be significant in understanding the experience of exclusion for this group of pupils. The present study does not deny the validity of attempts to understand exclusion in terms of these wider structures. For example, it is clear that there would be considerable value in examining exclusion within a critical perspective seeking to highlight the power differentials arising from social relationships based on ethnicity and gender. Attention has also been drawn to the importance of considering exclusion from school as an outcome of developments in educational and social policy (Parsons 1999). As Silverman (1989) points out, theoretical diversity is to be welcomed and should enhance understanding of the topic being studied.

Outline of the book

So far this chapter has presented evidence regarding the nature of the exclusion 'problem' as it is currently perceived and specifically in terms of the numbers and characteristics of children and young people who are known to be excluded from school. Chapter 2 will extend this discussion by probing in greater depth the reasons why exclusion is thought to occur. The literature relating to this will be linked to consideration of the way in which media debate on exclusion unfolded during the mid-1990s. Chapter 3 will then examine the design of the research. In Chapter 5 the characteristics of the 17 young people studied will be considered in relation to other evidence regarding both children looked after by local authorities and children excluded from school. Chapter 6 will present data from the study regarding the context of inter-agency work in the local authorities, and the way in which different professional roles and responsibilities were perceived by those involved. Chapter 7 then analyses the patterns of interaction between individuals in the cases studied. Following from this, Chapter 8 will examine in greater detail one of the main themes to emerge from the research, namely the problem of defining exclusion, and will outline a possible alternative typology of exclusion as it relates to the looked after group. Chapter 9 will consider the social work response in the 17 cases. Chapter 10 will conclude by considering the major findings from the study in relation to current policy proposals regarding exclusion and the education of children looked after.

2

Explaining Exclusion

Chapter 1 has presented evidence regarding the scale of the 'exclusion problem' and the pupils who are considered to be most vulnerable to this sanction, including those living in residential accommodation.

Some important contextual issues remain. Specifically, it is necessary to explain why exclusion has emerged as a particular problem during the early 1990s. Given the similarities between recent research and that which took place in the 1960s and 1970s about the type of behaviour described as leading to exclusion, it becomes difficult to understand the extent of current concerns regarding exclusion. In addition to the reasons being largely similar, exclusions appear to have been concentrated at the same age-groups as at present. This begs the question of why exclusion has become a matter of such acute concern during the mid-1990s.

This chapter will consider some of the explanations which have been offered for this concern. It will begin by examining research evidence about why schools exclude children. It will then go on to consider why use of exclusion increased over the last decade. It will trace the background to current concern and will consider whether exclusion is, or has been, a 'moral panic'. Finally, it will be argued that concern about exclusion must be linked to a changed policy context in education, which is thought to have had significant implications for schools' perceptions of unruly pupils.

It could be argued that these issues fall outside the remit of the present study, as explanations for the increased use of permanent exclusion are deserving of attention in their own right. However, some consideration of the context of exclusion is necessary. As Chapter 1 has explained, the main interest of this study is the social process of exclusion, as reflected in the interaction which takes place between the different individuals involved in this process. These interactions involve communication on the basis of the meanings which individuals attach to the young person's behaviour and the context in which they are operating. The consequence of this is that individual interpretations are informed by these broader explanations, and an understanding of these is necessary to the study.

Reasons for exclusion

Research into exclusion has proved remarkably consistent on the reasons for exclusion, in the sense of reasons collated by local authorities or stated on official letters of exclusion. There are, of course, difficulties in comparing findings as definitions of behaviour are inevitably subjective. York *et al.* (1972), examining pupils suspended from Edinburgh schools in the mid-late 1960s, found that the most common reasons were attacks on other children, intolerable temper outbursts and aggressive, disruptive or unco-operative behaviour. Galloway *et al.* (1982) described the most common reasons for exclusion as abuse/insolence to teachers, unspecified bad behaviour, refusal to accept discipline/disobedience, bullying or violence to other pupils and persistent absence. More recent studies have produced similar evidence. OFSTED's (1996a) survey of secondary school exclusions found that the main immediate reasons given were verbal abuse to peers, violence to other pupils, persistent failure to obey school rules, disruption and criminal offences committed at school. This last issue is one which – with the exception of drug possession and use – has perhaps been given too little attention. A survey of primary school exclusions in England revealed that the most common reasons were the refusal to comply with school rules, physical aggression towards other pupils, the verbal abuse of teachers and physical aggression towards other pupils (Hayden, Sheppard and Ward 1996). However, some LEAs also noted that the recorded reason for exclusion actually represented the 'last straw' in a series of misdemeanours culminating in an exclusion.

Thus, while very similar reasons are given for individual exclusion, there is considerable scope for difference in meaning in terms of what a child has done and for variation between schools about the nature of offences deemed deserving of exclusion. Official guidance has emphasised the need to reserve exclusion for the most serious offences, but where there is a long history of difficult behaviour it is unlikely that this will be easily dismissed. It is worth considering these findings in the light of other research on the type of behaviour perceived by teachers to be most troublesome. Studies by Wheldall and Merrett (1988; 1984) and Houghton, Wheldall and Merrett (1988) found a consensus between primary, junior and secondary school teachers respectively that 'talking out of turn' and 'hindering other children' were most problematic. The vast majority of teachers considered boys to be more problematic than girls. Verbal abuse and physical aggression were very seldom cited. The Elton Committee's enquiry, which included a survey of 3600 teachers in 470 schools, found that, while most schools were orderly, teachers in ten per cent of secondary schools and five per cent of primary schools felt that they faced serious discipline problems. However, physical attacks on teachers were found to be rare, despite the fact that this had been the main focus of teachers' concern. Instead, general classroom disruption was found to be the main problem. As with exclusion, the difference in standards of behaviour could only be partially explained by socio-economic differences between catchment areas (Department of Education and Science 1988).

'Disruptive' behaviour, the child and the family

The reasons schools give for exclusion provide only a very partial insight into the problem. Not only is the language used to describe 'disruptive' behaviour essentially subjective, but schools are constrained by the knowledge that the reasons they give must be acceptable in case of official scrutiny. It may therefore be helpful to examine the reasons why children are thought to present difficult behaviour in school, and whether the nature of the explanation given affects the sanction imposed.

Bird *et al.* (1981) demonstrate that teachers have a range of theoretical frameworks through which to explain behaviour which can be described as 'disaffected'. They note that the 'breadth and depth of their definitions of disaffection and its causes were indicative both of the enormous range of pupil motivation and behaviour, and of the teachers' awareness of the social and educational issues affecting their pupils' (p.53). Nor, they warn, do these definitions remain static, but change according to the amount of contact the teacher has with the pupil and the teacher's knowledge of the child's family circumstances. Teachers also recognise that pupil disaffection may constitute a 'rational' reaction to their experience of school life, or a rejection of the values of the educational system (Kinder *et al.* 1995; Bird *et al.* 1980). However, while pupils often see exclusion as unfair, or feel that they have been poorly treated by schools, it is not clear whether this – proportionately small – group perceive themselves as part of a broader disaffected group or as members of an identifiable pupil subculture.

Taking the evidence from the OFSTED (1996a) survey and Hayden, Sheppard and Ward's (1996) study of primary school exclusion, however, it would appear that the incidents giving rise to exclusion are rather more serious than the usual run of troublesome behaviour in the classroom. This may be linked to other evidence that many schools are reluctant to exclude and try hard to avoid doing so (Berridge *et al.* 1997; Hayden 1997). This should, however, be set against evidence that many exclusions continue to be the outcome of a build-up of problems within the classroom, with the decision to exclude triggered by a 'last straw' incident.

Explanations of disruptive behaviour have, on the whole, tended to be located within the child rather than in their wider social context (Galloway and Goodwin 1987; Cooper 1996). Galloway and Goodwin (1987) argue that it has been important to educationalists to be able to distinguish between behaviour that is simply disruptive and that which is 'disturbed'. This has typically been achieved through attaching pseudo-medicalised labels to the children concerned. Thus throughout the history of mass compulsory education such pupils have been variously described as 'maladjusted' and, more recently, as having 'emotional and behavioural difficulties' (EBD). However, these categories are essentially administrative and, as such, 'largely meaningless' (Galloway *et al.* 1982, p.5). These labels have, however, played an important part in the legitimation of the segregation of children within the educational system.

More recently, and in particular since the Warnock Report (Department of Education and Science 1978), the idea of the 'disturbed' individual child has been replaced by the concept of special educational needs. Thus the emphasis has moved from segregating children in special schools and units to that of 'integration' and meeting needs within the mainstream classroom. Children who are assessed as having EBD are entitled to receive support which will enable them to remain within mainstream schools. However, this concept has also been beset by problems of definition. Children presenting EBD are especially prone to such variations in diagnosis, as a satisfactory definition of EBD has proved elusive (Cooper 1996; Galloway, Armstrong and Tomlinson 1994; see also Farrell 1995; Peagam 1995). Although children defined as having EBD are included within the broader category of Special Educational Need (SEN), it has consistently proved difficult to specify the problems which a child with EBD may present. On the one hand it is acknowledged that such pupils may display behaviour which is disruptive and aggressive, while on the other they may become withdrawn and depressed (DFE 1993, para 4). The Code of Practice on Special Educational Need states the emotional and behavioural difficulties 'may become apparent in a wide variety of forms' including withdrawn, depressive or suicidal attitudes; obsessional preoccupation with eating habits; school phobia; substance misuse; disruptive, anti-social and unco-operative behaviour; and frustration, anger and threat of or actual violence (Code of Practice, para. 3:66). Commenting on the most recent guidance on school exclusion, Gray and Panter (2000) note that the analysis of the reasons for behaviour difficulties remains 'muddled' (p.6), describing children with EBD as being an 'at risk group for presenting behavioural problems.' Gray and Panter comment that this statement is understandable only if it is assumed emotional and behavioural difficulties originate 'within' the child. However, there is a recognition within a majority of the academic and professional literature that environmental factors – such as those relating to the classroom and home – will also affect the child's behaviour (Chazan 1994).

Assessment of EBD is therefore reliant on the 'subjective judgements of teachers and other professionals rather than on any agreed criteria' (Galloway, Armstrong and Tomlinson 1994, p.112) – though inevitably attempts have been made to extend and elaborate the different behaviours which underpin EBD (see for example Cooper 1996). The consequence of this is that the responses which professionals make to EBD will also be varied. Some research has shown that children presenting very similar social and educational problems may be directed into quite different services (Galloway, Armstrong and Tomlinson 1994; Malek 1993). Following from this, it is not difficult to see that distinguishing between behaviour that indicates a special educational need and that which is simply 'bad' is far from straightforward.

Recently – and indeed corresponding to rising concerns about difficult and disruptive behaviours – there has been a growing interest in the remedicalisation of behaviour problems, through 'discovery' of the conditions ADD (Attention Deficit Disorder) and ADHD (Attention Deficit Hyperactivity Disorder). Train (1996) describes ADHD as an inherited condition, which medical research suggests results from a malfunction in the chemicals which act as a communication system between nerve cells in the brain and which affect the individual's ability to concentrate. This can be corrected by the use of drugs such as methylphenidate (Ritalin). The diagnosis and treatment of ADD/ADHD have proved extremely controversial among the teaching profession in the United Kingdom, especially regarding the use of drugs for young children. Sociologists have also argued that this is another example of behaviour which has been socially constructed as a medical condition and is, in turn, being legitimated through the medical establishment (Tattum 1985). Others (see, for example, Cooper and Ideus 1995) argue that if a significant proportion of children are suffering from an undiagnosed condition that may have a psychosocial as well as an organic basis, then this should be taken seriously and educators fully informed about the issue.

An alternative way in which behavioural problems arise may be found in wider social changes. Rutter and Smith (eds 1995), for example, writing from a psychological perspective, have found evidence of an increase in psychosocial conditions among young people, which is not matched by similar changes for other age groups. They suggest a range of factors which might provide the bases for hypotheses regarding the causes of this, including changes in the nature of adolescence, shifts in moral concepts and values, and increased stress in family life.

Given that children spend rather more of their time at home than at school it is not unreasonable to suppose that a child's experience within the family will affect the way in which they behave at school. Chapter 1 has already presented evidence that the majority of children excluded from school have experienced high levels of social disadvantage including poverty, parental illness, bereavement and homelessness (Hayden 1997; OFSTED 1996a). Family background, including such factors as poor parenting behaviour and disharmony between parents, has frequently been identified as a causal explanation for educational disaffection and poor performance. This has often been linked to other aspects of social disadvantage, such as low income and poor housing.

That families are important to a child's education would not, generally, be disputed; indeed Furlong (1985) criticises the failure of other sociological accounts of school deviance for their apparent willingness to 'deny the validity of what to many other observers is common sense, the idea that difficult pupils often come from difficult or unhappy homes' (p.252). However, other commentators, from a variety of political perspectives, go further in identifying specific changes to family structure, which, it has been argued, are directly related to an increase in behavioural difficulties and involvement in crime. Dennis and Erdos (1992) reject the view that social disadvantage in terms of poverty and unemployment can be held responsible. Instead they claim that the absence of stable families where two parents are present, and in particular the absence of fathers, is directly linked to a weakening of cultural cohesion in some local communities and consequently families which do not offer their children a positive educational and social environment in which to grow up.

Inevitably, the identification of difficult behaviour among young people – as exemplified by increasing numbers of exclusions – with changes in the structure of family life has proved popular amongst politicians and the press. The families of excluded children are frequently portrayed as at best irresponsible and at worst shiftless. In turn this has been linked to a more widespread social malaise, involving a breakdown in family life and rising levels of crime. This view was perhaps encapsulated in the public debate following the murder of a London headteacher in November 1995 by a 15-year-old boy. Some months after the murder, the victim's widow instituted a campaign to raise moral standards among young people. This attracted a high level of support from politicians. The rhetoric accompanying this 'moral crusade' focused on the decline in moral standards which, it was claimed, pervaded the home and the classroom.

Exclusion and 'moral panic'

This brings us to the issue of the way in which exclusion has been constructed as a problem in the public realm. Blyth and Milner (1993) have argued that the level of attention which exclusion has attracted (attention which has, in fact, increased since they made this comment) constitutes a 'moral panic'. Cohen (1972) described this as a period in society when

> ...a condition, episode, person or group of persons emerges to become defined as a threat to societal values and interests; its nature is presented in a stylised and stereotypical fashion by the media; the moral barricades are manned by editors, bishops, politicians and other right-thinking people; socially accredited experts pronounce their diagnoses and solutions; ways of coping are evolved or (more often) resorted to; the condition then disappears, submerges or deteriorates and becomes more visible. (p.9)

Behaviour problems among children are far from new: a study of behaviour problems carried out in the 1930s reported 46 per cent of school pupils as displaying at least one 'behavioural deviation' (McFie 1934 cited in Galloway, Armstrong and Tomlinson 1994). Historical analyses also reveal a long-standing concern with attendance at school and discipline within the classroom (see, for example, Gleeson 1992). Equally, public perceptions of young people as increasingly delinquent have a long history. Pearson (1983) provides ample evidence to demonstrate that the 'teddy boys' of the 1950s and the 'hooligans' of the 1890s attracted similar public concern. The causes to which such behaviour was attributed are also strikingly similar, including, for example, the failure to use corporal punishment. Football, the cinema and rock music – and more recently children's access to violent videos – have each in their turn also been held responsible for a breakdown in discipline among young people.

The recent public debate about exclusion can be most easily traced to a set of anxieties relating to allegedly rising levels of disruptive behaviour and pupil violence which emerged during the 1980s. These led to the report of the Committee of Enquiry into Discipline in Schools chaired by Lord Elton (Department for Education and Science 1988). Concerns regarding disruptive pupils continued to emerge during the early 1990s, and a number of cases surfaced where teachers had been attacked by pupils (for example, *The Times* 15 August 1992). Teachers' unions continued to call for tougher measures to deal with disruptive pupils (*The Times* 27 May 1992), while government inspections revealed unacceptable levels of disruptive behaviour in certain schools. Importantly, concern was focused on disruption and classroom violence rather than exclusion per se.

Gradually, media attention has focused on 'exclusion' rather than disruption more generally. This trend was fuelled by television programmes (Panorama 1992; MORI, 1993) and the publication of surveys (DFE 1993; NUT 1992) and government reports (DFE 1993; OFSTED 1993). The annual conferences of teachers' unions also helped keep the issue at the centre of public debate over education. Statements from union leaders emphasised the risk at which teachers were placed by violent pupils, and claimed that current regulations afforded them little protection. Nigel de Gruchy, head of the National Association of Schoolmasters and Union of Women Teachers (NASUWT), stated at the union's 1994 conference that 'the problem is beginning to escalate and going further down the age range, even into the infant sector... Everything is stacked in favour of the disruptive pupil and the parent of the disruptive pupil. Parent power is often exercised by irresponsible parents.' Exclusion had therefore become a familiar term during the early 1990s and, by the end of the decade, a matter for policy intervention in its own right (Social Exclusion Unit 1998).

During 1995 and 1996 a small number of pupils achieved considerable notoriety through exclusion. The first of these was Richard Wilding, a 13-year-old pupil at Glaisdale Comprehensive School in Nottingham. Richard was reported to have been involved in 30 'violent and disruptive' incidents since September 1995. He was eventually permanently excluded in January 1996 for allegedly attacking a teacher. This decision was overturned by an independent appeals tribunal in March 1996. Members of NASUWT threatened strike action if Richard returned to the school. It was eventually agreed that Richard would return to the school, but would receive individual tuition there for half the week and would spend the remaining time at a local pupil referral unit (PRU).

The case of Matthew Wilson, a 10-year-old pupil at Manton Junior School in Nottingham, was remarkably similar. He had been excluded on a fixed-term basis on two previous occasions before being permanently excluded in the summer term of 1996. There are some contradictions in reports of the reason for Matthew's permanent exclusion, but his behaviour is said to have included bullying other pupils and on one occasion threatening them with a baseball bat, refusing to obey instructions and throwing things at staff. The school's headteacher was alleged to have stated that if Matthew stayed at the school the safety of other pupils could not guaranteed. Matthew's mother appealed against the decision and was supported by the school's governing body. It was eventually agreed that Matthew should return to the school to receive one-to-one tuition. Teachers then went on strike. Finally, after two months of feuding, Matthew's mother decided that he should move to another school (O'Leary 1996).

The final case to attract national attention was that of Sarah Taylor, a 13-year-old pupil at The Ridings School in Halifax. She was expelled in March 1996 for allegedly pushing a male teacher in the chest when he tried to break up a fight between Sarah and another pupil. However, she was reinstated by Calderdale LEA in a decision upheld by an independent appeals panel in June 1996. Thirty-one members of the NASUWT threatened to strike if she returned for the new term. The strike was averted when Sarah's mother decided to withdraw her from The Ridings, though the incident was to prove a precursor to a much larger 'exclusions crisis' at the school when members of the same union claimed that 61 children were 'unteachable' and should be excluded.

It has been pointed out that 'moral panic' is increasingly drawn upon as a convenient descriptor of any issue which attracts a sizeable amount of media and political attention, and that its sociological meaning has, in the process, become lost (Hunt 1997; McRobbie 1994). Hunt, in particular, notes that there is increasingly a confusion between the 'moral panic' and the 'folk devil'. The folk-devil is the 'scapegoat' onto whom public fears and fantasies are projected. In regard to the Mods and Rockers Cohen studied, the moral panic was not so much either of these groups than the post-war affluence and sexual freedom they represented. Thus, while moral panics relating to young people often draw on the same themes, they are likely to follow many different patterns and have the capacity to assume an 'infinite variety of tone and posture' (Watney 1997, p.43). Children excluded from school are perhaps more accurately described as the folk-devil of the piece, representing an ideal target for a whole range of public and political concerns regarding the state of education, crime and the family. The adaptability of the issue, therefore, makes it attractive to a wide range of interest groups and permits its manipulation by media.

The idea that children cannot be controlled even within the confines of the classroom can be utilised to indicate the degree to which control by 'legitimate' social institutions has been lost. The development of compulsory schooling has been associated with ensuring social control over, and conformity among children. Hendrick (1997) notes an ideological link between the evolution of the concept of juvenile delinquency and the compulsory introduction of schooling. While sociological attention has increasingly focused on the way in which children engage with and manage their social worlds, the schooling environment remains largely impervious to such manipulation (Mayall 1994), and the school has continued to represent a key agency of social control. It is therefore significant that media reports of exclusion have also included a number of cases where children in the early years of primary school have been excluded (for example, Charter, *The Times* 28 August 1996). The incidence of primary school exclusions has increased, but given the concentration of exclusions among secondary school pupils these reports may be seen as a misrepresentation of the nature of the problem. However, while such reports may be interpreted as 'teacher-bashing' – that teachers may be criticised for their inability to control mere infants – it might also be understood as emphasising the extent of the crisis. While adolescents have traditionally been viewed as potentially dangerous, younger children have tended to remain outside the orbit of such moral panics. The exclusion of five-year-olds as 'uncontrollable' also represents a significant challenge to widely accepted notions of childhood as a time of innocence and susceptibility to adult guidance.

The media discourse about exclusion has contained many, sometimes contradictory, elements. However, while concerns over the behaviour of young people may be a recurrent societal theme, exclusion has some different ingredients. The idea that the behaviour of a minority of children represents a significant problem has, in the past, typically led to their segregation and regulation in various institutions (Gooch 1997). The irony of school exclusion, of course, is that the erring child is not subject to increased measures of control, but is placed once more within the family – whose irresponsibility is nevertheless frequently blamed for the child's behaviour – and effectively given the freedom of the community.

Schools, education policy and exclusion

The 'moral panic' over exclusion should also be related to changes in the policy environment within which schools operate, which has also affected the construction of exclusion as a problem in political and media debate. Familial and individualised explanations continue to have currency as explanations for the apparently high levels of difficult behaviour resulting in growing number of exclusions in England's primary and secondary schools. However, schools also play an important part. It has also been vociferously argued that changes have taken place less in the behaviour of young people than in the wider political context and the effects of this on levels of social disadvantage generally – which are likely to affect the well-being of young people – and also the way in which schools respond to disruptive pupils. This can be traced back to the 1970s, when concerns emerged that pupils were failing to achieve sufficiently high standards in comparison with Britain's economic competitors. The 'Great Debate' on education inaugurated by Prime Minister James Callaghan emphasised the need for schools to become more effective in training young people for the workforce.

During the late 1980s the Thatcher governments introduced a radical set of policies which sought to restrict the role of the state in the provision of public services. Le Grand (1991) argues that the key element in these policies was the construction of market relations within public service provision. The state was no longer to act as both funder and provider of services, but would operate primarily as a funder, purchasing services from a variety of private, voluntary and public providers all competing with one another. The development of internal markets was evident in housing, health care, education and the personal social services, but progressed somewhat differently in each of these contexts. However, while in the past education policy had a degree of autonomy from other areas of policy-making, developments under the Conservatives resulted in a closer articulation between education and other fields of policy. Interestingly, this has continued since 1997 under New Labour, though this time under the guise of ensuring 'joined-up' government through improved co-operation between government departments.

The main instrument of change in the educational system was the Education Reform Act 1988 (ERA). Ball (1990) notes that while the Act is often interpreted and discussed in fragmentary fashion, there should be no doubt that 'at the heart of the Act is an attempt to establish the basis of an education market' (p.60). Four key elements of the Act can be identified: open enrolment, formula funding, local management of schools and a facility for schools to opt out of local authority control. Together these provisions placed schools in a competitive relationship to each other. Through formula funding arrangements, schools received funding allocations based on the number of pupils enrolled. As parents were given the power to choose which school their children attend, rather than being constrained by catchment area, schools must compete in order to attract pupils and consequently to maintain their levels of funding. The school controls how the budget is spent, and schools which have opted out of direct local authority control can receive grants directly from central government. The powers left in the hands of LEAs, therefore, have been severely restricted.

However, the education market is an imperfect one, diverging from the standard market model in a number of important ways. It has consequently been more accurately defined as a 'quasi-market' (Le Grand and Bartlett 1993; Le Grand 1991). Most obviously, such markets do not operate for profit and services are free at the point of delivery (Le Grand and Bartlett 1993). However, quasi-markets in education may also be distinguished from some other quasi-markets – for example those in social housing – by the fact that although the most immediate consumer is the pupil, parents (albeit usually in discussion with their children) are responsible for deciding the school which a child should attend. The operation of the market is also limited by the fact that purchasers are highly constrained by the distribution of providers, that is, schools. The amount of choice available to parents will depend, for example, on geographical location, which may mean that a local 'market' is dominated by a single school (Challis *et al.* 1994). Consequently the benefits of policies of choice are variable. David, West and Ribbens (1994) argue that choice is invariably mediated by geographical and social location, and that ultimately, the choice that is made is a compromise between limited options. The greatest benefits are likely to accrue to those who already possess considerable cultural capital in regard to their child's education (Gewirtz, Ball and Bowe 1995).

Glennerster (1991), drawing an analogy between education and health care services, has pointed out that it is critically important for any health care provider to exclude high cost, high risk patients from their group of users. A considerable amount of attention is given in marketing and in competition with other health care providers to ensure that a minimum number of these high cost patients are attracted. Similarly, in a situation where schools are required to market themselves on the basis of high performance in assessment tests and exams in order to attract pupils, he argues that 'Any school entrepreneur acting rationally would seek to exclude pupils who would drag down the overall performance score of the school, its major selling point to parents.' (p.1271). The consequence of this is that schools ultimately become more selective, catering for children in different bands of ability and from different social backgrounds. Further, given that socio-economic background continues to represent a highly significant, if not the major determinant of attainment, it is likely that those pupils who will be most adversely affected are those who are already socially disadvantaged.

Such an argument would cohere with the other evidence the numbers of exclusion taking place within such a context. Not only have the number of exclusions increased dramatically and concurrent with the implementation of the quasi-market, but the groups identified as most vulnerable to the phenomenon are those who have experienced significant levels of disadvantage. Researchers and others have argued that these changes have had a detrimental effect on the education of pupils with behavioural difficulties who are unlikely to enhance a school's public image, and that consequently a direct link can therefore be made with the increased number of exclusions taking place (Lloyd-Smith and Davies 1995; Parsons *et al.* 1994; Blyth and Milner 1993). Within the debates on exclusion in the media it is also possible to discern a perception of these children as essentially undeserving. In the cases of Richard Wilding and Matthew Wilson, these objections centred around the additional educational support given to these pupils following their reinstatement. One parent remarked that 'money is coming out of the budget for all the other children and it is our children who are losing out again because he cannot behave himself' (Charter, *The Times* 10 September 1996). Following the birth of Sarah Taylor's baby, a local councillor commented that 'at the age of 13, this girl has put nothing into society and is already starting to draw from it' (*The Express* 22 October 1996).

Schools have also been required to market themselves in order to attract pupils. The 1980 Education Act required schools to publish their exam results and hold compulsory open evenings for parents. Schools have become increasingly conscious of the image they present to the outside world, reflected in sophisticated school brochures and other forms of publicity. The rhetoric of parental choice permeates discussions on education, and advice on the best means by which to make the choice of school is widely disseminated. In such a situation, it is argued that the minority of pupils who are disruptive and disaffected are likely to be marginalised (Hayden, Sheppard and Ward 1996). Parffrey (1994) contends that such pupils are perceived as bad for the image of the school, bad for the league table, are difficult and time-consuming and upset and stress the teachers (p.108).

Children themselves have tended to have little voice in educational processes. While the Children Act 1989 requires local authorities to consult children in all major decisions affecting them, together with the right to make representations or complaints, this right is not present in education legislation. West (1994) notes that while the child's wishes were important to parents engaged in the process of choosing a secondary school, children had no opportunity to make any formal contribution and had no right to fill in or even sign the transfer form in the two boroughs where the research was carried out. The Code of Practice on the Identification and Assessment of Special Educational Needs, issued under the 1993 Education Act, confirmed and extended the non-statutory advice on the implementation of the 1981 Act that the concept of partnership should, as far as practicable, be extended to children and young people. In contrast, official guidance on exclusion does not contain similar advice, implying that pupils who are excluded are not perceived to have special educational needs. Indeed, pupils aged under 18 have no participation rights in the exclusion process – only parents have the right to notice, to appeal and to make representations to governing bodies and the LEA. Allen (1994) criticised this as a 'major failure' of this legislation, and it has not been addressed subsequently.

As parents are able to choose between schools, they can also decide to withdraw pupils – and consequently the funding associated with each pupil – from a school. Empirical evidence suggests that parents do sometimes exercise pressure on headteachers regarding a disruptive pupil by threatening to withdraw their own children, as in the cases of Matthew Wilson and Richard Wilding. Research into patterns of parental choice indicates that levels of school discipline are significant in parents' decision making (West 1994; Glatter and Woods 1993). School that can present themselves as offering a disciplined and orderly environment will therefore have a certain advantage against their rivals.

Another issue which tends to be managed locally is the nature and quality of the educational provision available to disruptive pupils. The reduction in the powers of the LEA can be a significant factor in finding another school place. This may be linked to the option for schools to opt out of local authority control. Opting out places further constraints on the relationship between schools and LEAs. In regard to exclusion the selection criteria used by grant-maintained schools may limit the options available to a LEA seeking to find a school place for an excluded pupil. So far only anecdotal evidence is available in relation to this problem. However, the lengthy periods of time a high proportion of excluded pupils spend outside mainstream school indicate difficulties in finding alternative school places. In areas where there is a significant number of grant-maintained schools, LEAs will be forced to direct excluded pupils to a limited number of maintained schools, which in turn experience the burden of a high number of disruptive and difficult pupils. In this respect, then, the operation of the education market significantly reduces the amount of choice available to certain groups, and militates against a balanced distribution of pupils between schools.

However, while the argument that a market in education disadvantages certain pupils is both logical and convincing, there are some problems. One issue which the model as it stands does not address is the consistent finding that no direct link can be made between exclusion rates and the level of socio-economic disadvantage in a school's catchment area (Hayden, Sheppard and Ward 1996; OFSTED 1996a; Dept. for Education 1995; Imich 1994). Equally, it does not explain the wide variations in exclusion rates between schools and between local authorities. Levacic (1994), drawing on findings from a study of the effects of formula funding on schools, claims that there was little evidence of 'cream skimming' of more able pupils in the schools she examined. She attributes this to informal agreements between headteachers to limit the amount of competition taking place, together with the inability of non-selective schools to 'fine-tune' entry requirements. Also, while changes in policy have frequently been viewed as marking 'the beginning of the end' (Reynolds 1993) for LEAs, case studies of individual local authorities indicate that LEAs continue to 'constrain and plan' their local markets, with significant effects.

It is therefore important to recognise that while the quasi-market in education undoubtedly carries the potential to marginalise and exclude difficult pupils, this will not inevitably occur. Local variations will exist, and generally, there is likely to be 'a complex interplay of planned, arbitrary, historical, spontaneous and producer and consumer factors' (Gewirtz, Ball and Bow 1995, p.93). As we have already noted, this is a quasi-market which diverges from the standard market model in a number of significant ways. However, pupils at risk of exclusion constitute one part of this market. In view of the fact that this group is costly to both schools and other services, they are a small but extremely significant group, and it is desirable that studies examining the operation of local education markets should examine their relationship to exclusion.

Improving standards

A further element of government policy which may contribute to explaining the increase in exclusion concerns the drive to improve educational standards. Education has always had an important function as a means to provide young people with credentials, but this has assumed a distinct shape under both Conservative and Labour governments in the 1980s and 1990s. While on the one hand reforms have given schools much greater autonomy, the powers of central government have also been increased through, for example, the imposition of a National Curriculum, a national assessment policy and statutory rules regarding the operation of governing bodies and the information which schools give to parents. Central regulation has also been extended through the replacement of Her Majesty's Inspectorate with the Office for Standards in Education (OFSTED). The regulatory function of OFSTED has shifted from the traditional acceptance of and adherence to professional convention to an emphasis on the setting of standards and the provision of information to parents (Challis et al. 1994). The inspection process has become noticeably more public and teams of managers have been sent to 'turnaround' schools which do not perform satisfactorily, and schools which have been found to be 'failing' have been closed. For pupils who experience educational difficulties, the National Curriculum represents a framework which offers significantly less flexibility in making curricular provision for pupils who may lack the ability to concentrate (Lovey et al. 1993). It has also been argued that the Curriculum emphasises academic targets at the expense of the development of social and personal skills, which are themselves essential if pupils are to learn effectively. More generally, the pressure on teachers to ensure that the range of the curriculum is covered that it may become more difficult to make special allowance for pupils who are disruptive, though this has been made more flexible under the most recent DfEE guidance (1999b). National 'league tables' detailing the exam results of secondary school pupils and the results of national assessment tests for primary school pupils are published annually. Discipline has also emerged as a matter for national regulation.

Debate over exclusion in many respects encapsulates the inherent tensions between quasi-market competition between schools and government regulation. Teachers' objections to policy on exclusion has centred on exclusion procedures and the balance of power between the school and the local authority. Specifically, the potential for exclusion decisions to be overturned on appeal has led to several bitter disputes; indeed, all three cases described earlier in the chapter resulted in such controversies. It is also reported that teaching unions have been involved in many more similar disputes which have not been given prominent press coverage (*Special Children* 1996). Thus one headteacher, following the decision by an independent appeals panel to overturn her decision to exclude, commented

> There is, however, a wider issue which needs to be addressed by the whole teaching profession. That is the forked tongue policy of the present Government which, with one tongue, instructs schools to raise standards in education. Meanwhile, the other tongue dictates legal procedures that effectively remove from schools the power to lay foundations for good behaviour.' (*The Guardian* 2 May 1996)

These concerns continue into the new millenium; at the NASUWT conference in 2000, David Blunkett, Secretary of State for Education, felt it necessary to reassure delegates that recent government policies designed to reduce the number of permanent exclusions did not reflect a tolerance of violent behaviour.

These policy changes have also included an increased emphasis on 'school effectiveness' or its political variant of 'school failure' (Galloway, Armstrong and Tomlinson 1994). This perspective is drawn from a tradition of educational research demonstrating the significance of school processes in influencing outcomes for pupils (White and Barber 1997; Reynolds and Cuttance 1992; Mortimore *et al.* 1988; Rutter *et al.* 1979). An important dimension of the debate has therefore been to place exclusion within the context of the organisation, policies and practice of the individual school.

By becoming more 'effective', therefore, it is argued that schools can reduce the number of exclusions taking place. An influential OFSTED report on exclusions unequivocally stated that low excluding schools are characterised by such factors as an effective behaviour policy, applying suitable rewards and sanctions, monitoring exclusions and providing pastoral support (OFSTED

1999). Thus Chris Woodhead, Chief Inspector of Schools, has commented that 'a good headteacher can always turn a failing school around' (*The Times* 2000). Similarly, Osler (1997) concentrated her research on practice within schools with low rates of exclusion and argues that this was achieved through good practice such as 'inclusive' discipline policies and the involvement of pupils in all aspects of the life of the school. This approach has also influenced government response to exclusion 'crises', most notably the prominent case of The Ridings School in Halifax. The news that this school intended to exclude some 60 pupils for disruptive behaviour attracted a high level of media attention. As the days passed, a story emerged of poor management, ineffective teaching and widespread chaos within the classrooms. A team of government inspectors was rapidly sent in and a new headteacher introduced. The subsequent inspectors' reports attributed the high level of exclusions to poor teaching and the lack of an appropriate disciplinary framework. It is still unclear how such factors explain the differences in exclusion rates which recent studies have identified between local authorities (Hayden, Sheppard and Ward 1996; DfE 1995).

However, the relationship between effective schooling and the rate of exclusions emerges less coherently in media and political commentary. A high number of exclusions in a school may be used to illustrate both a high level of discipline, equated with good management, and a total breakdown of discipline, as in the case of The Ridings. The positive portrayal of high excluding schools is evident in reports regarding the death of headteacher Philip Lawrence, lauded for his teaching abilities but also responsible for the exclusion of 60 pupils from his school. More recently, it was reported that a school which had been subject to 'special measures' for nearly two years had taken the drastic action of excluding 18 pupils. The headteacher responsible said that the action 'saddened' him, but also commented that 'there comes a point when you have to make a firm stand against anti-authority behaviour...and send a very loud and clear signal to others' (*Times Educational Supplement* 2000).

The idea that exclusions can represent a commitment to high standards and good discipline is also apparent if we examine news reports relating to exclusion in independent schools – usually termed expulsion in this context. While a succession of headmasters' conferences noted the rise in expulsions in the independent sector, this phenomenon was consistently linked to the use of drugs. In view of independent schools' overtly hard line on drug taking, it was argued that more sympathetic policies should be pursued. At the 1994 conference, for example, headteachers were being urged to be 'flexible' on pupil drug use. Again, in 1995, new guidelines designed to reduce expulsions were introduced. These were intended to help offenders 'kick the habit'. Reference to the relationship between drug use and the increase in exclusions is also mentioned in regard to state schools and it would appear that state schools have equally strict policies on drug use. However, the emphasis in the two debates is significantly different. Not only is no mention made of poor discipline or behaviour as a cause of exclusions at independent schools, but headteachers are being urged to be more lenient in order to reduce the number of exclusions taking place. This contrasts with the focus on poor discipline within high excluding schools in the state sector. In one context, therefore, exclusion is almost perceived as an example of good practice; in the other as evidence of lack of control.

Education policy and services for children looked after

Given that this study is the exclusion from school of children living in public care, it is important to consider some of the implications of shifts in education policy for this group. This may, in turn, help explain why children looked after are disproportionately represented among excluded pupils. It is also necessary to examine these changes in educational policy in the light of shifts in the pattern of services for children living in public care. Most obviously, there has been a dramatic reduction in the number of children looked after in residential care, from over 13,000 in 1987 to half that number in 1998 (DoH 1999). The proportion of children looked after in foster care has, in contrast, remained stable at around 30,000. Children's homes now care predominantly for adolescents, though many local authorities continue to make some provision for younger children under the age of 12 (Berridge and Brodie 1998; Sinclair and Gibbs 1998a). There has also been a shift in the pattern of residential accommodation, including the virtual demise of the voluntary sector of children's homes. Especially relevant to the present study, however, has been the loss of the tier of community homes with education (CHEs). The majority of local authority children's homes no longer provide education on-site. The exception to this trend are private homes, which seem more likely to have their own educational facilities (Sinclair and Gibbs 1998b).

As the number of children looked after in institutions has decreased, it appears to be the case that those left within children's homes and other institutions represent a 'hard core' who present more acute problems than in the past (Gooch 1996). The most common reasons for entry to care among adolescents are behavioural difficulties, the breakdown in relationships at home, and schooling problems (Berridge and Brodie 1998; Sinclair and Gibbs 1998a; Triseliotis et al. 1995). One study, for example, argued that two-thirds of children accommodated in one local authority, and 97 per cent of those living in residential care, showed evidence of psychiatric disorder (McCann and Jones 1996; see also Dimigen et al. 1999). Research also suggests that children living in residential accommodation also present a more complex combination of problems than hitherto (Berridge and Brodie 1998). Consequently, it appears that there is a higher concentration of children in residential care who are likely to experience schooling problems. This stands in tension to the quasi-market education system described above. Additionally, however, it has been argued that specific elements within education legislation conflict with the principles of welfare policy, and in particular the Children Act 1989 (Sinclair 1998; Sinclair, Grimshaw and Garnett 1994).

The Children Act 1989 is concerned with all children 'in need', that is, who are unlikely to achieve or maintain, or have the opportunity of achieving or maintaining, a reasonable standard of health or development without the provision for him of services by a local authority; where a child's health or development is likely to be significantly impaired, or further impaired, without the provision of such services; or where a child is disabled. The term 'development' includes physical, intellectual, emotional, social and behavioural development, and 'health' covers both physical and mental health. Children excluded from school clearly number among those whose intellectual, emotional, social and behavioural development has been impaired and the local authority has a duty to meet these needs, with the help of all relevant services. However, it has been argued that the emphasis in Conservative education policy on competition and achievement marginalised such pupils, and made it more difficult for different agencies to work together. Such collaboration has never been unproblematic; however, the changes which have taken place have resulted in a greater fragmentation of services. This fragmentation has occurred both between and within services, through such innovations as a purchaser-provider split. There are also tensions in the statutory responsibilities of different agencies. The net result is that services have been less likely to assume responsibility for young people presenting a range of problems (Roaf and Lloyd 1995). Under the Labour administration, there has been a shift in emphasis, with the problems associated with social exclusion generally and vulnerable youth in particular assuming a much higher profile, and becoming the subject of a range of policy initiatives. A key element of these has been to improve the way in which agencies work together – for example, the new Youth Offending Teams which include professionals from a range of backgrounds. These are encouraging developments, though at the local authority level many organisational and cultural barriers remain.

Conclusion

This chapter has sought to highlight some of the complexity which surrounds exclusion as a phenomenon. It is plain that there is no single factor which will explain either why children exhibit behaviour which can be described as 'disruptive', or indeed why schools resort to the use of exclusion as a sanction. It is, however, essential that a distinction is made between the different questions being asked in respect of exclusion. To present exclusion as a monolithic issue which can be addressed through a single strand of policy would be deeply misguided.

Schools exclude children for a wide range of reasons, not all of which are related to the young person's behaviour. That said, 'deficit' models (see Pitts 1998), where attention is focused on individual characteristics – such as family background or individual conditions such as ADHD – continue to have currency for educationalists and politicians seeking to explain disruptive behaviour in schools. These may become integrated into wider moral and social discourses regarding the behaviour of young people in society. Exclusion from school, encapsulating as it does a range of issues regarding the behaviour of young people, has been taken by a variety of groups as an indicator of social malaise.

It is no coincidence that exclusion has emerged as a matter of concern at the same time that major changes have taken place in education policy. It is important to remember that the numbers of permanent exclusions taking place in individual schools and local authorities are often very small. The processes which lead to exclusion also seem to be very similar to those documented in earlier research. Identifying what is new about exclusion in the 1990s is not easy. In the present study it is also essential to link changes in the educational context with those which have occurred in the pattern of residential care. The two sets of policies do not appear to be complementary.

This book acknowledges the importance of these wider social and policy frameworks in understanding the dynamics of the exclusion process. In examining the intricate dynamics of the exclusion process, those involved in the study drew on these frameworks in their attempts to explain their own experiences of managing exclusion. The next chapters will elaborate the theoretical approach and methodology of the research, which has sought to unravel some of this complexity.

3

The Research Design

Introduction

Discussion of the development and implementation of a research methodology is invariably wide-ranging, demanding consideration not only of the specific strategies adopted, but also the principles which underpin the research process (Bulmer 1984). As Chapter 1 has indicated, the theoretical stance of this study has important epistemological and methodological implications. In particular, symbolic interactionism emphasises the importance of methods which give precedence to the perspectives of individual actors, thus enabling the theorisation of social processes as occurring through symbolic exchange during interaction.

The theoretical perspective adopted is not, of course, the only consideration when developing a methodology. The topic and the groups being studied inevitably affect the way in which a study is undertaken. In regard to the exclusion from school of children looked after, the context in which the research took place was also important. As Chapters 1 and 2 have shown, exclusion from school has emerged as a matter of considerable public concern in recent years. The long neglected issue of the education of children looked after has also crept up the scale of professional awareness, to the extent that targets for the educational attainment of children in public care are now being developed (DoH 1998b). Consequently the subject of the research coincided with the emerging agendas of social services and education departments in the selected local authorities. While the qualitative nature of the study may have sometimes cast doubt on its potential value in practical terms, it was usually recognised that an improved understanding of the issue was essential for the future development of policy.

None of this can detract from the fact that exclusion was, and continues to be, a highly sensitive matter. However, it seemed that the nature of this sensitivity could vary for the different groups involved – namely young people, families, schools and children's homes. Young people are the group most obviously affected by the exclusion. Research evidence suggests that no matter how long the build-up, the interruption to schooling is an emotionally difficult one (Hayden 1997; Gersch and Nolan 1994). Caring for an excluded child can place considerable stress on a family, and may even be a significant factor in their entry to care (Hayden 1997;

Cohen *et al.* 1994; Parsons *et al.* 1994). The issue is also a sensitive one for institutions. Schools are often portrayed as anxious to be rid of disruptive and difficult pupils, and their effectiveness assessed on the basis of the numbers of exclusions taking place. However, contrary to the impression sometimes given by official statistics and media coverage, most schools experience only a small number of exclusions each year. For some of the primary schools visited, the case being studied proved to be the first exclusion in which they had ever been involved. The decision to exclude can therefore be an extremely difficult one for headteachers, and the process a stressful one for the entire school.

Other studies have shown that the use of a qualitative approach in the investigation of such issues can be extremely valuable. McKeganey, for example, commenting on qualitative research into drug use, states that such methods are especially useful where the social problem is sensitive for those involved, and where it is important for the purposes of the research question that individuals are able to convey meaning in their own terms (Cunningham-Burley and McKeganey 1990; see also Bloor, 1997). Layder (1993), in his classification of different forms of qualitative research, notes that qualitative methods have been fruitfully applied to the study of social problems in what he terms 'information gathering approaches'. He suggests that these studies do not aim to produce detailed ethnographic studies, but focus on segments of society or social processes about which there is a lack of information (p.47). In relation to the study of exclusion, while the individual characteristics which correlate with exclusion seem to be well established, there has been an absence of more detailed probing regarding the circumstances of social groups which are most vulnerable to being excluded. A theoretical approach which permits the contextualisation of individual experiences is helpful in this respect.

The present study has sought to contextualise children's experience of exclusion not only within the school, but also in relation to the children's homes. Unfortunately studies which seek to 'appreciate' the world of the pupil (Furlong 1985), have usually carried out their observations within the institution of the school, and consequently have not always made explicit links with the experiences of pupils outside the school gates. This study tries to capture something of the dynamic relationship between the experience of being looked after and that of being excluded, and how children perceive their experiences within these settings. Children's experiences of care may usefully be considered as a 'career', that is, a dynamic process in which young people who make the transition from a family setting to one of public care are engaged in the negotiation and renegotiation of their relationships with families, peers and carers. The options available at each stage of this career will, however, be informed by what has gone before (Millham, Bullock and Hosie and Haak 1986). This is also true of the choices available in relation to education, which will often be linked to the circumstances of the care placement (Fletcher-Campbell and Hall 1990).

This chapter explains in greater detail the methods used in this study and the principles underlying these. It begins by outlining the background to the study and the children's homes used. It then explains in greater detail the negotiation of access to the relevant agencies and the maintenance of field relationships during the study. The dissemination of research findings was an important component in this. The discussion will then turn to the specific strategies used, namely case studies, interviewing and use of documentary sources. In view of the involvement of children in this study, consideration of issues relating to research with young people is a crucial part of this. Finally, the methods used for the analysis of the data will be examined. It is important to point out that the research process itself may be regarded as an important source of data, and the issues arising from this have considerable relevance in relation to the final analysis.

Background

As Chapter 1 has explained, the potential for a study of the exclusion from school of children looked after by local authorities to be undertaken first became apparent while undertaking research for a national study of children's homes (Berridge and Brodie 1998). Although the research into exclusion was conducted separately, it was practically advantageous to build on existing relationships with local authorities and private agencies. This study was therefore carried out in six children's homes used by two local authorities which had participated in the children's homes research. The cases of 17 children 'excluded' from school were examined in depth through interviews with young people, social workers, teachers and other relevant professionals and through documentary evidence. Information was also collected from these individuals regarding their views on exclusion more generally, for example, if they found they were working with more excluded young people and if so, the reasons for this.

Three homes were located in a county authority in the south-west of England (Local Authority 1), and four were homes used by an inner London borough (Local Authority 2). Two of these were located in another local authority in the south-east (Local Authority 3). However, it should be emphasised that attention focused on Local Authorities 1 and 2 as the authorities with responsibility for the welfare of the young people. Although Local Authority 1 is a largely rural county, the three homes studied were based in its main city. The authorities selected varied considerably in terms of their social structure and it was felt that this would contribute to the diversity of the eventual sample and offer some scope for comparison. Local Authority 2 has a large minority ethnic population and, given the evidence that children from some minority ethnic groups are at particular risk of exclusion, it was thought to be important that there was an opportunity within the research design for such groups to be represented.

In Local Authorities 1 and 2 concerns had increased regarding both exclusion and the education of children looked after. The difficulties associated with understanding trends in the numbers of permanent exclusions taking place are evident when data from the two local authorities being studied is considered. In Local Authority 1 the number of exclusions taking place had risen considerably in the period between 1991/92 and 1995/96. As Figure 3.1 demonstrates, this rise had not been a steady one with dips in 1992/93 and 1993/94 and to this extent the pattern of exclusions in Local Authority 1 did not conform to national data. The increase between 1993/94 and 1994/95 was, however, considerable. In terms of specific trends, close parallels can be seen with the upward trend identified nationally. However, while recognising the increase in the number of permanent exclusions and expressing concern over this, a report by the Chief Education Officer also pointed out that the increase in the authority was half the national average.

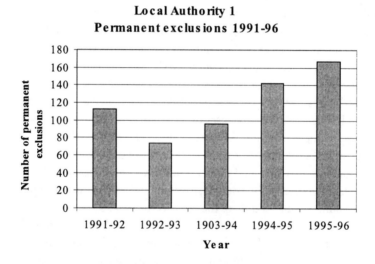

**Local Authority 1
Permanent exclusions 1991-96**

Figure 3.1 Total number of permanent exclusions in Local Authority 1 1991–96

In Local Authority 2 the picture is also somewhat uneven. As Figure 3.2 shows, a small increase in 1994–95 is followed by a considerable fall in numbers in 1995–96. As this was a London borough, concerns about exclusion were influenced strongly by their geographical location. In particular, there was some irritation regarding relationships with adjoining boroughs, specifically the difficulties in finding school places for children resident in this authority but excluded from schools in other boroughs. This problem was made particularly acute by the fact that the authority had several grant-maintained and single-sex schools, which tended to have more restrictive admissions criteria.

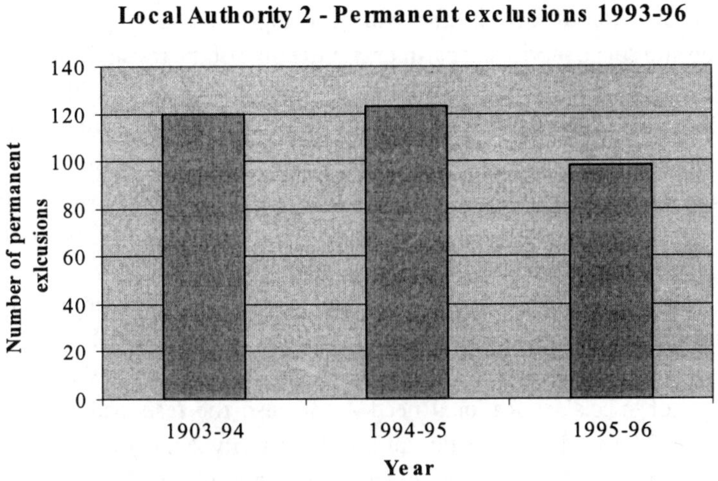

Local Authority 2 - Permanent exclusions 1993-96

Figure 3.2 Total number of permanent exclusions in Local Authority 2 1993–96

In terms of residential accommodation for children looked after, it is important to explain that Local Authority 2 had taken the decision to contract out its residential care to private agencies, with the exception a short-break home for disabled children. This was one of the four homes included in the study, while the remaining three were private facilities.

In terms of location, then, the homes were distributed as follows:

Local Authority 1	**Local Authority 2**	**Local Authority 3**
Home A	Home D	Home F
Home B	Home E	Home G
Home C		

The location of the six homes clearly had logistical implications for the management of the study. For example, the distances involved meant that it was not always possible to meet immediately with individuals on being notified that an exclusion had taken place. More important, however, were the different organisational structures operating in each authority to which access had to be gained.

The local authority arrangements for looked after children were very different. The children's homes studied in Local Authority 1 were all located in its main city, which made for considerable cohesion both in respect to care for looked after children and school exclusions. Although not always in agreement, the different agencies involved had mostly amicable working relationships, and systems of information gathering and liaison were perceived to work well on the whole. The education of children looked after had been high on the agenda of both the education and social services departments at the time of the research. The death of a young man in a joy-riding incident during 1994, while he was resident in Home A, had led to a report which highlighted the fact that the adolescent had been out of school when the incident occurred. The effect of this on professionals working in the city was evident in the frequency with which the incident was mentioned during interviews as part of this research. A joint education/social services working party had been established to examine the issue.

Organisation regarding looked after children was especially complex in regard to young people looked after by Local Authority 2 who were living in Local Authority 3 and whose education – if they were attending school or had statements of special educational need – was also the responsibility of Local Authority 3. The available statistics for Local Authority 2 suggested that in 1996 232 children were looked after outside the borough in 22 different local authorities, including children living in both foster and residential care. It should be noted that this does not include children placed in other London boroughs. The basis of these figures is also uncertain and it is possible that they over- or under-estimate the numbers of children involved. During the course of the research it consistently proved impossible to obtain up-to-date information regarding the educational placements of children looked after. Nor was any information held centrally about those residential placements which were known to exist.

In a report on the education of children looked after, the borough acknowledged some of the difficulties, noting that in the absence of a joint monitoring system maintained by the social service and education departments, some children looked after outside the borough had become unknown to the records of the education department. Consequently, neither department had a centrally held record of the school placements – and, of course, exclusions – of looked after children. This would be serious even if only a minority of children were concerned; in view of the numbers involved it is somewhat alarming. The issue was further complicated by the reorganisation of social work teams which placed greater emphasis on local area teams and reduced the amount of liaison and co-ordination between those teams. Furthermore, if a child was not allocated to a social worker, however, one could not be confident that anyone within the local authority would be conversant with arrangements for the individual's education. This was highlighted during one of the researcher's visits to the officer recently given responsible for liaising between social services and education in the borough, when she was able to inform him that one of the children's homes used by the borough had an educational unit on-site, a fact not apparently recorded. However, in recognition of the problem, a priority for the social services/education liaison officer was the setting up of a database for children looked after, to which both education and social services could have access.

Children's homes

Some introduction is also required to the children's homes where the young people were resident when the research took place.

Local Authority 1

Home A — a home catering for adolescents, situated on a council estate on the edge of the local authority's largest city. Six of the sample — Alex, Brian, Carl, David, Eddie and Hugh — lived in this home. Hugh had only recently moved there following a short placement in Home C.

Home B — this home catered for younger children, usually those who had experienced some form of abuse or who were being prepared for placement in foster care. Fred and Jack were both resident there, and Graham had also experienced two placements in Home B prior to his placement in Home C.

Home C — the aims and purpose of this home were very similar to Home B, and the two were closely linked organisationally. Of particular importance to this study was the fact that the two homes shared an educational co-ordinator. Ian and Graham lived in this home.

Local Authority 2

It must be remembered that Local Authority 2 had no residential accommodation of its own, with the exception of Home D, which provided short breaks for disabled children. Residential care was therefore provided by private agencies both inside the borough and beyond.

Home D — this home was situated within Local Authority B and offered short-term breaks for young people with severe learning disabilities and other health needs. Omar and Roland were both cared for here, though in many respects their educational experiences differed significantly from the other children who came to Home D.

Home E — this was one of several homes operated by an expanding private agency and situated within the borough. It catered for both adolescents and younger children, usually with severe behavioural difficulties, and offered a number of specialist therapeutic services including play and art therapy. Lewis had been resident here for four years.

Home F – Home F and Home G were both part of another large private agency, located in the south-east of England (Local Authority 3). It is important to note that this agency had established two educational units which provided schooling for a high proportion of residents. Places were also sold out to other private children's homes. Home F was formerly a large villa, situated in the countryside, which catered for younger children, most of whom had experienced abuse of some kind. Lee and Michael lived here, and Paul (Lee's elder brother) had lived here before moving to Home G.

Home G – this was based in the seaside town close to Home F, and provided for adolescents. As with Home F, most of these young people came from London boroughs. Nicki and Paul lived here.

The inclusion of Home D – the short-breaks home – in the sample should perhaps be given some explanation. The majority of children receiving care from this home were attending school. Most were physically disabled and/or had a severe learning disability. Exclusion from school, at least in the sense of official procedures, does not appear to have been a problem for this group, and it was not intended that the home should be part of this study, though the researcher had links with the home arising from the children's homes research (see below). In the course of discussion with the head of home, it was commented that exclusions did occur, albeit in a small number of cases. It was decided that as the focus of the study was on children excluded from school and living in residential care, there was no reason why children from Home D should be omitted. The Children Act 1989 includes disabled children, and local authority homes providing care for this group are governed by the Children's Homes Regulations (DoH 1989). Young people were as much affected by the interface between different agencies as children living in other kinds of children's homes. Eventually two cases were selected, though interestingly neither of these involved children whom staff in Home D considered 'typical' of their usual residents. The experiences of these young people proved extremely helpful in the development of this study's conceptual framework regarding exclusion (see Chapters 7 and 8).

Gaining access

The process of gaining access to the local authorities and the seven homes deserves some further discussion. Most empirical social research requires, to a greater or lesser extent, access to groups of individuals or organisations. However, this is not only a matter of obtaining permission to carry out the research; positive field relationships must also be sustained throughout the period of study.

The negotiation of access is often the most delicate dimension of the research process. This is especially true in qualitative research, which tends to be characterised by a closer relationship between researcher and researched (Bryman 1988a). It is doubtful, therefore, whether it can be 'left to chance' (Bryman

1988b), especially when the research can be described as sensitive. In view of the fact that permission was being requested for access to confidential information relating to children, as well as to interview young people, attention to ethical issues was essential (Alderson 1995). Initially managers in all three local authorities were approached and their agreement to the research obtained. The researcher's background was subjected to a police check and all adult participants were issued with a copy of this, together with letters of authorisation from social services and education departments. It was explained in a letter from the researcher and again at the point of interview that participation was voluntary and that confidentiality and anonymity were assured, with the exception of any case where it became clear that a child was being harmed. These efforts appeared to be appreciated by the adults involved. Some went further, checking with senior officers in their agencies that it was acceptable to participate. During the interview process itself, many asked for further reassurances regarding confidentiality before divulging information they defined as sensitive.

The initial stages of this study were greatly eased by its association with the wider study of children's homes (Berridge and Brodie 1998). The researcher was known to individuals – including some children – in five of the six homes, and had previously undertaken four days participant observation in two of these. Good field relationships also existed with the proprietors and heads of home in the two private agencies. Although this was a distinct and separate piece of research, managers in the children's homes tended to perceive the study of exclusions as a continuation of earlier work.

However, negotiation of access had still to be undertaken with educational agencies in the two authorities. In Local Authority 1 this proved relatively straightforward: existing organisational structures were efficient and officials from the LEA were helpful in securing rapid agreement to the research. Meetings were held first with the assistant education officer, who continued to be an important link throughout the research, and later with representatives of the local association of secondary headteachers, who in turn provided authorisation for the research.

In Local Authority 2 the situation was rather more complex, again due to the nature of organisation and specifically changes in the personnel and structure of the LEA during the period of the research. As individuals moved around the hierarchy, new relationships had to be built with their replacements. More important, and more revealing, however, were the nature of the links between the LEA and the residential care being used by the authority. This chapter has already that, with the exception of the single short-break home for disabled children, this was contracted out to private agencies. As it was anticipated that access to schools in Local Authority 3 would also be required, further negotiations with this LEA were also necessary. The lack of geographical and organisational coherence rendered the research process more complex and time-consuming, but was important in indicating the potential difficulties experienced by local authorities when using large numbers of private placements outside the county or borough. Equally, however, the need to negotiate with individual schools as well as with the LEA may be an indication of the changes wrought by local management of schools and, consequently, the increased independence of individual institutions.

Gaining access to an organisation does not, however, necessarily ease the forging of relationships with individual participants. In general, the latter was much more difficult. Local authority departments are notoriously subject to frequent re-organisations, often making it difficult to track down individuals with sufficient information to talk about a case. When individuals were identified as eligible for participation, arranging interviews proved highly time-consuming and often frustrating. This was true both of schools and social work offices. Difficulties in making contact were significantly greater in Local Authority 2, and were again related to frequent changes in personnel and the lack of clear organisational structures. The restructuring of social work teams during the period of the research proved especially problematic.

Obviously one must be cautious in generalising from those experiences, but sometimes these difficulties seemed to mirror those of children's homes. Residential staff in the three private homes where children from Local Authority 2 were placed complained bitterly about the problems they experienced in making contact with social workers. Equally, it is possible to empathise with the young person who commented regarding his social worker that 'she's never in'. Schools could be equally difficult to contact, despite the unfailing helpfulness of the majority of secretaries. In one case 16 phone calls and messages failed to reach a deputy headteacher. It would seem that the time spent in trying to make contact and the frustration engendered by repeated failure in this can help explain not only the many delays which emerge as significant in the exclusion process, but also individuals' perceptions of other agencies. Outright refusals to participate in the study were, however, rare and usually understandable. One school in Local Authority 2 refused access on the grounds that they were already participating in five other university or college research projects. Access to one children's home was also delayed for several weeks due to changes in management.

In negotiating access it was important for the researcher to be able to offer something in exchange for permission to carry out the work. This is perhaps especially important when a study focuses upon a social problem such as exclusion. A clear dissemination strategy is therefore important, and in this study both agencies were anxious that emerging results would be regularly fed into their decision-making processes. In Local Authority A regular meetings were held with the assistant education officer and representatives of the local headteachers' committee. In Local Authority 2 there were fewer clear channels of communication. However, updates on the progress of the study were directed to the education/social services liaison officer. In the latter stages of the study, all adult interviewees received a summary of research findings. In addition, more general dissemination was carried out via conference presentations and articles. This may also be important to those participating in the research in terms of indicating the status or the public profile of the research. Dissemination to children was more problematic. Some children had moved to other placements, one or two had returned home and one young man had, sadly, died following a move to another residential institution. It was eventually decided that no further contact would be made. Children did, however, receive a letter/card thanking them for participating in the research and also had the option of having a copy of the workbook questionnaire/interview schedule returned to them.

Methods

Case study

A case study approach was adopted for the study of the exclusion process. It is perhaps most helpful to see this as the organising strategy for the research, in the sense that case studies can incorporate a variety of methods (Yin 1994). However, it has been argued that this approach is useful in contextualising phenomena, especially where the boundaries between phenomenon and context are unclear (Stake 1995; Yin 1994). In the study of exclusion, where the nature of the relationship between the exclusion and the contexts of school and children's home has been uncertain, this strategy is therefore a helpful one. Use of case studies enables more in-depth examination and analysis of the exclusion process, and the value of such detailed information on specific cases has been illustrated by other work relating to exclusion more generally (Hayden 1997; Parsons *et al.* 1994). In addition, the use of a range of case studies, as in this research, also offers the potential to examine the way in which the exclusion process operates within a series of different contexts – that is, different local authorities, children's homes and schools as well as the varying circumstances of individual young people.

It was decided that 10 cases from each local authority would be selected, including children of both primary and secondary school age. These were identified via information gathered during the children's homes study and through contact with staff in the individual homes. It should be emphasised that, in accordance with the study's focus on the exclusion process, the concern was not to obtain a 'representative' sample. The aim of the study was to collect sufficiently detailed information on the exclusions of these young people in order to build up a picture of the different ways in which the exclusion process operates in relation to children looked after in residential accommodation. Diversity was, therefore, considered to be advantageous, both in relation to the individuals and the types of residential accommodation in which they were living. Nevertheless, the group shared many of the characteristics which research has shown to be common to excluded pupils – for example, in regard to gender and special educational needs.

Criteria for inclusion in the study, as outlined in access meetings and letters to children's homes, were the young person's permanent exclusion within the last 12 months. The researcher established links with an individual at each home and kept in regular phone contact regarding the current residents. However, the generation of the sample proved unexpectedly difficult. Cases were initially very slow to emerge. This was sometimes due to fairly practical matters, notably the care careers of young people which meant that some children changed placement or returned home quickly. Gradually, however, it became evident that significant difficulties surrounded use of the term 'exclusion'. Some of the cases referred were found to involve young people who were out of school but were not attending for other reasons. In another case the head of home insisted that a young person had not been excluded, yet on further questioning and examination of documentation from the school it seemed to the researcher that exclusion, albeit not in any official form, had indeed taken place. Residential staff appeared uncertain as to the boundaries of 'exclusion' and their definitions frequently did not cohere with those contained in official policies. It was evident, then, that the recent introduction of the term 'exclusion' did not prevent individuals from using the same language to describe quite different phenomena. It also became clear, as Stirling's (1992) work had previously shown, that 'exclusion' may be effected by a variety of informal means. The theoretical significance of this point will be developed in Chapter 7.

At this point several options appeared to be available. One of these was to retain the original criteria – i.e. official exclusion as demonstrated by a letter from the child's school within the last 12 months. However, this seemed to be at odds with the theoretical approach of the study, which emphasised the definitions of those involved. Yet it seemed that to widen the net to include all forms of non-attendance would extend the scope of the study to an unacceptable degree. As earlier discussion has shown (see Chapter 1), exclusion has assumed a recognisable public face. In this study it was important to capture the way in which macro issues were evident in the micro process of exclusion. This focus could be lost by examination of, for example, truancy. These difficulties are possibly inherent in research where existing empirical data is relatively scanty. Although residential staff had reported that exclusion represented a 'major' problem in their work, and while the vulnerability of this group to exclusion (especially informal) was noted in earlier work (Stirling 1992), other reports available at the beginning of this study acknowledged the difficulties of obtaining 'hard' information (for example, DfE 1994a; Bennathan 1993).

In view of these issues, it was decided that the study would continue to seek cases of young people permanently excluded from school as demonstrated by the existence of a formal letter of exclusion from a headteacher, as required by official guidance (DfE 1994a). However, cases of 'informal' exclusion would also be examined if one of the parties involved considered that the young person had been excluded. In other words, and in accordance with the theoretical approach outlined earlier, it was considered appropriate to accept individuals' definitions of what constituted 'exclusion' and to accept cases on this basis.

It quickly became apparent that the circumstances surrounding informal exclusion are enormously diverse. In relation to this problem it is perhaps helpful to take account of the work of Carlen, Gleeson and Wardhaugh (1992) regarding truancy. In this study a conceptual distinction is made in terms of whether the absence has been condoned and by whom. Thus we have a typology of non-attendance which focuses on the way in which the non-attendance is perceived by the different people involved 'in its production as a social phenomenon' (p.62), such as teachers, pupils, parents and other agencies such as education welfare officers. Absence from school may therefore range from that which is 'officially induced' – absences forced on pupils due to teachers' strikes and the failure of school buildings to meet legal requirements, to that which is 'internal and illicit', which involves absence from school even though the pupil may be recorded as 'present'. This could also apply to exclusion; temporary or permanent exclusions from school fall within the category of absence which is officially induced, while unofficial or informal exclusion would correspond with absence which is 'officially illicit but unofficially condoned'. These definitional issues will be examined in greater detail in Chapter 7.

Ultimately, however, the selection of the sample depended not on 'referrals' from residential staff to the researcher, but on negotiation between these individuals as to whether exclusion had taken place. In some cases, especially in Local Authority 1, the link person would sometimes contact the researcher to discuss whether a young person should or should not be included in the sample. Occasionally the young person was not yet out of school, but it was perceived to be likely that this would occur. While this approach does not correspond to 'objective' sampling procedures, it does accord with the approach taken by this study, namely that exclusion is a negotiated social process. This was clearly reflected in the identification of the sample. While the research process was undoubtedly made more complex by these issues, in retrospect such developments strengthened the theoretical base of the study.

Interestingly, this method did not increase the numbers being included in the sample. It had originally been planned that 20 cases should be included. Fieldwork began in October 1994, but by the end of 1995 this sample had yet to be achieved, even though the number of homes from which cases had been sought increased from four to seven. As personnel changed within the local authorities and children's homes it also became more difficult to sustain field relationships. Eventually, 17 young people were included.

Interviewing professionals

Interviewing was the principal method used in the study. Following the identification of relevant cases, interviews were first of all held with the young person, the head of the residential home and the child's residential key worker. Through these initial contacts, the researcher was furnished with the names of the other individuals who had been important in the educational experience of the young person. In all cases an attempt was made to interview the young person's social worker and a teacher from the school from which they had been excluded. However, the diversity of cases and the circumstances of individuals meant that there were some differences in the range of individuals interviewed for each case.

It had initially been intended to include parents as interviewees, taking social workers advice on whether this was advisable. In the event no parents were interviewed. To some extent this became a practical matter. Evidence already exists regarding the views of families whose children have been excluded, while much less is known about the perceptions of those working with children looked after. In view of the difficulties which emerged in making contact with all interviewees, it therefore seemed best to focus on the care dimension. Additionally, in this particular sample, a high proportion of the young people had also been looked after for several years, making it likely that parents played a less active part in educational issues. In some cases children had only recently renewed contact with one parent following child protection concerns. That said, there are obviously some disadvantages to the exclusion from the study of individuals who play such an important role in relation to their children's education. The perceptions of parents regarding care and educational experiences are also known to be quite different to those held by professionals and young people themselves (Fisher et al. 1986).

Participant observation is often seen as the 'pivotal strategy' of symbolic interactionism, and it is important to explain why this was not deemed appropriate. Observation is clearly attractive in offering the researcher the unparalleled opportunity to learn the shared meanings which construct the relevant social event and to watch the individuals 'in action' with relatively little intervention. However, the nature of the exclusion process seemed to render observation difficult, if not impossible. As it has already been pointed out, exclusion cannot be confined to any single location. While the school is obviously a critical site of interaction, interaction which is relevant to the exclusion may take place in a variety of settings and between a range of individuals. Exclusion is also a lengthy process occurring over time. The researcher intent on observing the exclusion process must therefore decide both what and when to observe.

It should also be stressed that other methods have also been acknowledged to be useful when using an interactionist framework, including semi-structured interviewing, life-histories and documentary sources (Denzin 1992; Plummer 1983; Blumer 1969). Inevitably, use of interviewing as the primary method carried both advantages and disadvantages. It has been pointed out that qualitative interviewing may be more difficult when examining research topics which are highly personal, threatening or confidential (Lee 1993; Brannen 1988). In such interviews the individual is being asked to divulge a considerable amount of personal information, and often to devote significant amounts of time and effort to assisting the researcher (Lee 1993, p.102). As described above, exclusion was potentially threatening for all those involved in the research. This threat was perceived to be considerable for the professionals involved, in that the nature of their involvement could be perceived as a reflection on their professional performance and the extent of their adherence to departmental or institutional policies.

Nevertheless, only five adults refused to be interviewed. Where a reason was given for the refusal, this usually related to lack of time. This is a remarkably small refusal rate given the sensitivity of the topic, and especially in view of the fact that professionals were being asked to discuss individual cases. However, a number of factors related to the nature of the research may explain the high level of co-operation. While sensitive, the overall topic of exclusion was easily recognisable by respondents as an issue requiring research. For some, notably the headteachers of primary schools, the exclusion being studied had been a highly significant and frequently stressful experience which they were anxious to discuss. Dissatisfaction with specific aspects of the exclusion process or social work procedures was also sometimes important. One primary school headteacher agreed to participate because she had not received any further information from social services regarding the outcome of a case which had involved child protection issues. Many expressed great liking for the young people whose cases were being discussed and clearly enjoyed the opportunity to talk about them in a confidential situation – sometimes they seemed to feel that the selection of a particular child conferred a kind of honour. Other participants were extremely conscious of the wider ramifications of exclusion and were pleased to have the opportunity to air their views. For some the enjoyment was obtained through having time outside their normal routine to discuss general issues, such as the secondary school head who remarked 'it's been good to sit and talk about education for an hour' at the end of the interview.

A further complication ensued from the fact that the individuals involved in each case worked with the other professionals being interviewed. Unsurprisingly, interviewees sometimes perceived the work of other agencies and individuals in a critical light. However, their willingness to express these views often depended on the amount of information which the researcher was thought to possess, and the extent to which they were associated with one or other agency. A small number of interviewees asked whom the researcher had interviewed, and occasionally – and in rather embarrassed fashion – asked what these others had told her. It was therefore essential that the researcher was viewed as independent, and that the opinions of other interviewees did not permeate the discussion.

Each interview was, therefore, in this respect a *tabula rasa* on which the interviewee could inscribe their account of the exclusion process. Within a symbolic interactionist framework it is important that the account provided by the individual is recognised as being significant in its own right. The variations in the accounts provided should not be interpreted in terms of bias or accuracy, as this would imply the existence of an objective process of exclusion which could be extracted from the accounts of participants. This means, in turn, that this study does not seek to present an idealised version of the exclusion as experienced by the individual child. This may, however, create certain difficulties when using a case study approach. Silverman (1986) criticises Denzin's (1970) claim that each account is a partial view and, by combining accounts and triangulating methods, a more complete picture can emerge. This view is also implied by this study's aim to explore and contrast participants' explanations for why exclusion occurred. Silverman argues that the sociologist's role is not 'to adjudicate between participants' competing versions' (quoted, p.105), but to understand the purpose and the role served by individual accounts. However, while the potential for the researcher to slip into a positivist paradigm is a real one, Silverman may exaggerate the difficulty. To contrast and even to compare accounts need not necessarily imply that one is preferred to another, but the observation of difference may help contribute to our understanding of the way in which the individual defines a situation.

Interviews were semi-structured in format. In order to ease discussion of the potentially more sensitive individual cases, interviews usually opened with a brief discussion of issues relating to exclusion and the education of young people looked after more generally. Regarding the individual cases, individuals were encouraged to describe the case according to their involvement and their perception of the way in which events had unfolded. Individuals varied greatly in the nature of their involvement with cases. Sometimes their information was second-hand – this was especially true for social workers in Local Authority 2, who were working with cases where there had often been long gaps in social work input and where the young person had been passed around a series of social workers. Interviews were also frequently, if not typically, retrospective and individuals were therefore engaged in a process of summarising and selecting information they perceived to be relevant to the interview situation. The extent and nature of contact with other agencies and the child's family, the individual's perception of the reaction of the young person to the exclusion, and what that individual would want to happen next were among the areas probed. The greatest reluctance appeared to surround questions about other agencies. Teachers were more concerned than other professionals that information was confidential, and on occasion asked for further assurances during the interview.

In total 78 interviews took place. Table 3.1 provides a breakdown of the spread of interviews according to different groups.

Table 3.1 Distribution of interviews and interviewees	
Interviewees	**Numbers of interviews**
Young people	11
Teachers/headteachers*	24
Residential social workers	23
Social workers	13
Other**	7
Total	78

*Includes teachers working in pupil referral units.

**Includes educational psychologists, educational welfare officers, and managers in both education and social services.

The majority of interviews took place in professional settings, specifically social work offices, children's homes and schools, though two were carried out in the homes of interviewees. There are obviously problems associated with interviews which are undertaken in the workplace: interviews were often interrupted by phonecalls, children arriving to show work to the headteacher or a crisis in another part of the children's home or school. Flexibility was therefore essential in order to obtain the information, and some interviews were inevitably more detailed than others. Some key individuals also provided information on a more regular basis – for example, the education support worker in Local Authority 1 provided numerous updates on the progress of young people. Contrary to what is now frequently regarded as standard research practice in qualitative research, the interviews were not tape-recorded. Instead, notes were taken throughout the interviews and written up in further detail as soon as possible afterwards. In one case where time was especially limited, an interviewee requested another interview schedule in order to expand upon her views. It is accepted that transcribed interviews do provide fuller accounts; this must be balanced against the aims and objectives of the research in question, together with the time and resources available. In this study, note-taking did produce detailed information which could be subjected to a qualitative analysis.

Research with young people

As described above, the issue of school exclusion is a highly sensitive one for both the adults and the young people concerned. Awareness of the rights of research participants has increased considerably in recent years; a shift in perspective perhaps best reflected in the description of those being researched as 'participants' rather than 'subjects'. However, the rights of children as research participants have taken rather longer to be recognised. Children are frequently ignored in standard texts on research methods (see, for example, Homan 1991) and in ethical guidelines (see Morrow and Richards 1996 for discussion). They may also be hidden in standard sources of statistical data (Quortrup 1997). Ensuring that these rights are recognised is not easy, and a balance must be sought between 'privacy for confidential data collection and an openness to public scrutiny for the protection of all those involved' (Hazel 1996). Also, while any researcher/researched relationship carries with it some form of inequality (Dean 1996; Finch 1984), research with children has the further dimension of the disparities in power which exist between children and adults (Mauthner 1997; Mayall 1994).

Further efforts were therefore required in order to enable young people to participate fully in the study. Interest in the issue of children's rights within the research process has undoubtedly increased (Ward 1997; Alderson 1995), at least partly as a result of the requirement of the Children Act 1989 that, according to their age and level of understanding, children should be consulted about decisions concerning them. The development of theoretical paradigms (James and Prout 1997) which recognise children as social actors in their own right and which consequently emphasise the centrality of children's own accounts in order to understand their social worlds, has also played a significant role.

However, ensuring that young people are giving informed consent to participate in a study is difficult; for example, children can easily misunderstand explanations regarding how they might withdraw from a study (Pole, Mizen and Bolton 1999). This is perhaps even more difficult when children are living within an institutional context such as a children's home, where they might regularly be required to attend case conferences and meetings with other professionals. In order to protect young people and to demonstrate the bona fide nature of the research, children were approached via their key workers, who were asked to talk to the young people about the study and to provide them with a brief letter of introduction, written in 'child friendly' language, which explained the background to the research and what they would be asked to do. This usually appeared to have taken place and most children were prepared for the interview. In the case of one 10-year-old, the researcher's visit had been written up on a weekly planner in his bedroom. This letter also emphasised that children need not participate if they did not wish to and that information was confidential, unless the young person disclosed that they were being harmed in any way. The researcher gave a second verbal explanation on meeting the young person. As a further safeguard, young people could also choose to have another adult present during the interview, and three younger children requested that their key worker be in the room. Eventually 11 of the 17 children were interviewed. Of the six who did not participate, three refused and in three cases the researcher was advised that, due to the problems surrounding the young person's current educational/home circumstances, professionals preferred that they should not be approached.

As Chapter 1 has noted, research specifically focusing on the views of excluded children and young people – as well as pupils experiencing other kinds of problems at school – is an area of growing interest (Cullingford and Morrison 1996; de Pear and Garner 1996; John 1996; Marks 1995; Gersch and Nolan 1994). As Cooper (1993) comments, it is increasingly recognised that there is a need to take seriously the perceptions of pupils if appropriate responses to disaffection are to be found.

During the interviews questions focused on the exclusion, experiences at school and the nature of the help they had received. It was accepted that children might choose to talk about their families and the problems that had led to their becoming looked after. Some questions were also asked about placement changes and living in a children's home. Most of the interviews took place within the children's home, with the exception of one 17-year-old who was interviewed at the Intermediate Treatment centre he attended. Marks (1996), whose interviews with young people took place within a school setting, comments on the need to ensure that these young people were not further stigmatised by their involvement with her research. This issue was less relevant in this research where some young people – including the peers of the child being interviewed – already knew the researcher. Attention spans tended to be short, and some young people were easily distracted. One adolescent spent a large part of the interview trying to gain access to the desk drawers in the office. A joint interview was carried out with two young men, who tried to persuade the researcher – unsuccessfully – to allow them to smoke in a building where this was not permitted. Such situations are unpredictable, but it is important that researchers seeking to interview young people are aware that the usual canons of interviewing techniques may well prove ineffective. The idea of 'rapport', for example, can assume quite different meaning in such circumstances.

The way in which the relationship between the researcher and young people is negotiated is therefore of considerable importance. Mauthner (1997) notes that the researcher's role can 'take on elements of both teacher and mother figure as disciplinarian and carer – blowing children's noses and filing broken nails' (p.22). Fine and Sandstrom (1988), in their discussion of participant observation with young people, suggest that roles of supervisor, leader, observer and friend are all potentially available. Invariably, the researcher cannot disclaim all responsibility for the young person or persons being studied. However, the way in which she is perceived may have significant implications for the amount and quality of data which is obtained.

In this study it was notable that two of the children who refused to be interviewed had not previously met the researcher. For the five who had done so, she was viewed as a familiar face, and already had a role to which they could relate. Importantly, this included the recognition that she was essentially independent and not a member of staff. In the adolescent home, young people who had already been interviewed sometimes talked to their less enthusiastic peers on my behalf, for example telling them that they could swear during the interview. As McAuley (1996) emphasises, prior preparation is frequently crucial. If this is not possible, sufficiently good working relationships with those close to the child are an important intervening factor.

It was recognised that the interview methods would necessarily have to be modified for younger children. Other researchers have testified to the value of more imaginative methods, including role play, vignettes and story telling formats (Hill 1997 for a general discussion of participatory research with children; Hill, Laybourn and Borland 1996; McAuley 1996). In this study it was decided to retain the format of the semi-structured interview, but to facilitate this a workbook-style questionnaire was developed and piloted with three under-10s, one of whom was assessed as having moderate learning difficulties and another who had been excluded on a fixed-term basis on a number of occasions. The workbook incorporated questions about the same areas covered in the interview schedule for adolescents; that is, regarding the child's likes and dislikes about school, friends and teachers as well as their account of the exclusion. The key difference was in presentation and the participatory format; children were given the option about whether to write/draw in the booklet themselves or have the researcher do this on their behalf. 'Face pictures' were also used to help children describe feelings about school and about their exclusion. Young people generally enjoyed the booklet, and it was successful in holding the attention of children whose key workers had predicted would not be able or willing to participate. It is doubtful whether the same amount of data could have been elicited using standard interviewing methods, and it is possible that similarly imaginative techniques could have been effective with some less articulate adolescents.

During both the more standard interviews and the workbook-based sessions, it became apparent that the researcher had to probe carefully the meanings which young people attributed to their experiences. Not only may children and adolescents have different meaning systems to adults, but some of the concepts involved – most obviously, 'being excluded' – can be described very differently. For example, in some schools exclusion can mean being sent to work in a different building. Such probing is not easy; in a discussion with a none too articulate adolescent it may be tempting to accept at face value the 'Yes' supplied or even to interpret facial expressions as having a particular meaning. Discussion of the pictures used in the workbook was also important; this quickly became obvious when a face picture the researcher included on the grounds it suggested 'sadness', a child described as 'angry'.

Documentary information

While interviews constituted the main method used in the study, it is important to explain the role given to information collected from documentation. The main source in this aspect of the research were the case files of individual young people. These were usually located in children's homes; in some cases, however, social workers held additional information to which they provided access. Other research has found the case files of children looked after to be poorly organised and often lacking in important information. For example, Farmer and Pollock (1998) express concern at the frequent absence of information relating to children's experience of sexual abuse and/or abusing behaviour. The lack of educational records, such as evidence of assessment for special educational needs, has also been noted (Jackson 1987; but see Berridge et al. 1997).

In the 17 cases studied here, the situation was highly variable, with the education sections of some files overflowing with documents while others were practically non-existent. Generally it seemed that the information available on the education of these young people was somewhat better than is true for the majority of children looked after; this can be attributed to the complexity and problematic nature of many of these cases. It is important to acknowledge, though, that the amount of information was not necessarily an indication of the quality of record-keeping. It must be recognised that files have developed over time, and the fact that a variety of individuals have been involved in their compilation. Where the care history of the young person had been lengthy, and changes of placement frequent, documents and information often appeared to have been lost along the way. This was especially true of young people from Local Authority 2 living outside the borough, for whom there was often no written documentation regarding which schools they had attended and the number of reason for their exclusion. It must be recognised that case files, however useful, are constructed through a social process which will involve decisions about what should be included and what can be omitted (Packman, Randall and Jaques 1986). This information should not, therefore, be regarded as 'objective' any more than the interview accounts of individuals.

Even where the information was limited, case file information was useful in making chronological sense of the narratives of individuals, providing details of times, dates and the names of relevant individuals. This data also provided a useful reference point for comments made by interviewees, for example regarding the details of statements of SEN. It is important to note that, during interviews, some individuals also made use of the information from case files in order to help fill gaps in memory or even knowledge. It was interesting to observe that this information sometimes proved new and/or surprising to these individuals and caused them to speculate on the difference in the picture of the young person portrayed there.

In addition to case file information, documentation was also collected relating to the policies operated by schools and local authorities relating to exclusion. This information was usually patchy; however, it is notable that during the period of the research both local authorities introduced initiatives relating to the education and/or exclusion of young people looked after. School brochures and other publicity material was also helpful in terms of contextualising the information provided by teachers and other educational staff.

Methods of analysis

Qualitative data is not easy to analyse, mainly because researchers taking this approach reject the view that data is not neutral or representative of an 'objective' social world. Rather it has been subject to multiple processes of interpretation, on the part of the researcher, the researched and many other unnamed individuals who have contributed to the construction of documentation or providing information to research participants about the subject matter. Silverman (1993) comments that the primary issue for researchers working in the tradition of symbolic interactionism is 'to generate data which give an authentic insight into people's experiences' (p.91). Even while methods of data collection are recognised themselves as involving a symbolic interaction between the researcher and the research participants or documents, this does not discount the possibility that knowledge of the social world beyond the interaction can be obtained (Miller and Glassner 1997).

The data produced by this study primarily took the form of accounts of children's experiences of exclusion, together with further, more general, individual views about the problem of exclusion as it affects schools and children's homes. It was decided that this should be analysed manually, rather than by using – as is increasingly the case – a computer package such as NUDIST. Although such packages are considered to have several advantages, including greater ease in the retrieval of data and management of information, concerns have also been expressed – for example that the researcher can be distanced from her data. Others (see, for example, Buston 1997) argue that the question of whether use of computer packages is positive or negative is less important than that the researcher is aware of the analytical process and is clear on the various stages of this (Mason 1996). In the present study it did not seem that there were any particular advantages to a computer-aided analysis and that the amount of data, though substantial, was amenable to manual analysis.

Following the 'grounded theory' approach described by Glaser and Strauss (1967), the view was taken that there should be an ongoing, dialectical relationship between the emerging data and the development of theoretical categories. Throughout the research process there were different kinds of questions to be asked which contributed to the development of these categories: for example about the the chronology of the exclusion process and how this related to policy, who took decisions and with reference to which agencies, when contact was made and not made between professionals. Crucially, however, the research was interested in finding out how individuals interpreted the exclusion process and the meanings they attached to different elements in this.

Although the study began with some ideas about the issues which could be important, the grounded theory approach emphasises that data should not be forced or selected to fit pre-conceived or pre-existent categories (Strauss and Corbin 1990). Instead there was an interplay between the aims of the research and new issues which emerged as the data accumulated.

One problem in the analysis, resulting from the case study approach, was how to retain a focus on the experience of each child while developing analysis of individual explanations about the problem of exclusion in the local authority and national context. Themes were therefore identified within interviews and also across each case. These themes related to issues which emerged consistently from the data. This does not, of course, mean that the opinions of participants were identical, but rather that these were recurrent issues which interviewees themselves defined as important. Thus, for example, professionals did not always agree that there had been an increase in the number of exclusions taking place, but consistently expressed concern at the effects of local management of schools (LMS) on the ability of schools to work with troublesome pupils. Additionally, these themes often overlapped with aspects of the research process, such as the difficulty in identifying a sample. There was consequently an interaction between the views of participants and the experience of the researcher. To this extent, it would be mistaken to suggest that the coding of themes was driven 'purely' by the data, thus highlighting the multi-layered processes of interpretation which contribute to the analysis of qualitative data.

Once initial themes were identified and coded, these were further sub-categorised. Thus, for example, 'admission to schools problematic' could be sub-divided to make the further categories 'private homes: absence of links with schools'; 'concentration of looked after children'; 'stigma of looked after children'. Some of these themes were descriptive, for example relating to the educational or care experiences or young people prior to exclusion, while others – for example the issue of how exclusion is defined (see Chapter 7) – were more abstract. As themes were developed, the task of the researcher is to identify the relationship between the different categories.

Conclusion

Methodologically this study might be criticised in that it follows the well-trodden path of symbolic interactionists in maintaining an interest in those on the receiving end of policy making, groups which to a lesser or greater extent could be viewed as disadvantaged in this process (see Dean 1996). In focusing on the exclusion process as it operates within and between schools, children's homes and other services it could be argued that the management or mismanagement of exclusion at the 'grass roots' is emphasised at the expense of processes at higher levels of management and policy making. Meanwhile these policy makers have shown themselves anxious to disclaim responsibility and to place this on the shoulders of 'failing' schools (see, for example, OFSTED 1998a) and social services. However, the research process itself has shown that the definitions held by the individuals responsible for managing the exclusion are variable and, consequently, may have considerable significance in terms of the management of the young person's experience. This proved to be an important starting point for the analysis of the data, and perhaps contributed to a more wide-ranging analysis than would otherwise have been possible.

4

The Young People

Introduction

Having outlined the theoretical and methodological background to this study it is now necessary to introduce in greater detail the 17 young people whose experiences of 'exclusion' formed the basis of this research. While it is important to stress that this is not a representative sample, the characteristics of the group will be considered in relation to other evidence regarding excluded pupils and children looked after. This general information provides an important backcloth to the more detailed analysis and discussion of the main body of data which will be presented in subsequent chapters.

As Chapter 3 has explained, information about the sample was obtained through social work files and, where details were missing, by asking social workers and carers. Unfortunately, these methods did not always prove sufficient and there were aspects of the histories of the young people – usually in respect to their schooling and specifically regarding the previous exclusions which they had experienced – which eventually had to be labelled 'unknown'. In accordance with other research findings (Berridge and Brodie 1998; Berridge *et al.* 1997; Triseliotis *et al.* 1995; Fletcher-Campbell and Hall 1990), the amount and quality of information contained in the education sections of the files of this sample varied greatly.

The young people

The 17 young people studied were in many respects a diverse group, but nevertheless shared many of the characteristics which other research has identified as being common to excluded pupils. Table 4.1 summarises details of age, ethnicity and educational background, including – where available – previous fixed-term and permanent exclusions.

Table 4.1 Details of age, ethnicity and educational
backgrounds of the sample studied

Case	Age at interview	Ethnicity	Assessed as requiring a Statement of SEN*	Previous fixed-term exclusions	Previous permanent exclusions	School from which most recently excluded
Alex	13	White	No	3	None	Mainstream
Brian	15	White	No	None known	None	Mainstream
Carl	16	White	No	1	None	Mainstream
David	15	White	No	None known	2	Mainstream
Eddie	16	White	Yes	1	1	Mainstream
Fred	10	White	Yes	1	None	Mainstream
Graham	9	White	Yes	2	1	Mainstream
Hugh	13	White	Yes	1	1	EBD day
Ian	10	White	No	1	None	Mainstream
Jack	7	White	Yes	None known	1	EBD day
Kris	16	African-Caribbean	Yes	None known	2	EBD day
Lee	11	White	Yes	None known	None	EBD day
Michael	6	African-Caribbean	Pending	1	None	Mainstream
Nicki	13	White	No	None known	None known	Mainstream
Paul	15	White	No	None known	None	Mainstream
Omar	7	African-Caribbean	No	None known	None	Mainstream
Roland	15	White	No	None known	None	FE College

*At the time the research was initiated, the Code of Practice on the Identification and Assessment of Special Educational Needs (DfE 1994b) was in the process of being implemented. The special educational needs of this group had therefore been assessed under different arrangements, and it is therefore, unfortunately, necessary to restrict details of special educational needs to possession of a Statement.

As the table shows, all the group were male, with ages ranging from six to 16. Throughout the period of the research, no cases of excluded girls were identified. As Chapter 1 has explained, it is now well established that a much smaller number of girls are excluded from school, though it is also true that less attention has been given by researchers and policy makers to the experiences of girls who have been excluded (Hayden 1997). Fourteen of the group were white and three – all from Local Authority 2 – African-Caribbean. One young man, also from Local Authority 2, was Portuguese and English was not his first language. The absence of any pupils from minority ethnic groups in Local Authority 1 is a reflection of the ethnic composition of that authority.

In regard to the nature of the exclusions experienced by the group, it is important to remember that the definition of exclusion being adopted in this study encompassed both 'formal' and 'informal' exclusions (see Chapter 3). This means that the most recent exclusions of the children and young people studied had not necessarily been 'officially' excluded according to the procedures outlined in Circular 10/94 (DfE 1994a), though they might have been excluded in this way at some other point in their educational careers. In terms of the most recent exclusion, eight of the sample had a letter of official exclusion held in a social work or children's home file, though this was not always seen by the researcher and may therefore be an under-/over-estimate.

In all the cases studied it was clear that, without exception, all the young people had disrupted schooling histories, and 11 of the 17 had experienced a previous exclusion on either a fixed-term or permanent basis. This may well be an underestimate, as carers and social workers were frequently unclear about the details of previous exclusions and files were also lacking in such information. Exclusions were also frequently referred to in euphemistic terms, such as being 'sent home' or 'cooling off'. Even so, this is a very high proportion and an indication of the seriousness of the educational problems many of the young people were perceived to present prior to their most recent exclusion. It is clearly a matter of concern that children who had already experienced fixed-term and permanent exclusions did not yet have a school place appropriate to their needs. Unfortunately there is an absence of comparative information on the extent to which exclusion from one school increases the likelihood of exclusion from another. However, as the stories of these 17 young people unfold in the rest of the study, it will be possible to see how different experiences of being out of school interact.

Using the broad definition of exclusion, the majority had been excluded from mainstream schooling, six from secondary and five from primary schools. Exclusions had occurred at almost every stage, with some children excluded very early in their primary school careers. However, three – two from Local Authority 1 and one from Local Authority 2 – had been excluded from schools for children with emotional and behavioural difficulties (EBD). Another had been excluded from a school for children with MLD (moderate learning difficulties) which was based in Local Authority 3. One 16-year-old with MLD and whose first language was not English had been excluded from a college of further education. While the evidence is sparse, it seems that exclusions from 'special schools' have increased, apparently in response to the same trends which generated an increase in exclusions from mainstream education (Association of Metropolitan Authorities 1995; DfE 1995; Stirling 1991). However, exclusion from a special school can be especially serious in that other forms of provision – such as PRUs – are not always willing to accept young people whose needs have already been recognised as requiring special expertise. Hugh and Kris had already been excluded from mainstream secondary schools before their exclusion from EBD day schools.

Seven had statements of SEN for EBD at the time of their exclusion, and in Michael's case a statement for EBD had been pending. This raises a number of questions, most obviously why exclusion occurred if statements were in place or assessment ongoing. Assessment for SEN and where appropriate the provision of extra support for a pupil is intended to prevent later exclusion (DfE 1994a; DfE 1994b). The fact that these pupils were later excluded could be taken to mean either that they displayed such extreme behaviour that schools felt they had no choice but to exclude, or that the extra support provided through the statement came too late or was deemed inadequate.

The relationship between exclusion and the assessment of SEN is a complex one. For this group of young people, the degree of mobility which most had experienced in their school careers was also potentially significant in terms of whether the assessment process had been initiated and in ensuring that the provisions of a statement were in place. In a small number of cases, young people had experienced an extremely high level of disruption in their schooling. Alex and Fred, for example, had experienced many changes of school due to their fathers having service careers. Fred – aged 10 – thought he had attended 10 schools, but while his social worker was aware he had moved around a great deal, it was impossible to corroborate any of the details. Assessments had been started in several schools but had never been completed. Consequently, in his final year of primary school, he was still without a statement and the support he needed.

Care careers

Changes in care placement were also important, and Table 4.2 provides a summary of these. Discussion of the education of children in care has frequently stressed the disruption which may ensue when changes in care placement also mean a change of school (Fletcher-Campbell and Hall 1990; Berridge 1985). For example, in their survey of 400 children looked after in both foster and residential care, Fletcher-Campbell and Hall set the educational careers of young people against their care histories. Over a third of the children in this sample had experienced changes of school for reasons other than routine transfer from primary to middle or secondary school.

One consequence of a disrupted care history can also be that important information, including that relating to schooling, is lost along the way. This was certainly true for Nicki, whose educational history had effectively vanished. The records which existed indicated only that he had attended a primary school just prior to entering care at age eight, and that he had been enrolled in a secondary school for some three weeks, but had only attended for a few days. On re-entering mainstream school aged 13 it seemed almost inevitable that there would be problems. In other cases more details were available. Eddie had attended three primary schools and was to be excluded from his third secondary school. Hugh had attended five primary schools, and remained at only two of these for more than a year. Meanwhile he moved between his mother, other relatives and a series of foster placements.

Table 4.2 Details of the care histories of the sample

Case	Length of current care episode	Number of foster placements	Number of residential placements (including current)	Legal status	Reasons for entry to care
Alex	1 week	None	1	Accommodated	Relationship and control problems; delinquency
Brian	1 year	2	1	Accommodated	Control problems; school problems
Carl	7 months	3	2	Accommodated	Neglect; relationship problems
David	4 years	9	2	Accommodated	Physical abuse; neglect
Eddie	1 month	None	1	Accommodated	Family stress; control problems; solvent abuse
Fred	1 year	2	1	Care Order	Physical abuse
Graham	2 years	None	3	Accommodated	Emotional abuse; control problems: relationship problems
Hugh	10 years	6	1	Care Order	Physical abuse; emotional abuse

Ian	1 year	4	1	Care Order	Control problems; relationship problems
Kris	4 years	None	1	Accommodated	Inadequate care; control problems; parental illness
Lee	5 years	None	2	Care Order	Physical abuse; neglect
Michael	19 months	2	1	Interim Care Order	Sexualised behaviour; emotional abuse
Nicki	5 years	Care history unknown	Care history unknown	Accommodated	Relationship problems; control problems
Paul	4 years	None	2	Care Order	Physical abuse; neglect
Omar	18 months	None	1	Care Order	Physical abuse; neglect
Roland	1 year	None	1	Accommodated (short-breaks)	Family stress

In terms of their legal status, the group was almost evenly split; seven young people had been accommodated through a voluntary agreement with their parents and two according to a series of placements ('respite care'). Seven were subject to a court order and one to an interim order which later became a full Care Order. The proportion of those with Care Orders is high, though it is worth noting that these were concentrated among younger children and those who had been looked after for some time. Abuse of some kind was a primary reason for entry to care in all the cases where a court order had been made.

As Fisher *et al.* (1986) comment, it is a 'dangerously misleading question to ask why a child has come into care' (p.32), and the summary above may seem at odds with the emphasis of this study on the interactional nature of experience. It is therefore important to emphasise that the table above does not pretend to capture the complexity of the circumstances leading to accommodation and care, but is intended only to indicate the seriousness of the problems which this group had experienced.

Ten of the young people were known to have experienced some kind of abuse or neglect. This proportion is very high, though recent research suggests that the proportion of children looked after in children's homes who are known to have experienced abuse has increased (Berridge and Brodie 1998). This is partly due to heightened public and professional awareness of the problem. The effects of abuse on a young person's experience are difficult to measure, but research into sexual abuse, for example, has found evidence that educational performance may be adversely affected (Kendall-Tackett *et al.* 1993). Children who have been physically abused are more likely to show behaviour problems at home and school and have problems in their relationships with peers. Cognitive development can also be adversely affected (Gibbons *et al.* 1995). Other research into children looked after has also shown that there is a strong statistical relationship between experience of abuse and educational difficulties, including exclusion (Farmer and Pollock 1998).

Relationship and control problems were the other main reasons for entry to care. Other research into residential accommodation has also shown that the breakdown in family relationships and the young person's behavioural and schooling difficulties are the key issues, especially for adolescents (Berridge and Brodie 1998.; Sinclair and Gibbs 1998a). Interestingly, there was little evidence of involvement in offending in the group; only one young man was known to have been in trouble with the police prior to his exclusion, and then for vandalism.

Interestingly, school factors were not cited as the primary reason for entry to care either in case files or by social workers or carers, though, with the exception of Paul, all the young people had experienced some forms of schooling diffi-culties prior to entry to the children's homes where they were resident at the time the research was undertaken. There are a number of possible reasons for this, including the degree of significance which social workers attach to education as a reason for social work intervention (Borland *et al.* 1998; Aldgate *et al.* 1993). There are also likely to be many overlaps between such matters as control and relationship problems and schooling difficulties (Triseliotis *et al.* 1995). Addition-ally, where abuse is cited as the key reason for entry to care, less importance may be attributed to other factors. The number of primary-school-aged children in the sample is especially important in this respect, as younger children appear to be more likely to enter residential care for reasons related to abuse (Berridge and Brodie 1998; Sinclair and Gibbs 1998a). In some cases, educational problems had also spiralled during the young person's care career, and this is obviously important in relation to young people who had experienced a lengthy time in the care system. An alternative explanation could be sought in the different per-ceptions which individuals may hold regarding the reasons for entry to care. The absence of parental views in this study may be important here, as some studies suggest that while social workers and young people considered behaviour in the community and difficulties in family relationships to be most important as reasons for becoming looked after, parents perceived schooling problems to be much more serious (Triseliotis *et al.* 1995).

Nevertheless, the problems at school which some young people had experienced should not be underestimated. The majority were considered to have some form of literacy or numeracy problems. In the cases of younger children, developmental difficulties were also sometimes noted – for example, Graham, aged nine, still found using scissors difficult and his concentration span was considered to be very limited. Jack's concentration span was so low that his teacher described him as almost hyperactive, and she considered it dangerous to take him on school trips outside the classroom. Interestingly, some problems which were recorded in case files were not raised by professionals. Eddie's file contained evidence showing that early in his secondary school career he had been a victim of a neighbourhood 'hate' campaign which had led to his being branded a child molester. His educational social worker had noted that he was 'a prisoner in his own home' and that 'school became untenable because of the ill-feeling towards him'. Eddie had subsequently moved schools and had been excluded because of his disruptive behaviour. While there are dangers in making direct causal connections, it is striking that such stressful experiences were either not known to the professionals interviewed or were not considered relevant to his later problems.

Most of the sample had been looked after for a lengthy period of time. Fourteen had been looked after for a year or more, and, surprisingly, seven had been looked after for four years or more and Phil had been looked after for ten years. It is important to stress that this is atypical of the care population as a whole, as most young people spend a shorter period of time in care than in the past. The majority of adolescents, in fact, will return home within a few months (Berridge and Brodie 1998; DoH 1999).

Other research evidence shows that, although care episodes now tend to be shorter than in the past, young people may still experience several placements (DoH 1999). Berridge and Brodie (1998) found that the care careers of adolescents were particularly unstable, with young people experiencing an average of more than three placements. Sinclair and Gibbs (1998a) found that over 40 per cent of their sample of adolescents had lived in two or more care settings. For six young people, the current residential placement was their first. Most of this group, however, had not remained in the same placement throughout this time. Two children had experienced one other foster or residential placement and four two other placements. The remainder had lived in another four or more care settings, the record being held by David who had experienced nine foster placements and a stay in another children's home in addition to his current residential placements. There was little clear distinction between younger children and adolescents in terms of care placements, though children living in private homes were notable in having generally stable care careers (see also Berridge and Brodie 1998). Young people included in the sample had been living in their current placements for anything from a week to four years. This, coupled with the individual's previous care history, had important implications for the way in which carers were able to respond to a young person's immediate educational needs.

Conclusion

The children and young people studied had clearly experienced a range of very serious social and educational difficulties. As other research has also shown, this group appeared to present not just one but a combination of significant problems. Many had been subject to a high level of disruption both inside and outside school. These transitions had been managed against a background of considerable personal stress, including abuse and the breakdown of family life. In the light of these problems, it may not be surprising that children were excluded. Equally, however, it is surprising that, given knowledge about these prior difficulties, action was not taken to avoid more disturbance in the young person's life.

It is important that, amid attempts to find explanations for disaffection outside the individual, that the impact of prior emotional damage is not forgotten. Furlong (1991) argues that while there are some pupils who will be damaged by the experience of schooling itself and who will consequently find some means to oppose it, there are other pupils who are already emotionally vulnerable and for whom even the 'most mundane' demands of school may be too much. This is not to excuse weaknesses of the care system, but rather to draw attention to the extreme nature of the problems which young people have experienced which, unsurprisingly, have all too tangible effects on their lives. There is some support for this in one of the few studies to focus on the causes of low educational achievement of children looked after, which involved a longitudinal study of young people looked after in foster care and a 'comparison group' of children receiving social work support while remaining with their parents. Heath, Colton and Aldgate (1994) found that even where children were living in stable foster placements, their educational progress in maths and reading tended to be slower than for the comparison group. The researchers concluded that the educational input for these young people needed to be significantly greater than for other children if the effects of early experience were to be neutralised. More studies like this are needed if the complexity of the issue is to be understood.

The next three chapters will examine in detail how the decision to exclude came to be made, and how this was influenced by different aspects of the family, care and educational experiences of the young people.

5

The Inter-Agency Context

Introduction

Chapter 4 has introduced the group of 17 children studied and described their characteristics. It is clear that all these young people had extremely troubled family and educational backgrounds, which other research suggests may increase their vulnerability to exclusion from school (see, for example, OFSTED 1996a; Hayden 1997).

The premise of this study, as previous chapters have explained, is that this decision to exclude results from the nature of interactions between a range of professionals and young people themselves. While professionals intervene in the lives of all children, the nature of this intervention and the quality of relationships between professionals becomes even more pivotal when children are looked after. It is important, then, to identify the areas of practice which relate to the young person's experience during exclusion and which involve different agencies.

Interaction between professionals does not emerge from a vacuum; the way in which individuals respond to a situation is likely to be influenced by the contexts in which they are operating (Goffman 1974). The purpose of this chapter is to examine the local authority contexts in which interaction between professionals took place in the three local authorities where cases were studied.

At this point it is important to make some comment on definitions of 'inter-professional' work. There appears to be little agreement on the terminology surrounding this, and a wide range of descriptions of the associations between different professional groups are available (see, for example, Leathard 1993; McGrath 1991). Hallett (1995), in a review of the literature, notes that terms such as 'collaboration' and 'co-ordination' are sometimes used synonomously, while other writers have sought to develop taxonomies of the relationships which might be associated with different terms. A further problem is that collaboration/co-ordination and so on may be applied both to relationships between individuals, but also between disciplines and organisational structures. Perhaps significantly, much of the literature in this area relates to inter-professional working in health and social services and frequently in relation to child protection; much less has been written about variations in the relationships between social services and schools or other education services. In this study it is acknowledged that while useful distinctions can be drawn between, for example, co-ordination – 'working independently but in harmony' – and collaboration 'working together' (Booth 1981, p.25) these processes will tend to occur to varying degrees. Throughout this chapter, no particular classification of styles of working will be adopted, though different terms have been used to describe different types of relationships between professionals and organisations.

Local authorities also operate within national guidelines and policies, which are likely to influence local practice. As in other areas of social care, policies relating to children have increasingly emphasised the value of inter-agency working. However, while the principle that co-operation and collaboration between different professionals is not only desirable but necessary is widely accepted, an array of reports have criticised the fact that this occurs on only a limited basis and that the quality of relationships between agencies is often poor (House of Commons Health Committee 1998; Social Services Inspectorate/OFSTED 1995; Audit Commission 1994; Social Services Inspectorate 1993). Inquiries into the deaths of children following abuse have consistently pointed to the failure of inter-agency communication as a contributing factor to these tragedies (Reder, Duncan and Gray 1993; DoH 1991a). Additionally, while the value of inter-agency working has been emphasised, other aspects of government policy during the late 1980s and 1990s arguably diminished opportunities for collaboration. It has been argued that, for example, the introduction of the purchaser/provider split in social services and the development of quasi-markets in schools have led to a greater fragmentation in services for children (Jones and Bilton 1994).

This chapter will begin by examining the provisions of current official guidance regarding inter-agency practice during the exclusion process. It will then outline other areas of policy relevant to the experiences of the sample group and which have implications for inter-agency co-operation. The next part of the chapter will describe the way in which each of the local authorities had developed policy relating to exclusion procedures. The discussion will then turn to the perceptions of individual teachers, social workers, residential staff about the way in which different agencies related to each other and how they defined their roles in relation to the education and exclusion of children looked after.

Exclusion procedures and inter-professional interaction

At the time the research for this study was undertaken, the main piece of procedural guidance regarding exclusion was the DfE Circular 10/94. It is therefore necessary, in analysing the data, to focus on this guidance, while acknowledging that the more recent Social Inclusion: Pupil Support guidance (DfEE 1999b) places even greater emphasis on the role of external professionals, especially in preventing exclusion and managing difficult behaviour. The law relating to exclusion has, however, remained substantially the same, and in both circulars the headteacher, the pupil and the pupil's parents are the main players in the procedures associated with the decision to exclude. A guiding principle is that parents have a duty to secure the education of their children (see also Section 36 of the Education Act 1944), and to this extent it could be inferred that those acting *in loco parentis* for a child looked after in residential accommodation would have an important part in the exclusion process.

Circular 10/94 also indicates that other processes may be important when an exclusion is being considered. It is advised that pupils who show signs of behaviour which cannot be managed within the provisions of the school's behaviour policy should move to the school-based stages of assessment outlined in *the Code of Practice on the Identification and Assessment of Special Educational Needs* (DfE 1994b) and Circular 9/94 (DfE 1994a) on the education of children with EBD. This in turn implies the involvement of other professionals outside the school, in that it is anticipated that using these frameworks will permit schools to draw on 'increasing levels of support and expertise to meet children's needs' and that in the later school-based stages 'expertise available outside the school, in particular educational psychology and teaching support services' may be used (para 4).

As exclusion is intended to be a last resort, Circular 10/94 makes clear that 'all reasonable steps' should have been taken to avoid this most extreme of sanctions. According to this document, this is essentially a matter of talking to the pupil and his/her parents, possibly negotiating some kind of agreement about the young person's behaviour. Sometimes, though not usually, the police or social services will be involved. Regarding the decision to exclude, the headteacher will gather facts about the pupil from other staff members and, in addition to notifying parents of the exclusion and of their right to appeal, will also keep school governors and the LEA informed. According to Circular 13/94, when a child is looked after the first point of contact for a school should usually be the care-givers. Following exclusion, and if the child has been out of school for a considerable period of time, then support agencies such as education welfare services, may be involved in planning the young person's return.

It is evident, then, that even within the fairly narrow definition of exclusion adopted in the Circular, there is scope for the involvement of a range of individuals both inside and outside the school. However, beyond the duties for the headteacher to inform the governing body and the LEA, there is no requirement that other agencies should be involved. In the context of this type of guidance it is possible that such a requirement would be inappropriate, in that the difficulties which eventually lead to exclusion frequently have complex histories and will not necessarily require the involvement of another agency. At the same time, the evidence suggests that a high proportion of children who are excluded are already in contact with another professional agency, and to this extent it might be argued that a requirement for consultation where such a link existed would not be inappropriate. However, in the light of the present discussion, it is interesting in presenting us with a scenario where there is scope for considerable negotiation in the way in which other agencies will be involved in the exclusion process. Accordingly, the number and type of interactions which may take place between individuals prior to, during and following the exclusion are likely to vary quite widely.

Child welfare and inter-agency working

The research evidence that has been presented earlier in this study has shown that children at risk of exclusion tend to be experiencing multiple problems and a high proportion are already in contact with external agencies. Their needs are, however, often exacerbated by the exclusion itself – for example by increasing the stress on families (Parsons 1997; Cohen *et al*.1994;). Many children who are excluded from school are therefore already 'children in need' according to the Children Act 1989. The Act's definition of 'need' refers to all aspects of a child's health and development, and 'development' is in turn defined as meaning 'physical, intellectual, emotional, social or behavioural development' (Section 17 [10] Children Act). The Act also states that

> it shall be the general duty of every local authority (a) to safeguard and promote the welfare of children within their area who are in need, and, (b) so far as is consistent with that duty, to promote the upbringing of such children by their families, by providing a range and level of services appropriate to those children's needs. (Section 17 [11])

This definition of need would appear to embrace children excluded from school, whose intellectual development is impeded by the limited amount of education they tend to receive (Sinclair 1997). Also relevant to the experiences of the sample of children in this study are processes relating to special educational needs and child protection, both of which are explicitly multi-disciplinary in orientation. Section 166 of the Education Act 1993 also enables LEAs to request the help of district health authorities or social services departments if this will assist in the exercise of the LEA's duties under the Act regarding children with special educational needs.[1] Help from other agencies can therefore be requested at any stage in the assessment process.

Child protection is perhaps the best example of an area of social work practice which requires a sophisticated level of inter-agency working. The associated guidance states that the responsibility for protecting children should not fall entirely on one agency, and that collaboration will be enhanced by awareness of the roles of other agencies (Home Office *et al* 1991, para 4:1). The agencies which may be involved in this process include health services, the police and education services as well as social services. It is envisaged that social services will take the lead role in the child protection process, but inter-agency co-ordination is key to practice. Importantly for this study, schools frequently have a vital part to play. Gibbons *et al.* (1995) found that schools were the agency most likely to refer children because of child protection concerns (see also Cleaver and Freeman 1995). Teachers may also have an important role in monitoring the well-being of children, and their knowledge and observation of children is especially valued at initial case conferences (Hallett 1995).

As part of the increased emphasis on inter-agency co-operation, policies have also been introduced to ensure better integration in planning at local authority level. An amendment to the Children Act 1989 requires local authorities to produce a plan for children's services which should be made in consultation with a range of other agencies, including health authorities and trusts, LEAs and voluntary organisations. These Children's Services Plans are intended to help local authorities identify groups of children 'in need' within a local area, and adjust services accordingly. Children experiencing educational difficulties should therefore be included in these definitions of need (Sinclair 1998; Sinclair, Grimshaw and Garnett 1994). Children's Services Plans should also be complemented by the new duty on LEAs to draw up and publish plans showing their arrangements for pupils with behavioural difficulties (DfEE 1998).[2]

However, the Children Act definition of need is undoubtedly wide, and the way in which it is applied carries important resource implications (Colton, Drury and Williams 1995). The inevitable consequence of this is that some groups of children in need will have higher priority than others when resources are being allocated. It has been argued that, in general, adolescents in need have been given lower priority than child protection and families with young children (DoH, 1996; DoH 1995). The latter report recommends that local authority policies for teenagers must be developed and that central to this should be inter-agency working, in line with Section 27 of the Children Act.[3] This is important in view of the fact that the majority of young people excluded are of secondary school age – though, of course, some of their problems may be of long standing.

In similar vein Roaf and Lloyd (1995) argue that groups of young people with multiple problems are especially vulnerable to 'falling through the net' of local authority provision. Interestingly, they include young people experiencing educational difficulties whilst in local authority care as one such high risk group. They locate this problem firmly within the arena of inter-agency relationships, claiming that differences in statutory responsibilities and the dominance of organisational structures militate against collaboration and strategic planning and preventative work.

Therefore, while children who are excluded from school and are also looked after by the local authority are indisputably children in need, the complex and varied nature of their problems – as is well illustrated by the 17 young people studied – may act against a collaborative effort on the part of the different agencies which could potentially be seen as having a contribution to make. It is, perhaps, impossible for any guidance or policy to deal adequately with the whole range of problems which may help precipitate an exclusion. However, mechanisms which involve inter-agency co-ordination in regard to young people at risk of exclusion have been introduced in a number of areas. Indeed, this has been a central plank in New Labour policies regarding the issue. In Scotland, for example, there have been a number of initiatives, called Youth Strategies, which have sought to create more systematic structures through which to co-ordinate professional responses to children presenting an array of needs (Kendrick 1995).

In practice these processes are not, of course, unproblematic. As Gilligan (1998) remarks, there had been a 'chasm' in children's services between schools and teachers on the one hand and non-educational services on the other. Development of good practice in this area requires efforts on both sides: social workers need to recognise the importance of education as a protective factor in the face of other difficulties (Triseliotis *et al.* 1995) and also the pressure which teachers experience in their professional lives, while teachers need to understand the skills of social workers in other areas of work with young people.

Inter-agency working at local authority level

Having considered the way in which inter-agency work is embedded in legislation and official guidance relating to the 17 cases, the discussion will now turn to the arrangements which existed within the two local authorities for children excluded from school and living in children's homes.

There was a widespread recognition in all the local authorities that school exclusion was a major issue. As Chapter 3 has shown, this could not be directly related to a change in the numbers of exclusions taking place, though there was a recognition of the way in which exclusion rates were increasingly being used as a measurement of school and LEA performance. No one, it seemed, wished to attract the kind of publicity around exclusion which had emerged in The Ridings school in Halifax and elsewhere (see Chapter 2). Both local authorities had introduced procedural guidelines, largely coinciding with those contained in Circular 10/94, regarding exclusion. For maintained schools these included the requirement that exclusions be reported to the Education Officer. As a result both local authorities were building up their data bases regarding exclusions.

Discussion in Local Authority 1 about the nature of inter-agency working in regard to excluded pupils had been spurred by the death of a young man living in residential care and also excluded from school. In 1996 a joint education/social services working party had reported to the Education Officer, setting out a strategy for an inter-departmental approach to tackling the problem of disaffected pupils and exclusions. This paper reveals two main concerns, namely the behaviour support provided within schools for pupils at risk of exclusion and the alternative educational provision available to pupils following exclusion. There is a recognition that an inter-agency response to the problems of disaffection and exclusion is desirable; reference is made to the potential value of the French 'social crime prevention' and the fact that within this model responsibility for young people is not assumed only by a criminal justice agency. Two of the children's homes had also produced staff guidelines relating to the education of children looked after. These provided clear guidance for the support of children who were attending school – for example, attending school functions and events – and those who were excluded. Practical suggestions were also made within these guidelines for liaison with school, from checking school correspondence to sharing relevant information about the child on a 'need to know' basis and making appropriate arrangements for inviting schools to reviews and meetings, such as providing sufficient notice for teachers and the clarification of the information which would need to be available beforehand. The working party had also considered the possibility of producing fact sheets for schools and children's homes which would cover the practical 'parenting' responsibilities of the local authority in regard to the education of children looked after.

The situation in Local Authority 2 was generally less advanced. Communication between agencies in regard to exclusion was facilitated by the fact that all the main education support services – the education social work service (ESWS), education psychology service (EPS), special educational needs, an exclusions officer and the education/social services liaison officer – were located in the same building. The exclusions officer reported 'excellent communication' with the ESWS, though contact with social services itself was more sporadic. However, these benefits were not always available to children looked after, most of whom were located out of the borough, and this was reflected in the absence of any centrally collected statistics or information on the placements (care and educational) of this group. Indeed, an in-house research report noted that while 11 per cent of children looked after were reported as having been excluded from school, 37 per cent appeared to have no school placement. The exact nature of their educational circumstances were unknown to the education department within the borough, and social services had no central record. Responsibility for the educational welfare of these young people consequently lay almost entirely in the hands of individual social workers.

Policies and procedures within schools

As Chapters 1 and 2 have pointed out, research has repeatedly shown that there are significant differences in the rates of exclusions between local authorities and also between schools (OFSTED 1996a; DfE 1995; Imich 1994; DfE 1993; OFSTED 1993). The response to this finding has been an increased emphasis on the development of good practice in regard to both discipline and also in terms of teaching standards. This study does not cover this latter area; however, teachers were asked about the way in which breaches of discipline or behavioural problems would be dealt with in school. School organisation and policy has also been argued to be an importance factor in structuring the build-up to exclusion. Galloway *et al.* (1982) suggest that the nature of organisational decisions within the school can result in problems moving up the hierarchy of authority, with the result that 'relatively minor issues could escalate from a dispute between a subject teacher and pupil to a confrontation between the head and the pupil, culminating in exclusion or suspension' (p.158). Other factors within the school which have been identified as significant include the quality of the pastoral care system, support within the school and relationships with parents (Mortimore *et al.* 1988; Rutter *et al.* 1979). Improvement in these areas has been highlighted by official advice on good practice in preventing exclusion (OFSTED 1996a; DfE 1994a; OFSTED 1993).

Research has shown that persistently disruptive behaviour, including rudeness and insolence to teachers and classroom interruption, is perceived as most difficult by teachers (see, for example, Wheldall and Merrett 1988). This type of behaviour has consistently been found to be one of the most common reasons cited for permanent exclusion. While this study seeks to move away from a mechanistic model which suggests that any exclusion has a single cause, or that exclusion can be explained purely in terms of the individual child, the importance of perceptions of behaviour to an understanding of the phenomenon cannot be ignored.

While current concern regarding exclusion may lead to a sense that schools exclude too often and too quickly, this was not perceived to be common practice in the schools visited. During the research 16 schools were visited, including mainstream primary and secondary schools, PRUs, again catering for both primary and secondary pupils, an EBD day/boarding school and an Intermediate Treatment Centre. In all the schools visited staff felt that behaviour was a matter given high priority and something at which they worked hard. All the headteachers interviewed made reference to behaviour and discipline policies, and were able to describe in detail the different aspects of these. Practice in schools typically consisted of a series of layers: problems were initially dealt with at classroom level, at which point parents might also be invited into the school, then moved up the school hierarchy. Detentions and extra tasks such as tidying litter were the most common sanctions used. At a more serious level, fixed-term exclusions were considered useful as warnings and, as one secondary head remarked, in 'making a child come to his senses'. SEN provision was perceived as an important resource in dealing with behavioural problems, and the Special Educational Needs Co-ordinator (SENCO) was often the first port of call when significant difficulties first emerged. To this extent it could be said that in these schools emotional and behavioural difficulties were perceived to be examples of special educational need. Such problems were explained in terms of the child being naturally 'difficult', or linked to family and home circumstances, or indeed placement in a children's home. Teachers also considered broader social trends, such as the increased disruption in family life, to be relevant. This coheres with other research – described in Chapter 2 – which has found that teachers tend to explain behavioural problems in terms of the child's home environment or individual pathology (see, for example, Peagam in Farrell 1995)

Most teachers provided a very detailed description of practice within the school concerning behaviour. In one primary school, for example, the headteacher explained that

> any misbehaviour in class and their names go on the board. If they misbehave more than twice in one day they go automatically into detention next morning... Two detentions in one term mean a letter to the parents. If a child persistently misbehaves at lunch times then they will be suspended from lunch times for two weeks. (Headteacher)

Primary schools appeared to have a greater range of rewards and sanctions available to them, perhaps due to their smaller size and more personalised approach. More reference was also made to strategies used within the classroom, important in view of other research showing that much of the interaction relevant to behaviour will take place within the confines of the classroom or within the peer group (Delamont 1976; Hargreaves *et al.* 1975). This was reflected in a greater emphasis on the need for social education. Methods such as 'circle time' [4] were being used in three of the schools visited. Reference was also made to counselling; in one school the headteacher stated that so much counselling was taking place that the local school council had suggested employing a counsellor. This had been rejected on the grounds that

> we have a system in place and the teachers know the children better. We are always willing to support parents who are having problems. We don't think children's lives are just about between nine and three. We have meetings with parents and home-school books where teachers write in how the child has been behaving. (Headteacher)

Another school had made it a priority to work with the community, applying methods of mediation to help reduce levels of aggression. Overall children in primary schools seemed to have greater involvement in the running of the school, either through school councils or peer mediation.

Secondary school staff were more familiar with exclusion and the processes associated with this. Staff were also much more clear cut regarding the circumstances in which exclusions would take place, defining these in much more formal language. In Local Authority 1, for example, reference was made by headteachers to county guidelines on the use of exclusion and the need to 'follow these to the letter'. However, this should not suggest that secondary schools were uncaring in their approach to those pupils at risk of exclusion, or that they did not make efforts to retain a child in school. It was emphasised that parents were usually involved at an early stage, though it was pointed out that many parents found the young person quite as difficult to manage as teachers, and that help with parenting from another agency might have been helpful.

Despite their efforts, however, all the headteachers and teachers interviewed felt that there would always be a very tiny minority who could not be maintained in mainstream school, no matter how effective their behaviour policies. While exclusion rates varied in the schools visited, there was no sense that frequent recourse was made to exclusion as a sanction. Indeed, exclusion was viewed essentially as an extremely rare event which occurred only after many other attempts to deal with the child's behaviour had been made.[5] A primary school headteacher commented

> We have a great many problems, I'm not saying that we haven't. We work very hard on behaviour and if we didn't we'd exclude a lot more. (Headteacher)

As one educational psychologist commented, 'Most schools are desperate to keep them in'. This was especially true for primary schools, perhaps understandably in view of their smaller size and more personalised approach. One headteacher stated that Samuel's exclusion had only been the second in 15 years. Jack's headteacher had to find out what exclusion actually involved, as this was the first time the school had excluded.

The emphasis placed by school staff on preventing exclusions and positive approaches to behaviour might appear contradictory to more general views expressed regarding exclusion, in that all teachers and headteachers agreed that the number of exclusions had increased. This may be explicable by the fact that the majority believed that changes in education policy, rather than internal school organisation, were responsible for the increase in the numbers of exclusions taking place. Competition between schools resulting from the publication of league tables was cited as being especially important in making schools less tolerant. Teachers and headteachers also pointed to the pressure wrought by the National Curriculum and lack of specialist support. There was also a sense among secondary school teachers that schools now had fewer options available to them in controlling behaviour, due to such changes as the removal of exclusion on an indefinite basis. The view was also expressed that 'taking the cane out means exclusion occurs much more quickly', and that regardless of opinions about the desirability of corporal punishment, it had represented another disciplinary option.

Perhaps inevitably, accounts of policy and practice within schools and of the efforts made by teachers with individual pupils, can contribute to a sense that the behaviour of the pupil was so extreme that exclusion represented the only option available. However, such a conclusion would be premature. As the following discussion will demonstrate, factors other than behaviour were perceived to be important. Also, the nature of the exclusion process itself sometimes led to the establishment of a consensus between the different individuals involved that exclusion represented a rational and desirable course of action.

Schools and children looked after

As well as the pattern of organisation regarding discipline and special educational needs within the school, it is necessary to examine the perceptions held by teachers regarding children looked after. It has sometimes been suggested that children living in residential and foster care are stigmatised in school, and that this affects the way in which discipline is applied (Shaw 1998; Kahan 1989; Page and Clark, 1977). The issue of how much information about children's family circumstances should be shared, for example, can prove contentious; children can feel either that teachers know too much and use this information in ways that disadvantage young people, or alternatively fail to make allowances in the light of their knowledge.

Perhaps the key issue, however, is the fact that schools may have limited experience of working with children looked after in children's homes. In the present study, with the exception of an EBD school in Local Authority 1 and two schools in Local Authority 3, most education staff had only rarely worked with children looked after. Schools typically reported that there were children in care within the school, but that the numbers were small and the time these pupils spent in care usually very brief – a few weeks at most. Views were mixed regarding the extent to which these children had distinguishable needs and they were often grouped alongside other pupils experiencing family problems which could result in emotional stress (see Berridge et al. 1997 for similar findings). Some teachers placed this in the wider context of communities where there were high levels of social deprivation or of a society in which there has been an increase in divorce, unemployment and other disruption to family life. It was not considered inevitable that children looked after would be problematic or indeed that contact with carers would be necessary.

Teachers tended to have a better knowledge and understanding of foster care – unsurprisingly, in view of the much greater proportion of children looked after in this way (DoH 1999). Sometimes the term 'foster care' also appeared to be used to describe children living in residential care. Where a comparison was made between foster and residential care, the latter was perceived much more negatively. This was not necessarily related to experience of the care provided by a children's home, but sometimes to views about the acceptability of placing a child in an institutional environment. One primary headteacher, who at the time had three looked after children attending her school, commented

> To be honest, we weren't very happy about the children who came from the children's home. It's like sending someone to prison. They learn things from other children. Normally, if they go into foster care, their behaviour improves, because many foster carers do a sterling job. They are wonderful. (Headteacher)

Another primary headteacher held similar views.

> I can honestly say that when they are in foster care they honestly improve. Ian was placed with various sets and most of them were very good. Ian went from a situation where mum didn't care to people who really loved him. If anyone deserves medals in this country it is foster carers. But the rule is that they try to get them back to their families. (Headteacher)

The positive views expressed regarding foster carers could be related to the greater involvement of some foster carers in the life of a school – carers' own children might attend, and some teachers cited individuals who were governors or members of the PTA. Where a child was placed in residential care, teachers usually felt that residential staff tried to be supportive and helpful, but lacked the appropriate training and were working in a difficult and stressful situation. However, some aspects of the organisation were considered to be problematic, most usually shift working and the difficulty of making contact.

> They try. They don't have strong enough rules homewise. When you have all these miscreants together you need to have clear boundaries. The helpers aren't always strong enough, but they do try to be supportive. There should be a set of bullet points which RSWs enforce about home and school. (Secondary school teacher)

There was also criticism of the attention given to education by residential staff. Jack's class teacher commented:

> I know they [the children] have social problems. Possibly if more attention was given to education, it would take their minds off other things. It would help in the school, then it has a knock-on effect on their self-esteem – and that's what is usually the main problem. I said that to the care worker, 'can't you get him into something he's good at?' After all, he was quite a sporty child. It's giving them the

same chances as children in families... At the Christmas concert we had to really ask if someone would come to take him home. Jack wanted to read, which caused all sorts of problems, but we let him. And there was no one for him there. All the other children are taken home afterwards by a parent. You feel that you're always having to say 'why don't you, why don't you'. (Teacher)

The sense that the school had to take the initiative was also remarked on by another primary school headteacher, who said

If you don't push, you don't get anything. I had to write to tell them what Graham's plan was – they should have invited us to the home, to show us where he lived and what the arrangements there were... It all depends if the school can be bothered. (Headteacher)

The implication of this is that the carers in question did not demonstrate a commitment to the school and were not perceived as 'good parents'.

Teachers in special schools and units were, if anything, more critical about the way in which children's homes were run. While the present study can only speculate on the reasons for this, it is important to note the greater experience of these schools in working with social services. In the day/boarding EBD school visited, for example, 25 of the 80 pupils were looked after in foster or residential care. The headteacher acknowledged that residential staff tried, but said that, nevertheless

When a child is moved from foster to residential care, we throw our hands up in horror. The instability, the constant changeover of staff, the difficulty of concentrating a group of very difficult children in one place, just leads to chaos. Children feel the chaos, and these kids are already chaotic. (Headteacher)

To some extent, then, the picture which teachers presented of children's homes was of an environment characterised by lack of discipline and expertise on the part of those working there. Some homes in a local authority appeared to have built up negative reputations which seemed difficult to overcome. Others were perceived to try hard, but even these seemed to be viewed as somewhat ineffectual. Fortunately, however, there were some more positive glimmers of individuals' experiences of children's homes. For example, it was considered helpful that in Homes B and C there was an educational co-ordinator who could be contacted rather than residential staff. In Local Authority 2, it was pointed out that there was huge variation in the quality of care provided by children's homes and similarly in their reliability regarding matters of schooling. However, in some homes improvements had been discerned. Teachers appreciated residential social workers who ensured that young people were punctual and notified the school about absence, but there seemed to be considerable variation in practice.

It depends on the children's home. [Home D] is very good at attending reviews, keeping in touch and responding to problems. Most children's homes are not good at telling us if a child is not going to turn up or is sick. Sometimes they say 'we just couldn't get them out of bed'. (Head of PRU)

Aside from residential staff, schools had regular – sometimes daily – contact with social services and viewed such frequent access as essential. However, this did not mean that they viewed the relationship as especially positive. Headteachers were particularly critical.

The main problem with social services has been communication, confusion over meetings, which meetings we [the school] should attend and the times of meetings. (Primary school headteacher)

Social services are the worst [of all the other agencies]. They are obstructive, over-protective and fail to recognise the seriousness of the school's position. (Secondary school headteacher)

However, where there were avenues for contact these were valued. The situation could also vary depending on different levels of the hierarchy, and good relationships were felt to result more from individual effort than from established inter-agency relationships. One primary school headteacher, for example, had found that contact with an individual social worker had proved very positive, but attempts to obtain information from the team leader had been unproductive. Generally, in fact, the key message was that relationships with individuals could work well, but it could not be said that relationships with either social services as an agency or with children's homes as institutions were positive. Again, this seemed to offer scope for some fluidity in the negotiation of individual exclusions. At the same time, previous experiences could have a negative impact on the way in which schools responded to the approaches of a new social worker or member of residential staff.

Residential staff and schools

Of all the groups interviewed, residential social workers were most likely to feel that children looked after in residential care were stigmatised, or 'singled out' in school. While social workers tended to feel they lacked evidence to support such assertions, residential staff were insistent that stigma not only existed, but made it more likely that young people would be excluded. Comments from RSWs such as 'If a child is living at home then they are less likely to expel because of the hardships on the family'; 'Some schools send these young people home much more easily than young people whose parents are working all day'; or simply

'...schools don't want to know about these kids' problems' were frequent. It was also suggested that this stigma was evident when children's homes and social workers were trying to find a new school place for a child. One member of staff in Local Authority 1 who had special responsibility for education explained:

> Sometimes when I've had difficulty in getting placements for new referrals several schools have turned us down with varying excuses. Once some of our children have actually gone to the school and had support I have heard the comments on more than one occasion that the children are no worse than a lot of others they have already got in the same class or school. Schools do seem to be put off by children from children's homes – maybe this is more linked to them often having behavioural problems though as opposed to actually the fact that they are 'in care'. Also, past relationships with social workers and social services may not have helped the situation. (Education co-ordinator)

It is almost impossible, outside evidence from individual cases, to discover the extent to which schools discriminate against children because they are looked after. It is not, of course, unimportant that those working with young people in the care system and young people themselves frequently feel that this is the case. Such views would appear to carry the potential to have an impact on the relationships between schools and residential staff.

The major concern of RSWs in regard to education was when children were excluded or out of school for any other reason. This was perceived to have a negative effect on other children who were attending school, and also placed considerable pressure on staff. One RSW also felt that exclusion 'gives a home bad publicity'. The way in which roles were perceived varied considerably – sometimes it was considered to be the role of the children's home to liaise with schools and, where a child's education had broken down, to find another educational placement. Indeed, there was a considerable overlap between the descriptions of the role of the children's homes and the way in which field workers perceived their responsibilities. However, there tended to be little consensus about how education would be managed even within the same home, even in regard to such issues as whether young people would be permitted to watch television during the day (see also Berridge and Brodie 1998). It seemed that residential staff often felt that they stood in the crossfire regarding education – required to care for children who were out of school, but with little resources to change these situations. This led to considerable dissatisfaction, and the sense that too much was expected of staff.

> Education thinks social services can do more than is actually the case…there needs to be more consistency for staff – education must have clear guidelines, and before entering a school some kind of agreement should be made about what is to happen if attendance fails. (RSW)

Social work roles and responsibilities

Social workers tended to be more cautious than their residential colleagues in their assessment of schools' attitudes to children looked after. Perhaps surprisingly, they were also less convinced that the number of exclusions had increased, occasionally suggesting that the issue of special education more generally was more important. They did not feel that they were dealing with large numbers of exclusions.

It has been argued that social services have on the whole failed to prioritise education and that this is one way in which children looked after are disadvantaged in terms of their educational experience. In this study only one social worker voiced the opinion that emotional needs should be given attention before schooling, and stated that while social services did pay attention to education, they would not necessarily do so immediately. Another admitted that, as a parent himself, he sympathised with schools when they excluded a child whose behaviour was disruptive for other pupils. The majority of social workers emphasised that they considered education to be a key element in planning for a young person. It was pointed out that attendance at school provided stability, a sense of belonging, and the opportunity to develop skills. Almost every social worker pointed out that schools were always invited to reviews, though it was sometimes complained that schools did not always attend even when given considerable notice.

Interestingly, however, no social worker made any comments regarding positive academic achievements. A small number had made extra efforts to make links with school staff; one, for example, was involved with an education welfare officer (EWO) in developing child protection training in schools. However, as with teachers vis-a-vis social services, relationships with schools were thought to be variable, with some schools 'bending over backwards' to help a child while others were only too anxious to exclude. Again, this finding corresponds with other research (see, for example, Borland et al. 1998; Berridge et al. 1997; Kendrick 1995; Fletcher-Campbell and Hall 1990).

Education was perceived to be one of the main components of a child's welfare and therefore something for which social workers had a responsibility. Social workers tended to feel that they had the key role in terms of planning and organising a young person's education. An important aspect of this was considered to be finding educational placements for a young person, and the majority of the social workers interviewed had found this problematic, and in Local Authority 2 this was exacerbated by the number of grant-maintained schools which existed. It seems likely that this reflects the number of children looked after who are out of school, but also raises questions as to whether social workers possess enough expertise or have sufficiently good links with schools to carry out this role effectively. One social worker in Local Authority 2 liked the fact that all the residential homes she worked with had education on-site, but said she did not know enough about 'quality issues' in education to ask questions about, for example, the extent to which the National Curriculum was covered. Social workers also stated that they had an important role as advocates for the young person, and were much more likely than residential staff to point out that families had a continuing responsibility for their children, and that parents should be encouraged to be involved in education. Social workers 'represent the interests of the child in partnership with parents' and can 'help young people and their parents be heard in the education system.'

It appeared that social workers' intentions regarding schooling were benign, but it was not always clear that they would have sufficient information, or indeed power, to act when problems emerged. None of the social workers interviewed knew of any policy or local authority procedure relating to exclusion or the education of children looked after.

The involvement of other services

Research into children looked after in residential accommodation has at the same time indicated the problems presented by the majority of young people but the lack of specialist treatment or support in dealing with these difficulties (Berridge and Brodie 1998; Farmer and Pollock 1998). Similarly, in the 17 cases studied, there was generally a lack of active involvement by other groups. The involvement of other professionals was greatest, however, in cases of younger children – namely Michael and Fred – who were also involved in child protection processes.

In a small number of cases, other professionals did play a more significant role. Educational psychologists were especially important. In Local Authority 1 an educational psychologist was seconded to social services and children looked after were frequently referred to him. These sessions tended to focus on the nature of the child's inter-personal relationships. However, this psychologist was a source of information and advice which was valued by the heads of homes, especially those working with younger children. Teachers saw psychological services as a potential source of extra support, but complained that

> Ed psychs spend all their time doing paperwork and we don't feel they are making good use of their time – we would prefer time to be spent with the children. (Teacher)

However, it appeared that educational psychologists were likely to have limited opportunity for such work – one of those interviewed was linked to approximately 30 schools. He saw the main locus of his work to be in primary schools, where he saw his role as spending time with teachers to give advice about behavioural management. The same psychologist commented that this was a

...frustrating area of work. I get asked in to say what a difficult child this is, isn't he awful. Trying to get them [teachers] to change is very difficult. Children often need quite a different style of classroom management and so sometimes I'm asking them to change the whole way the classroom is organised. (Educational psychologist)

As other studies have shown, educational psychologists can wield considerable power regarding the resources which may be allocated or in the decisions made by schools (Galloway, Armstrong and Tomlinson 1994). Social workers agreed that educational psychologists played a crucial role in helping obtain funding, especially if a residential school placement was being sought. However, educational psychologists and managers with responsibility for special educational needs voiced concerns about the emphasis given by social workers to extra resources.

There is a tendency in social services to think that a classroom assistant is the answer to everything. There is also a small number who think they are experts in education. We are very happy to take social services advice on social work, but not on education – and I will send back appendices that say 'Kevin needs a full-time classroom assistant' because they have not seen him in the classroom. It doesn't happen often, but it is very important that we respect one another's professionalism. (Senior manager)

Similarly, an educational psychologist argued that in regard to exclusion, there was

a great danger in setting up an assumption that every child excluded is in need of an educational psychologist... We don't want to set up a system where an ed psych must be involved, for example to go to a school ed psych as a last hurdle. It's not necessarily always appropriate. (Educational psychologist)

Conclusion

In the absence of any written policy regarding exclusion, and in a situation where there is little information about the young person or clear guidelines about what should happen next, it is unclear how the exclusion will be negotiated. Schools have a clear set of procedures to follow in the event of a child presenting behavioural difficulties and at the point when the decision to exclude is made, but there is no mandate for the involvement of other professionals. Much will depend on how the young person's behaviour is defined. There is, however, no automatic procedure which is triggered when a child is experiencing difficulties at school which may result in exclusion. There is therefore considerable scope for 'creative management' of the situation by the different professionals involved (Crawford and Jones, 1995). This contrasts with the framework for child protection. Hallett (1995) comments that

> ...widespread routinised inter-agency co-ordination was central to child protection practice. While there were occasional reported lapses and certainly some frictions and difficulties in the process, the automatic mode of operation at referral, and if cases progressed further into the system, at the investigation and critical child protection conference stage was a multidisciplinary one. This was reflected in a routinised and relatively clear division of labour among the key agencies, operating largely sequentially, particularly in the early phases of the construction of a case of child abuse. (Hallett 1995, p.324)

This brings us back to the central question of the study, namely how the exclusion process is managed when a child is also looked after in a children's home.

The evidence presented above suggests that none of the parties concerned have clear expectations of the roles which other agencies should play, or even perceive other professionals to be particularly relevant to exclusion per se. Importantly, however, the majority of those interviewed had experienced good relationships with some schools or with some social workers, though there was a strong sense that these were 'down to individuals rather than organisations and departments'.

Additionally, there appeared to be a reserve of good will and cross-agency sympathy which could potentially ease the way for collaboration. Despite the probably inevitable tensions, there was a mutual recognition of the pressures under which all were labouring. It was widely acknowledged in all local authorities that social services were under considerable pressure, and they were often praised for what they managed to achieve.

> They do wonders with what they have. They are overwhelmed with work and hidebound with regulations. (Teacher)

> Budgets are a problem – social services have borne a large brunt of this and I feel sorry for my colleagues who are doing their best. Relationships with them – well, they are people too. But in the main we know each other fairly well and we understand their frustration. (Teacher)

Similarly, social workers felt that teachers faced a difficult task. Nevertheless, such sympathy could serve to reduce rather than to enhance contact. In one school, the headteacher stated that she would 'only contact social services in dire emergencies' because they were working under such pressure. On the other hand, such sympathy could help elicit a higher degree of professional consensus regarding a case. In such situations it is also important to consider the organisational level at which negotiation is taking place.

6

Interactions Between Professionals and Young People

Introduction

So far the discussion has examined the context of inter-agency relationships in which the 17 case studies were to unfold. Chapter 5 has shown that, while there is a strong rationale for inter-agency collaboration in child welfare, no specific mechanisms exist in the policy framework relating to exclusion which would make such collaboration a matter of course. Some conditions, such as the placement of children from Local Authority 2 in private children's homes some distance away, actually appeared to militate against such work. There is therefore considerable space for negotiation within the exclusion process.

This chapter will examine in detail the way in which one part of the exclusion process, namely the build-up to the decision to exclude, was negotiated in the 17 case studies. As previous chapters have explained, the theoretical basis of the study is that this is an interactional process, which therefore emerges through symbolic communication between individuals. This communication may take place through face-to-face interaction, or through telephone calls, letters or other forms of official documentation such as reports. Importantly, symbolic exchange may also occur through 'non-interaction'. Ignoring a message or failing to respond to a telephone call can convey a great deal about the recipient's attitude to the information (Reder, Duncan and Gray 1993). Such behaviour may also have origins in existing organisational or professional practice, as discussed in Chapter 5. The methodology for this study did not, of course, permit the recording of every moment of interaction which took place. Everyday discussions in staff rooms and the offices of children's homes, which may be of immense important in the formation of individual and group perceptions of a young person's behaviour, were unfortunately outside the researcher's purview.

The following discussion will therefore consider further the concept of exclusion as a process which incorporates both temporal and interactional dimensions. It will focus on the time prior to the decision to exclude, and the relationships which were perceived to exist between professionals during this period. It will be argued that this is a critical time for negotiation, in which the power relationships which exist between different professionals have an important bearing on the development of a pattern of interaction. Particular attention will be given to the significance of the young person's entry to – or exit from – residential accommodation and the implications of this for professional interaction. In addition, the chapter will consider how agreement about the child's education is negotiated and maintained, or, alternatively, how tensions and conflicts are managed. While the most detailed information about these issues was obtained from adults, young people are key players in the process, and their perceptions will also be examined.

Anticipating exclusion: defining the starting point

Chapter 4 has demonstrated that the backgrounds of the 17 young people studied were in many respects troubled. All had experienced considerable social disadvantage, and it had emerged that eight children had suffered various forms of abuse. In regard to their education, over half had been excluded previously on either a fixed-term or permanent basis, and seven had statements of SEN due to either EBD or moderate learning difficulties. It might therefore be argued that these problems made these children more vulnerable to exclusion from school and, in turn, that the decision to exclude could not be considered unexpected. However, such circumstances do not make exclusion inevitable and by no means explain the lack of surprise with which the adults working with these children – and the young people themselves – greeted the eventual decision to exclude. As later chapters will demonstrate, several of the children later settled happily in other schools or education units. They were not, therefore, intrinsically incompatible with school. This begs the question, therefore, as to what happened in the relationship between school and pupil which led to the decision to exclude being made.

Other research, usually focusing on the type of behaviour exhibited by pupils, has shown that, while exclusion will sometimes result from a single and perhaps momentous incident, it is more often the result of a 'gradual build-up of tension' (Hayden 1997; Parsons et al. 1994; Galloway et al. 1982). Interviewees in this study supported this position. One headteacher interviewed described exclusion as usually resulting from 'ongoing things in the classroom, constant interruptions, not letting teachers teach and other children learn'.

Individuals also explained the eventual decision to exclude as the culmination of such a build-up in tension, using such phrases as 'we were at the end of our tether' and 'the school had really had enough of him'.

The existence of such a period of anticipation has important implications for professional practice. If it can be shown that exclusion is predictable, then it would seem that there is scope for preventative action to be taken or alternative plans made. The research process certainly appeared to demonstrate the possibility for such prediction, in that more than half of the cases studied were often notified to the researcher prior to exclusion taking place. Hugh's case, for example, was first identified six months before his exclusion. Interestingly, none of these early notifications turned out to be false alarms; professional instinct was always correct and exclusion occurred in all those cases.

This period of build-up highlights the temporal nature of the exclusion process. However, to say that exclusion occurs over a period of time is not entirely original nor, in itself, particularly helpful. Specifically, it tells us nothing about how individuals might interact with each other during this period. Conceptualisation of the exclusion process must somehow incorporate an interactional dimension. A useful concept which combines these dimensions is that of trajectory, as deployed by Glaser and Strauss (1965) in their study of dying patients. This concept refers to the clearly defined period between the diagnosis of a forthcoming event – such as birth or death – and the actual event. Trajectories imply anticipation of the event, and therefore lead to a certain pattern of interaction, which is in turn determined by the 'awareness context' – the degree of awareness on the part of all actors within an interactional episode of the existence of the trajectory, and their knowledge of each other's awareness. Glaser and Strauss suggest that there is a range of awareness contexts from a situation of 'closed awareness' where the patient is unaware of his or her impending death, though everyone else is, to 'open awareness' where all those involved know that the patient is dying and act on this quite openly. It should also be noted that it is by no means inevitable that a trajectory will exist – sudden deaths, for example in accidents, will frequently occur and make it impossible to anticipate the event.

Some potentially important parallels can be discerned between this process and that of exclusion. For example, it is possible for a 'sudden death' exclusion to take place. Headteachers and teachers, in their accounts of school policies relating to exclusion, stated that certain behaviour, such as carrying a weapon or selling drugs, would automatically lead to an exclusion. Equally, it might be expected that if key actors within the exclusion process were fully aware that exclusion was possible or likely, then one might assume that action would be taken to prevent this. In turn this could lead, in the absence of empirical evidence to the contrary, to the suggestion that young people who are excluded represent the cases which 'slip through the net' and have been the object of a process of interaction during which key actors were not aware of the extent of the problems or where views have remained static.

The build-up to exclusion: patterns of interaction

However, the 'starting points' to the exclusion only assumed significance when these were associated with a changed perception of the young person's behaviour on the part of at least one of the individuals involved with the case. They were also associated with a shift in the pattern of professional interaction surrounding the young person. This is unsurprising in those cases where, for example, the starting point involved entry to a new school or children's home, thus introducing new actors to the situation. Similarly the fluctuating nature of social work input in several of these cases meant that the professional network was flexible and amenable to changes in perceptions of the young person, as new individuals entered and added their contributions to the process.

As Chapter 5 has argued, there is no multi-disciplinary process associated with exclusion which can be triggered when a particular constellation of stress factors is perceived by one or more actors to heighten the risk of exclusion. This potentially creates difficulties for the interactional process through which exclusion is negotiated. Hargreaves (1975) argues that interactional situations vary along a continuum of the degree to which there is a structure inherent in the situation. This structure concerns the 'mutual orientation' of participants and their awareness of how they should behave in the situation. When there is a high degree of structure, participants in the interaction are fully aware of the role that each should perform, the goals of each actor and the timing of their respective contributions. Conversely, when structure is low, the interaction will be surrounded with uncertainty, confusion or ambiguity for the actors concerned. Similarly, Goffman (1969) argues that the way in which individual actors manage the complexities of social interaction is through an understanding of the roles they are expected to perform. In terms of written policy and procedure, it would appear that schools – and specifically headteachers – have the clearest agenda for action. The roles of other professionals seem much less clear, and the way in which they will interact with colleagues from other agencies relatively uncharted territory.

Analysis of patterns of interaction is not easy. In their study of child abuse deaths, Reder, Duncan and Gray (1993) present a typology of ways in which professionals enter and exit a child protection case. This is based on the concept of 'boundary permeability'. It is argued that there is an optimal level of inter-professional contact which balances stability of personnel with a sufficient degree of openness that permits professionals to enter and exit the process at appropriate points. It is proposed that boundary permeability operates on a continuum. At one end of this continuum is the 'closed professional system', where a group of workers developed a fixed view about a case and would not admit any contrary information or observations. At the other end of the spectrum are cases where 'polarisation' occurs, that is where a schism developed between two groups of workers, which in time led to the emergence of two distinct groups of workers whose views about the case increasingly diverged.

This model is an attractive one, particularly in that it offers scope for the flow of individuals in and out of a social process such as exclusion. This flexibility is important in regard to the present study, especially in view of the disrupted nature of the schooling and care histories of almost all the young people studied, which revealed a lack of stability in their social networks. However, the model is also problematic in that it is somewhat deterministic. The nature of personal contacts between individuals is less important than the maintenance of the 'system' in which it is embedded. The model also seems to present us with an inadequate conceptualisation of power relationships in the inter-agency network. Yet, as described in Chapter 5, these relationships exist prior to the development of the individual case and are often embedded within the cultures of professional groups. For example, as analysis of official guidance demonstrated, the decision-making process relating to exclusion is also located within the school, leaving little room for the intervention of external individuals. Indeed, the way in which the appeal process operates in respect to parents has been subject to criticism (Harris 1995; Allen 1994). To this extent the balance of power could be said to favour the school, though this is not necessarily true in practice – such as those cases where a school is directed to admit/readmit a pupil by the governing body or the LEA.

However, Reder, Duncan and Gray do draw attention to the potential importance of the way in which consensus is reached during a process in which individuals from different professional backgrounds and agencies are involved. It appears that problems can emerge both from the lack of any consensus and also consensus that results from the inability or failure to criticise by some of the individuals involved. Hallett (1995) also comments on the significance of consensus in decision making in the child protection process, remarking that 'A dominant finding was that despite the varied professional backgrounds and agency functions of those concerned, decisions were characterised by consensus rather than dissent' (p.329).

This does not, of course, mean that relationships between professionals from different agencies in the child protection process are always unproblematic (DoH 1995). Hallett suggests that the high level of consensus may be attributed to a range of factors, which include the existence of a relatively stable local network of professionals who are likely to have to collaborate again in future. The procedural system devised for processing cases can also act to limit disagreement. Additionally, in a context of considerable anxiety where there is a fear of making mistakes, there will be a tendency for some professionals to defer to others who are perceived to have greater expertise, thus also reducing conflict.

The nature of consensus in the exclusion process might represent one way of understanding the different patterns of interactions found in the cases of the 17 young people studied, and it is striking that the majority of cases exhibited a high level of agreement from all those involved that exclusion was both inevitable and desirable. However, the consensus was not always maintained, or, alternatively, early tensions gave way to high levels of agreement. The remainder of this chapter will seek to identify the different social conditions which were perceived to affect the quality and quantity of interaction between professionals and the way in which this related to the views of young people about their schooling.

Entry to residential accommodation

To say that the young person's entry to residential care was an important point in the build-up to exclusion could be considered tautologous, in that this was a group of children resident in children's homes. It is important to remember that this study aims to examine the interactions between individuals. Entry to residential accommodation is an important aspect of this, though it is recognised that there are other points in the care and educational experiences of this sample which are also significant. Certainly, in identifying a 'starting point' to the child's most recent exclusion, interviewees drew attention to an overlap between changes in the young person's relationship with his family and entry to or changes in care placement. Interestingly, schools were always aware of these new circumstances. The head of year at Carl's school, for example, suggested that the fact his mother was about to remarry could help explain the deterioration in his behaviour. This issue was not raised by his social worker or residential key worker.

It is also necessary to consider the relationship between the young person's behaviour and entry to residential care. As Chapter 4 has shown, the majority of the 17 children had histories of behavioural problems. In a minority of cases, one or more professionals felt that living in a children's home had further exacerbated these difficulties. For example, Ian, aged 10, had suffered repeated rejection from his mother and all those interviewed agreed that a further rejection following a placement at home explained most of his educational problems. His behaviour at school had become increasingly difficult, but his headteacher felt that entry to Home C had made matters worse still.

All of these issues are important in helping explain the escalation of the situation to the point of exclusion. More often, though, professionals did not think that the child's behaviour at school had changed significantly following entry to residential accommodation. On the other hand, entry to a children's home for the first time, or indeed a change of placement, affected the amount and nature of professional interaction and had the capacity to bring an already difficult situation to a climax. As professionals began to interact with each other, concerns about education were articulated and the possibility of exclusion raised.

In these cases schools already perceived the young person's behaviour to be extremely problematic and had usually tried to work with him, for example through special needs support. Teachers nevertheless felt that the prognosis was gloomy. The young person's entry to residential care offered schools a new channel for their concerns, and access to a different group of professionals.

Alex's case is a good example of this. On entering residential care – due to relationship and control problems – his school perceived the situation to be at crisis point, and he had already been excluded on a fixed-term basis on three previous occasions. The teacher described his behaviour as 'uncontrollable' though at times he could be perfectly polite. There had been suggestions that he was involved in drug taking but this had never been proven. The school was frequently contacting Alex's mother, to the extent that she was in danger of losing her job. There were also problems in the community. As the school found Alex's behaviour increasingly difficult to deal with, he was gradually withdrawn from classroom learning. Initially a teacher accompanied him to classes and he then began working alone in a teacher's office. The head of year acknowledged that he behaved while doing this, but she felt he was being 'babyminded' rather than learning. During this time the attempt was made to contact social services, but without success – 'everyone was away on a course, and although a message was left, no one phoned back'. The same teacher believed that had extra support been forthcoming earlier in the process, the crisis point might not have been reached.

A similar pattern is evident in Hugh's case. However, unlike Alex, this was not because there had been no professional network in existence, but because this had been inactive. According to his social worker, Hugh's behaviour had deteriorated as his foster placement had broken down and, simultaneously, contact had been renewed with his mother. However, it was seven months after problems had first emerged that Hugh's headteacher contacted social services and, according to the education co-ordinator at the home where he was later placed, demanded that something be done.

Hugh's current social worker – who had entered the process at approximately the same time – felt that there had been a decided lack of activity on the part of social services, and blamed this on the previous social worker who was renowned for 'not doing anything about anything'. She felt that accounts of Hugh's education changed considerably following his placement in residential accommodation; while in foster care the education reports presented at reviews had been quite bland, but on entering the children's home 'he was being presented as a child who was absolutely horrendous at school'. The social work definition of the situation had therefore undergone a significant shift, while teachers had been able to raise their concerns in a new arena.

Analysis of the sample showed that the child's entry into residential care could lead to three patterns of interaction between professionals: negotiation, strategic collaboration and estrangement. Each of these will be described in some detail below.

Negotiation

A build-up to exclusion characterised by negotiation tended to involve a considerable amount of contact between professionals. At the time the young person entered residential care, schooling difficulties were already reaching a crisis point. It is important to point out that in these cases the school was the stable factor, while entry to the children's home was either the result of the breakdown of family relationships or of a previous care placement. The input of social work professionals seemed to permit the containment of the situation for a period of time, but it was clear to all concerned that the young person's educational difficulties were not being solved in the longer term.

An important consequence of a child's entry to residential care was that this could provide additional resources to the school. Social workers and residential staff assumed a supportive role and, crucially, did not challenge the school's definition of the young person's behaviour. Meetings which were held when the child entered the children's home were important for interaction between professionals and set the stage for what was to follow, but social workers appeared to be essentially recipients of information regarding the educational situation of the young person. They might then seek to persuade the school not to exclude, but there was an underlying agreement that the child's behaviour was serious and an acceptance that exclusion was both possible and justifiable. In terms of the Glaser and Strauss (1965) model outlined earlier in this chapter, the situation was one of 'open awareness' in that all participants were cognisant of what was happening and the likely outcome, namely the removal of the young person from the school.

Within a few days of his entry to residential care, Alex had thrown a chair at a teacher. The school contacted the children's home, asking a member of staff to collect him. A review was then held at which Alex's year head said that they were at 'the end of their tether' and saw no future in Alex's continued attendance at the school. The social worker said that since coming to the children's home, Alex seemed happy and asked that the school hold the situation a little longer. He 'prevailed' on the school to give him one more chance, saying that he had arranged for him to see an educational psychologist and thought it best to wait for his report.

However, neither the social worker nor the residential key worker disagreed with the school's assessment of Alex's behaviour. The social worker thought that Alex was an attention seeker, disruptive and cheeky in class, and disrespectful to teachers. He felt that Alex was encouraged in this behaviour by other pupils. The key worker thought that Alex's behaviour was the main problem at the school and considered that the school had worked hard to keep him as long as they had, commenting that the year head 'did seem genuinely concerned about his welfare' and had tried to avoid confrontation. Neither the social worker nor the residential key worker felt that much more could be done. Both the children's home and the social worker consequently assumed a supportive stance towards the school, collecting Alex when requested and considering the school's position to be a reasonable one. This was perhaps inevitable in view of their involvement in the case – there seemed to be no time and no resources by which an alternative set of goals could be formulated, and consequently the definition of the situation presented by teachers remained unchallenged. In turn the school felt that the children's home had been very supportive, for example in allowing Alex to stay at home for a few days to 'cool down' when there had been problems.

In Hugh's case a strategy meeting took place the day after he had been sent home for being verbally abusive and physically assaulting a teacher. Accounts of this incident were somewhat confused: Hugh claimed his behaviour had been provoked, the education co-ordinator at the children's home thought that the incident had been poorly handled by the school, while the acting headteacher was increasingly incensed by Hugh's behaviour. At the strategy meeting the school representative expressed considerable concern at the situation; however the school was 'persuaded ' to give him a 'fresh start'. At this point the education co-ordinator felt that, regardless of the agreement, Hugh was at the 'end of the line' and needed to do very little before he would be excluded. Her prediction proved accurate when, at the start of the following week, he was sent home once again (though still not excluded) for persistently disruptive behaviour. Indeed, the extent to which he was actually participating in the life of the school was very limited, and during this period Hugh's social worker pointed out that 'now [school] know they can pick up the phone and say "come and get him" which they wouldn't do for a child in foster care'.

In the meantime, the number of professionals engaged in the case had markedly increased. His social worker had contacted another educational psychologist, who saw Hugh and agreed that there was a problem, but that he would have to link in with the school psychologist. Child guidance had also been contacted and an assessment of family relationships took place.

In Ian's case, residential staff attempted to provide extra support and a care worker went in to the classroom with him. This was viewed quite positively by the class teacher as a gesture of support, but at the same time she felt that it had proved relatively ineffective. She explained

> Once he was in the home he started part-time at school with a care worker with him. It was very difficult, obviously, but they'd come in, present him on time. By this time it was very difficult and they often ended up taking him out of the room. Even with the care worker with him, he was still shouting abuse and he was able

to hurt other children. They [the care workers] were always helpful – we worked out what he was going to do each day and strategies about what to do when such and such happened…[but]…'The care workers were not really trained sufficiently to deal with him in the classroom.' (Teacher)

The fact that such support was offered was sufficient for some schools to wait before making the decision to exclude, but it seemed to be insufficient to halt the build-up in the longer-term. It appeared that the momentum towards exclusion had gathered such pace that these attempts to contain the situation had come too late.

The only remaining question seemed to be when exclusion would occur. Very little interaction appeared to surround this. Indeed, in Alex's case communication between the professional actors seemed to break down altogether. Shortly after the review, Alex's social worker went on holiday, and on his return found that Alex had been, in his words, expelled. However, his head of year viewed the situation differently, and explained that as the school had 'come to the end' of what they could do for Alex, they had asked the children's home to find another school. Alex was therefore transferred to another secondary school within the local authority, from which he was soon also excluded.

Hugh was excluded six months after the possibility of exclusion had first been raised at his review. By this time he had been moved to another children's home, and the additional support which he had been receiving from a teacher employed by social services was withdrawn. The exclusion was triggered by another incident in the classroom. Containment therefore came at a price, namely sustained high input from all the adults involved. When this diminished or was removed, the decision to exclude became more likely.

This was highlighted in cases where the child's return home was perceived to contribute to the escalation of the build-up to exclusion. In Graham's case, for example, residential care was considered to be helpful educationally, and following his return home after a placement in Home B his school placement became much more tenuous. His social worker and residential staff agreed that Graham's education had always been problematic; however, during his time at the children's home he had moved to a new school and had found some stability there. On returning home problems emerged once more. His social worker explained that social services had opposed the attempt at rehabilitation, but this had been dictated by the courts. The education co-ordinator also pointed out that when Graham returned home, the links which had been established between the school and the children's home were broken. His mother lived some distance from the school, had never had much involvement and would not provide the same sort of support. She had no transport and therefore could not act as an 'emergency service' as the children's home had done. Graham then returned to Home C and was, in time, excluded.

A common element in these cases is the clustering of professionals around a crisis point. To this extent they have some similarity to the model proposed by Dennington and Pitts (1991) in regard to young people entering secure accommodation. This suggests that when a young person's behaviour first arouses significant concerns, there is an increase in professional involvement and the 'professional network' expands. At this point in the process the stakes are high, and professionals therefore opt for a 'safe' option in the form of secure provision, which removes the young person from the crisis situation and also means that this extended network need take no more responsibility for the young person. The professional network then diminishes in number until investment in the process is reduced to what is arguably an inadequate level of support. Similarly, in regard to professional involvement in the child protection process, Birchall and Hallett (1995) found that when an abuse inquiry is instituted, the level of inter-agency co-operation was high, though often operated through informal consultation. However, as the child protection process progressed, collaboration declined, and Birchall and Hallett found that in two-fifths of cases where a child protection plan was produced, social services had assumed sole responsibility for implementing the plan.

In the cases described above, the issue is not simply the amount of contact which took place between professionals. Certainly, this seemed to increase at the point of the young person's entry to residential accommodation and the (re)awakening of social work interest in the case. This was especially true for adolescents; in the cases of younger children a larger professional network tended to be in place already. The perception of the problem which the school had developed carried greatest influence. The definitions subsequently developed by residential staff served to confirm this view of the young person's behaviour, and thus the perception of exclusion as the most favourable, and indeed the 'only' option was reinforced – in the cases of Hugh and Ian as incidents which occurred within the school permitted the accumulation of evidence which made a convincing case for exclusion. Agreement was also thus maintained between the professionals involved.

Strategic collaboration

In other cases, schools saw the revitalised professional network more strategically, that is, as a means by which to achieve specific ends. The idea of exclusion as a sanction which can be used strategically has been discussed by Kinder, Wilkin and Wakefield (1997), who identify three main rationales for taking the decision to exclude: removal, reprisal and remedy. These rationales are not necessarily mutually exclusive, but nonetheless have important distinguishing features. Exclusion as removal suggested a viewpoint which emphasised the rights of the majority of the school community. Exclusion was often undertaken reluctantly in such cases, and was accompanied by concern that the young person's needs would not be met through use of the sanction. Exclusion as reprisal, on the other hand, involved what the authors termed a 'symbolic denunciation' (p.31) of inappropriate behaviour. The involvement of other parents was an important factor when exclusion was used in this way. Finally, those who took the view 'exclusion as remedy' felt that mainstream school could not meet the needs of some children, though perhaps only for a temporary period of time.

In the present study, the idea of 'exclusion as remedy' dominated in those cases where professionals saw themselves as working together to achieve a specific outcome. In these cases, field social workers rather than their residential colleagues appeared to play a more significant role; indeed, it is noticeable that for these young people, most or all of the build-up to exclusion occurred prior to entering the children's home.

Jack's case is a good illustration. Aged seven at the time of exclusion, he had been looked after in foster care since the age of three and a half. He was excluded from his first primary school within a few weeks, and was then placed in the primary unit of a day EBD school. Jack's teacher had always found his behaviour extremely difficult to manage. However, concerns regarding his education became highlighted only when his foster placement broke down and a new social worker entered the case. At this point the professional network expanded rapidly. A social services psychologist came to test Jack and he also began receiving psychotherapy. A review was held at which the question of Jack's schooling was discussed and the proposal made that a residential school placement be sought. There was a widespread agreement that his current placement could not be sustained. In one report his teacher describes Jack's behaviour to be so extreme that he had to be held for much of the time in class. He was said to be aggressive towards other children and could not concentrate on a task for any length of time. His statement of special educational need notes that psychological assessment proved very difficult as Jack's level of distractibility reached a state almost of hyperactivity. His class teacher recalled

> I remember that was a huge relief for us – you know, you keep going because you don't want to let the child down. From then on they were looking for an alternative placement – it took some time. (Teacher)

In Michael's case, concern regarding his behaviour at school was interlinked with child protection concerns. During Michael's first year at school his behaviour became highly sexualised, and he also became increasingly aggressive. The headteacher used fixed-term exclusion as one means to signal to others the seriousness of the situation. This highlights the significance of exclusion as an event with meaning beyond the child's behaviour, the threat of which is a potent tool in relationships between professionals.

Concern grew when social workers began observing his behaviour at school, and a gradual consensus emerged that Michael could be placing other children at risk. Throughout this time there was also a high level of communication between the school and other professionals, though according to the school's headteacher this varied according to the seniority of the social workers involved:

> On the child protection side we had the police, a doctor and the school nurse. His mum also had a lot of things attached to her. On the child protection side we worked together well, because then we had to focus on Michael and what he needed... Michael's social worker was very good and she made a point of keeping in touch. We made an arrangement to phone every week – she would phone me or I would phone her – but we always talked. Further up the hierarchy, with the team leader, it was much less good and we were kept in the dark most of the time, constantly fighting for information. The social worker tried to bridge the gap. (Headteacher)

Michael then became looked after by foster carers within the local authority. However, the school did not feel this was entirely satisfactory, as he had been placed some distance away from the school and was constantly late.

In these cases professionals tended to see themselves as working together collaboratively. However, achieving the desired outcome tended to depend on the support of managers, and it was this aspect of the process which frequently led to difficulties. It is also important to stress that maintaining consensus about a particular strategy depended on the stability of the professional network. Graham's case presents us with a situation in which relationships between professionals were initially positive, but gradually changed as a new – and key – actor entered the process. Graham, aged nine, had a history of family problems and had displayed extreme behavioural difficulties throughout his school career. He had already been excluded from one primary school when a place was found for him at Downside Junior School. His social worker had approached the school following a chance conversation with a colleague, who had told her that the school was very sympathetic to admitting excluded children. At this point Graham was placed in Home B. As explained above, and in contrast to several other cases, his schooling tended to become more stable when he was living in residential accommodation. On returning home problems emerged once more. His social worker explained that social services had opposed the attempt at rehabilitation, but that this had been dictated by the courts. The education co-ordinator also pointed out that when Graham returned home, the links which had been established between the school and the children's home were broken. His mother lived some distance from the school, had never had much involvement and would not provide the same sort of support. She had no transport and therefore could not act as an 'emergency service' as the children's home had done.

The school saw these issues as much less significant than Graham's aggressive behaviour, which following his return home deteriorated still further. His class teacher stated that he was bullying and assaulting other children and required constant supervision. Even one-to-one work with a classroom assistant failed to meet his needs. Graham then re-entered the children's home, but there was little improvement in his behaviour. The children's home education co-ordinator and the school agreed that mainstream school was probably inappropriate; Graham was referred to the educational psychologist and was placed on the waiting list for the local day EBD school. As with cases where negotiation was the dominant pattern of interaction, as described earlier in the chapter, the deepening crisis brought with it an expansion in the professional network. In this case it seemed that the educational psychologist was being used to help legitimate a consensus regarding the desired course of action.

The pattern of interaction then shifted. The headteacher of Graham's school, who had been absent for much of this time, then returned to the school. She felt strongly that the school was the right place for Graham and insisted that he remain. However, his behaviour deteriorated still further and other parents began removing their children from the school. In the meantime Graham's social worker and the educational psychologist continued to argue that exclusion should take place, on the grounds that Graham was 'a danger from the child protection point of view'. Eventually the headteacher felt that she could no longer justify her position, commenting

> The parents just couldn't take his level of violence to other children – I almost had placards at the window…in the end the parents were right and the other children were getting a raw deal. (Headteacher)

It was agreed that Graham should leave the school, though no formal exclusion took place. In the meantime, Graham's name had been removed from the waiting list for the EBD school. Consequently he had to wait for over a year before gaining a part-time place at this school. In retrospect, residential staff regretted the way in which the situation had progressed, while acknowledging that the school had sought to act in Graham's best interests. Throughout the process leading up to Graham's exclusion there was a high level of interaction between all the professionals concerned. This had permitted consensus in the early stages of the process, but gradually the introduction of new actors – first the headteacher, and later parents, shifted the definition of the situation in important ways. The pattern of interaction also shifted from one characterised by negotiation to a strategic approach.

However, in the majority of cases where problems emerged for professionals working strategically, difficulties resulted from tensions further up the hierarchies of education and social services departments. These problems were especially acute when professionals took a 'strategic' view of the case and were collaborating with a particular end in view, such as finding an alternative school for the young person. To achieve such outcomes they depended on the support of managers. Thus in Hugh's case the social worker commented

> To the best of their abilities the different services have worked together quite well. But if we look at the needs we have identified for Hugh, we can't have them. We have identified that he needs a 52 week residential placement, more a behavioural therapy unit – not psychotherapeutic. But he can't have it – [Local Authority 1] won't pay for any out-of-county placements. (Social worker)

In these situations, exclusion was used by schools as part of the attempt to force action from managers. Jack's case demonstrates this particularly well. His teacher recognised and valued the support being offered by his new social worker and by children's home staff. The breaking point came when tensions emerged in relationships with those with authority over funding, further up the social work and education hierarchy. Eventually the school lost patience.

> I think it was finding that the date for the new placement had been put forward again. The headteacher [of the EBD school] was backing me, give him his due. Part of me thinks I should have hung on, but at the time it seemed an endless 'hanging on'... I don't think it was a good thing to do, but what else was there to do? It might have been the best thing for other people, but not the best thing for Jack. [The social worker] was certainly in agreement. [Home A] didn't really have a choice. They were being asked to provide extra support, so there was a funding implication there. They were saying they would only take him if there was adequate [educational] provision. (Class teacher)

However, the decision to exclude was not perceived as negative by the other professionals involved, in that it was felt something had to happen if progress was to be made. It was agreed by his teacher, social worker and the educational co-ordinator at Home A that Jack was not appropriately placed either at the EBD school he attended or in Home A. At the same time that the school felt increasingly unable to cope, plans were being made to find Jack a long-term therapeutic placement. There was also a sense among the professionals involved that exclusion, formal or informal, was necessary if funding difficulties were to be overcome and a new placement found. The school had also recently experienced similar difficulties with another child from the same children's home, which led the teacher in charge to believe that with Jack they had to be 'more forceful'. She explained that 'we excluded him really to push the system...'. Jack's social worker and key worker agreed with this interpretation, and overall it seemed that there had been a high degree of collusion among the different professionals. All the individuals who had worked together during the build-up to the exclusion were full of praise for their colleagues. The discrepancy in power, therefore, seemed to relate to hierarchical relationships within the local authority rather than between professionals working on the ground. This process seems similar to cases where exclusion is used as a means to push forward assessment for SEN. Galloway, Armstrong and Tomlinson (1994) found that out of a total of 30 assessments, in nine exclusion was used to force the pace of assessment. In ten other cases exclusions were made to signal a school's unwillingness to readmit a child whose needs were being assessed. In this study, the special needs of the child were accepted, but existing resources considered inadequate, especially given the needs of other children in the class or school.

Estrangement

As the discussion above has shown, the growing seriousness of the young person's problems tended to attract a considerable amount of professional attention. Professionals reached agreement about the nature of the problem and what might be appropriate action through meetings and regular contact by telephone. However, in some cases an apparent lack of communication between social worker, residential staff, school and young person if anything made exclusion easier. In these cases interviewees often disagreed about how much contact had taken place.

Estrangement most obviously characterised children living in private homes. This was consequently further exaggerated by the geographical distance which existed between the chief professional actors. As Chapter 5 has explained, Homes F and G had limited contact with either the local education authority and few links with local schools. Decision making could therefore more easily occur without the knowledge of other key professionals.

Interestingly, and in contrast with the pattern of interaction where children remained at the same school and changed care placement (see the section on negotiation above), estrangement tended to be associated with a change of school rather than entry to a children's home. As Chapter 4 outlined, several of the sample had experienced frequent disruption in their schooling and entry to a new school for reasons other than the move to secondary school was important for three of the sample. The educational problems resulting from high levels of mobility in schooling can be considerable. One of the educational psychologists interviewed noted the difficulties associated with moving school, remarking that if middle-class, stable families talk about the major impact of this, it must be 'many magnitudes greater' for children whose lives are already disrupted. Research into children living in bed-and-breakfast accommodation (Clark 1996) and traveller children (OFSTED 1996c) emphasises that schools will also encounter problems when dealing with children who have attended several schools and who may enter the school at unusual points in the school year. The most recent guidance on school exclusion also identifies pupils transferring schools outside normal entry points as being at particular risk of disaffection (DfEE 1999b).

When pupils have moved frequently, it is possible that schools do not perceive them to be 'permanent'. This issue became especially apparent in Local Authority 3, where large numbers of pupils from Local Authority 2 – and indeed many other local authorities – were placed. The care population in Local Authority 3 was therefore very large, and this in turn had implications for schools in the area. In one secondary school, briefly attended by Nicki, as many as a quarter of the total roll of 414 children was looked after, mostly in foster care. These pupils were described as 'casual admissions', a telling indication of their transient status. The head of pastoral care in the school explained:

> In many cases, children arrive with no educational information. Foster carers only have a bit of the story and children frequently have had no education. The onus is put on the foster carers and it is in the interests of the agency to get them into school. Our governors' policy is to talk to those who seek admission. We are under-subscribed and so we have little choice. Some other schools in the same area have the same problems. (Teacher)

The problems were especially acute where children had SENs. Although the school tried to admit only those with whom they felt they could work, the lack of information meant this was not always clear. A further difficulty was that Local Authority 3 did not always accept statements of SEN from elsewhere. The same teacher cited one girl with a statement who had attended a special school in her home authority. On arriving in Local Authority 3 she was pronounced fit for mainstream. The school felt unable to meet her needs, but this inevitably left this pupil without education.

Both Nicki, Lee and Paul entered new schools within this context, and the links which were formed between the young people concerned and their new schools were decidedly fragile. Residential staff believed that it was unlikely that exclusion would have occurred if changes of school had not taken place. In both cases the children's homes involved (Homes F and G) had objected to the attempt to place the young people in mainstream school. The preparation for entry to school had been non-existent, even though Nicki and Lee had extremely limited experience of such a setting, and had previously been attending the agency's own education unit. Meanwhile the schools concerned had received little or no information about their new pupils, and were not aware of the potential difficulties. Inevitably, however, problems quickly emerged.

Both Nicki and Lee were moved to new schools following the decision of managers in Local Authority 2 that the education they were receiving at the onsite unit of the private children's home was unsatisfactory. Residential staff played an important role in finding a new school place, as the social workers concerned did not know the area. In both cases, problems emerged very quickly indeed. In Nicki's case, the assistant headteacher insisted there had been some contact with the children's home at the point when difficulties began:

> My impression was this was another child who had no prior experience of mainstream school and probably no experience of the educational or social norms of the secondary school... To be fair to those responsible for Nicki, I made contact with carers when problems started to emerge and they did respond positively. Nicki also had academic problems. My gut reaction was that he had serious emotional problems in socialising with his peers. He only spent a couple of days here so we never had a chance to come to terms with his academic problems. (Assistant headteacher)

For the key worker and head of the home, however, the first contact with the school had come when, only two days after starting at the school, a letter had been received from the assistant headteacher stating that Nicki had punched another pupil in the stomach during a PE lesson. Nicki's key worker met with the headteacher, but Nicki was asked to leave. The senior teacher responsible for pastoral care stated unequivocally that in this case there were no grey areas. Home F tried to persuade the school to have Nicki back, but staff were told that this was too much of a risk.

Lee's case reveals what was probably the highest level of conflict in this respect. He was resident in Home F (a privately owned establishment) in Local Authority 3. Lee, aged 11, had been living there for four years with his two brothers. He had suffered physical, emotional and sexual abuse from his parents and also – allegedly – while living at another residential institution prior to his placement at Home F. Throughout his time at the children's home he had attended the linked education unit, and he had been assessed as having learning and behavioural difficulties. An education assessment which had taken place shortly after his entry to Home F (aged seven) stated that academically he was still functioning at a pre-school level. An educational psychologist's report (an educational psychologist was employed on a consultancy basis by the private agency) assessed Lee as mid-way between having moderate learning difficulties and having low average intelligence. When Lee was ten, however, the education department in Local Authority 2 decided – in consultation with Lee's social worker – that he should no longer attend the private unit. Home F alleged that they had not been invited to the meeting at which this decision was made. Instead, the social worker telephoned this decision to Home F. The service manager of the home immediately responded with a letter expressing considerable concern about the proposed change in placement, and also that there had been no consultation with residential staff. The headteacher of the onsite unit also wrote to the education department, complaining at the lack of consultation and stating that she did not think it was in Lee's interests to be moved. Home F called a meeting which was attended by the social worker. Local Authority 2, meanwhile, argued that they could not continue to pay for an educational placement in a unit which was not registered by the DfEE.

> It was really out of the blue – we were stunned by it. However, these things do sometimes happen and we thought it would all blow over, then realised it wasn't going to. We just couldn't believe it. It was clearly the wrong thing for Lee. I wrote a report and the ed psych wrote a report making our views clear. Social services and education just weren't prepared to listen. They had taken the decision and that was it. (Headteacher of education unit)

> Our school was in the midst of the registration process – we had interim approval. Lee was doing very well…[Local Authority 2] took the decision to move him and place him at another school. It was a political decision – that's what it looked like. (Manager, Home F)

The social worker took charge of finding Lee a new school, and eventually he was placed in a local EBD school. Problems quickly emerged. Four days after starting he had been given a detention and a week later the taxi firm which had been transporting Lee to and from school refused to take him home. Within the children's home his behaviour is recorded as being increasingly abusive and difficult. After only three weeks the school phoned Home F to say that Lee was not to return for the following week.

These cases are interesting as examples of situations where the structure of residential care, and specifically the relationship between local authorities and private provision, contributed to the development of a situation where exclusion became much more likely. The official responsible for the education of children looked after in Local Authority 2 had a low opinion of the quality of education offered by the private agency; meanwhile, the relationship between the agency and the education department in Local Authority 3 was extremely weak. Those interviewed appeared to consider these issues to be more significant than any assessment of the young person's education. In each of these cases, residential staff saw themselves as following a strategy which was in the best interests of the child, but felt that they had been powerless against the decisions of the local authority. The local authority consequently became the 'bogeyman', while the children were construed as victims of an unfeeling and arbitrary bureaucracy. Interaction between all professionals involved was highly dispersed, and indeed almost confined to the communication of extremely important decisions. Both the local authority and the school apparently had sufficient power to make these decisions without consultation.

In these cases (Nicki and Lee) it is also significant that the children's homes involved had little commitment to their being placed at these particular schools. While acknowledging some regret that the exclusions had taken place, they also felt strongly that, had their views been listened to by the local authority, the young people would have remained in the educational unit attached to the private agency. Lee's former teacher at this unit described her reaction, saying

> When he was excluded, the education department had to say 'O God, they were right'. I must admit my behaviour wasn't very professional, but I phoned up the education officer and said 'surely to goodness, you must realise he has to come back here'. But it was all very childish. He [Lee] was then out of school for more than a year. I think it's criminal, I really do. (Head of education unit)

The head of home felt that she had essentially been blackmailed by the local authority, in that she had been told that if a mainstream place was not found for Nicki, his placement at the home would also be ended. Although the school place had been found, she insisted that it had been bound to fail.

In Paul's case, exclusion was to occur without any apparent awareness on the part of those involved that the situation within the school placement was serious and likely to result in exclusion. Aged 15, Paul had lived in Home G for only a few months; prior to this he had been cared for at Home F with his two younger brothers. His primary school career had been, from all accounts, relatively unproblematic. During his first year of secondary school, however, he became a school refuser. Residential staff attributed this to the failure of Local Authority 2 to find a foster placement for the three siblings, although they had been looked after in residential care for some three years. The fact that Paul had now reached adolescence, together with the learning difficulties and severe behavioural difficulties of the brother next to him in age, made it unlikely that a joint foster placement would ever be found.

It had been decided that, in view of Paul's long-standing absence from his first secondary school, an attempt should be made to look elsewhere. The children's home took responsibility for this, on the basis that they knew the local schools. This was not easy, but a place was found at Hilltop school. Early reports from teachers included such comments as 'Paul is a loner. Many of the tutor group don't have a good word to say of him.'

The senior teacher involved considered that Paul was not motivated to do well either socially or academically, and that although he had been new to the school, other entrants had contrived to settle down and make friends successfully. His conclusion was that ultimately Paul was a 'shallow character'. Paul also claimed that he had never wanted to go to the school, as he did not know any of the other pupils. However, his attendance continued to be erratic, though there was little, if any, contact between the children's home and the school in regard to this and no other service – such as the education welfare service – became involved. No contact took place with the social worker. Early in the Autumn term a letter was sent from the senior pastoral teacher at Hilltop to the head of Home G requesting that Paul should not return to the school. Meanwhile, the head of home felt that the school had tried hard and agreed that Paul's return to school was unlikely. No formal decision was made to exclude. Paul himself concurred with this situation – he had not wanted to go to the school and had not enjoyed the time he had spent there.

In many respects this case appears to have been more a matter of drift than active consensus about the exclusion. None of those involved had a strong commitment to Paul going to the school, but there was no debate or disagreement about the placement. The ending of Paul's time there consequently appears to be less exclusion than a petering out of a placement to which no one had ever attached any great importance.

Young people: strategy and collaboration

So far this chapter has focused on the relationships and the patterns of interaction which operated between professionals during the build-up to the exclusion. This must be complemented by consideration of the role which young people themselves played in this process.

Perhaps significantly, remarkably little comment was made by professionals regarding the views of the young people themselves. Younger children tended to be perceived more sympathetically, and were sometimes seen as victims of the process. This was especially true of those caught up in a build-up to exclusion which involved tense or conflictual relationships between the professionals involved. However, as has already been suggested, in professional relationships characterised by negotiation or strategic collaboration, there tended to be agreement on the 'deviancy' of the young person and the fact that they were not best placed in mainstream school.

It is important, when examining children's perceptions of exclusion, to distinguish this from their views on school. All those interviewed liked some aspects of school and enjoyed being with their friends and the majority also liked some subjects at school. Younger children, indeed, frequently appeared to enjoy the entire curriculum. Teachers were viewed less positively, with some children complaining that teachers 'nagged' or were 'grumpy' – though one 10-year-old qualified this by noting that 'it depends on whether she's had a good day or not'.

In terms of their exclusions, the four younger children interviewed were not always clear on what had happened, or perhaps did not feel able to talk about the incident during interview. On asked about their feelings on leaving the school, two had felt happy, one 'not bothered' and the other angry. Lee said frankly 'I was actually glad I left, to tell you the truth.' Two also said that they had not been surprised at being excluded and knew that they had been in trouble many times before.

Adolescents had adopted a more strategic approach to the situation and insisted that they had deliberately sought to be excluded. At the same time they felt that they had been unfairly treated within school. What came first – that is, their dislike of school or the school's desire to have them excluded – was difficult to disentangle. Alex, for example, liked being with friends at school, but did not like teachers. He claimed that he was picked on at school, and could 'fill a book' with all the things he was blamed for, which had included the accusation that he was taking drugs. He had not been surprised when excluded on a fixed-term basis, and had been unconcerned when this happened – 'I just sit and laugh at them.' To this extent he seemed able to distance himself from the situation, and even to be able to use it for his own ends. He wanted to be expelled and to have home tuition. Similarly, Hugh liked seeing his friends and also enjoyed some subjects such as maths and cooking, while condemning humanities and English as 'boring, completely boring'. He also felt that he had been unfairly treated, but his resentment related mainly to his placement in an EBD school. He wanted to return to mainstream and therefore wanted to be excluded. On being interviewed after his exclusion, he explained that he

'...just didn't like the school. They said I couldn't cope in a mainstream school and I said if they gave me five weeks in a mainstream school I'd prove it. I hate small schools, don't like the kids.'

He agreed that in the meantime he had behaved badly:

'...hitting teachers, throwing chairs around, breaking the computer, anything you can do... I did it on purpose. I wanted to get kicked out, that's why I kept on kicking off.'

Unfortunately this strategy had somewhat backfired, as Hugh acknowledged. He disliked the children's home in which he had been placed and was opposed to the plan that he should go to a residential boarding school. 'There's no way they're getting me to a boarding school. They'll need all the coppers in the world.'

Eddie acknowledged that the language he had used to his head of year was appalling and thought that this had been the main reason for his exclusion; at the same time he agreed he had been in trouble many times before. This, he suggested, was due to 'mood swings'. However, views varied as to whether the exclusion was fair. Adolescents were more likely to feel that they had been blamed for the misdeeds of others or simply 'picked on'. Kris also strenuously denied that he had been a problem. 'They said I was swearing at teachers and fighting. I wasn't at all. I never once fought at that school. So I just left. Kicked out.'

In wanting to be excluded, the views of these young people came to complement those of the professionals working with them, and to this extent exclusion was made easier. It is interesting to observe, though, that the adolescents at least felt that while they were unable to change teachers' attitudes towards them, exclusion was something they could control through their actions.

The group of children whose views were most closely aligned to those of staff were those living in private homes, and who had moved into a school – only to be excluded after a short time there – following the decision of managers in Local Authority 2. In these cases the young people themselves did not perceive placements at these schools to be positive. Lee stated unequivocally that he had hated attending the school and had been angry at being made to do so. Similarly, Paul said that he had found it very difficult to settle in his new school. Both he and Nicki stated a preference for attending the on-site education unit, but, in Paul's case at least, realised that this was unlikely to happen. Paul and Nicki also thought that the children's home staff had worked hard on their behalf.

Overall, then, exclusion appeared to be no more of a surprise to the young people than it was to professionals. Some children saw exclusion partly as an inevitable consequence of the way they were perceived within school and partly as a result of their own deliberate actions. Others knew that they had been in trouble but did not suggest that they were personally involved in the decision to exclude.

Conclusion

This chapter has focused on the nature of relationships between professionals during the exclusion process. Three patterns of interaction have been described: interaction characterised by negotiation; interaction involving strategic collaboration; and interaction which involves estrangement between the relevant professionals.

A great deal of information has been covered and it is necessary not only to highlight the issues which appear to be of most importance, but also to consider these in relation to earlier chapters. Chapter 4 presented data regarding the family and care backgrounds of the young people, making the point that educational difficulties might well be exacerbated by the troubled nature of their prior experiences. Chapter 5 went on to suggest that, despite the existence of a legislative framework, there is no standard procedure which can guide the actions of teachers and other professionals in the time leading up to an exclusion. At the same time, the teachers interviewed did outline the different levels of sanctions which existed within schools and the resources available to provide support in the event of a pupil experiencing behavioural difficulties.

In the present chapter, it has become clear that the experiences of young people prior to an exclusion are both varied and extremely complex – to the extent that they may often appear arbitrary and hard to classify. Clearly, however, for most of the 17 young people, exclusion was predictable. The individuals involved were, for whatever reason, aware that exclusion was likely to occur. This situation required delicate management if the episode was to be brought to a close perceived as satisfactory by professionals.

Descriptions of the behaviour presented by the young people supported other research into the issue, but it was not always clear that any significant deterioration had taken place. However, it is striking that while many young people had long-standing behavioural problems, professionals – and most often teachers – were usually able to point to a particular event or change in circumstances which they felt to have resulted in an escalation of these difficulties. Events in the care careers of the young people frequently played a part in this. More detailed examination of the significance of the care process in relation to the eventual decision to exclude will take place in Chapter 8.

It is important to point out that the predictability of exclusion did not necessarily make it easy for schools to make the decision to exclude. As Hayden (1997) points out in relation to primary schools, an exclusion could prove very stressful for the staff concerned. One class teacher, reflecting on Ian's exclusion, remarked that 'Schools always feel guilty – we carry this huge guilt complex about having excluded someone. Even though you know in your heart that it's best for the other children.'

On the other hand exclusion could also be a huge relief. Michael's teacher commented 'I remember it was a huge relief for us – you know, you keep going because you don't want to let the child down.'

A number of important findings emerge in relation to the relationships between professionals during that period prior to exclusion. In particular, and given much current rhetoric on the value of inter-agency working, it seems that finer distinctions should be drawn between the amount of interaction which takes place between professionals and the quality of that interaction. Care must also be taken in drawing a direct relationship between close inter-professional relationships of high quality and the prevention of an exclusion. As has been shown in relation to the present sample, in many cases where exclusion occurs there is consensus between adults – and often with the concurrence of the young person – that exclusion is the desirable course of action. However, the measures taken to prevent exclusion in these cases appear to be variable. The gradual severance of links between the young person and the school is particularly noticeable in this sample, and casts some doubt on the value of 'cooling off' periods as a means of support. Consensus also seemed to be based on considerable disparities of knowledge between the individuals concerned, and carers in particular were only rarely in a position where they were able – or saw their role as involving – advocacy for the young person concerned.

7

Exclusion
An Alternative Definition

Introduction

Understanding the reasons why exclusion takes place is at least partly dependent on an accurate definition of what exclusion means. The evidence so far presented in this study suggests that exclusion is a much more heterogeneous phenomenon than is sometimes apparent from descriptions of the problem. As the previous chapter has shown, the decision to exclude is also mediated through different kinds of professional relationships, which may be managed through negotiation, strategic collaboration or estrangement.

As a result, exclusion is much less amenable to definition than might appear from the way in which it is presented in the public realm. Indeed, as Dean (in Macdonald 1997) has commented in regard to the concept of 'underclass', the term 'exclusion' 'does not so much define a tangible phenomenon as symbolise socially constituted definitions of failure' (p.57). Rather, its significance lies in the manner of its construction and debate (Mann 1994 cited by Dean in Macdonald 1997). Similarly, exclusion from school has come to represent the failures of teachers, parents, government policies and young people, depending on the social and political discourse being adopted.

While this study argues that official definitions of exclusion are inadequate, it is impossible to dismiss the high profile which exclusion per se has assumed in media and political debate about education. However, the gap between the public definition of exclusion and the way in which individuals understand the situations of young people has been a recurrent theme in this study. The issue first emerged in the data collection phase of the research, when it proved difficult to identify cases which fulfilled the initial criteria for inclusion in the study – namely permanent exclusion as indicated by a letter of exclusion sent by a headteacher to the young person's parent or carer (DfE 1994a; see also DfEE 1999b). The absence of cases conforming to the political definition of permanent exclusion suggested that exclusion covers a much more varied range of circumstances than those contained in official guidance and legislation.

Chapter 6 has examined the nature of relationships between professionals and young people during the build-up to the exclusion process. This chapter will develop this discussion further by considering how these relationships affect the way in which a young person is excluded. It will begin by considering which groups of children can be placed within the category of those who are 'excluded'. It will then examine the issue of the distinction between formal and informal, or official and unofficial, exclusion. Although 'unofficial' exclusion is recognised as a matter of concern, there has been little research investigation of this.

However, it is important to move beyond the question of such distinctions if theoretical understanding of exclusion is to be developed. Also, if it is correct to say that 'exclusion' fails to do justice to their experiences, it is necessary to find an alternative classification of their problems. This is not easy; a striking feature of the experiences of the 17 young people studied is the wide variation in the exclusion process as applied to each case. This is especially true in regard to professional involvement in these cases; as Chapter 5 has already shown, social workers, residential social workers and teachers frequently remarked that the action taken 'depends on the individual'. This chapter will suggest, however, that common features can be identified in the problems presented by the group studied, some of which can be directly or indirectly linked to their experiences of public care.

'Excluded' children

A theme which has flowed through this study is the problem of defining when an exclusion has taken place. Early in the process of finding a sample, it was discovered that, contrary to the expectations of the researcher, it was difficult to identify children living in children's homes who were officially excluded. This has also been the experience of other researchers in this area (Jackson 1995, private correspondence). At the same time, however, residential staff continued to claim that exclusion represented a significant problem in their work. Two observations can be made in respect of this apparent contradiction. First of all, as Chapter 8 will discuss in greater detail, exclusion was a major problem when it did occur. Secondly, more intensive questioning during interviews revealed that 'exclusion' was often used as a shorthand for a range of problems relating to children who were not attending school.

Stirling's (1992) research into the exclusion from school of children looked after in children's homes has proved instrumental in demonstrating the existence of a category of 'informal' exclusions, where children are discouraged from attending school but where no official procedures are followed. Booth (1996) takes this further still, arguing that any children who are outside mainstream schooling may be considered to be excluded. He therefore includes children educated in special schools, truants, and pupils for whom English is a second language in the 'excluded' category. This definition of exclusion as a problem has the merit of emphasising that exclusion represents a social phenomenon which is defined and negotiated by the different individuals involved. However, the disadvantage of this 'all or nothing' approach is that it detracts from any idea of exclusion as an issue which has assumed a distinct dynamic in a specific socio-political context. Crucially, the experiences of some of the groups of pupils Booth describes as 'excluded' are mediated by quite different social and bureaucratic arrangements.

Examination of the present sample reveals, equally, that their problems were defined in very different ways and these too were mediated by the relationships between professionals who were also working within quite different structural contexts. Analysis of the data suggests that there were four different sets of problems identified by professionals as reasons why children were not in school, all of which call into question a focus on 'exclusion' as an object of concern regarding children looked after in residential accommodation. The inclusion of young people within these different groups should not of course suggest that their experiences were identical; rather these categories serve as 'ideal types' which contribute to an understanding of the different relationships which may exist between the young person and the school and so permit exclusion, in the broadest sense, to take place.

Exclusion by non-admission

The first group to be considered includes three of the sample – Roland, Omar and Fred. For these young people the initial problem centred on the fact that they did not have a school place. This is not to suggest that they did not present behavioural problems; in Fred's case, for example, his behaviour was among the reasons that the school explicitly stated to be a reason for his non-admission. However, their education had been disrupted for other reasons, including changes in care placement, the decision of the local authority that they should no longer receive their education from private agencies, and in one case coming to the UK from another country. No school or even the relevant local education authorities appeared to be taking responsibility for their education, and consequently the role of social services personnel was crucial in terms of their subsequent educational careers.

It is hard to evaluate how far difficulties in gaining admission to schools can be attributed to being in residential care. Most residential staff, as Chapter 5 has described, did feel that young people were stigmatised by their care status and this extended to admissions to school. One interviewee, for example, had contacted 13 schools before finding a place for one young person. She said that the school had expressed strong reservations related to the fact that the child was looked after. This problem was equally pertinent to private homes. The result was that children's homes and social workers would tend to target efforts at schools where they already had contact, or, in some cases, schools which found it more difficult to refuse access because they were under-subscribed. This will be especially difficult where pupils have a history of exclusion; two of the sample had been permanently excluded at least twice, and four more had been permanently excluded once before.

Exclusion on admission

The second group also includes three young people – Paul, Nicki and Lee. For these children, exclusion occurred remarkably quickly, within a few weeks or even a few days of the child's entry to the school. The pupil's behaviour was almost immediately defined as intolerable, and accounts of the young person's time at the school recast in quite dramatic terms by the teachers involved. The pathology of individual pupils – in being 'odd' or 'a sociopath' – tended to dominate in the school's explanations for the rapid decision to exclude.

The speed at which the exclusion occurred is striking when considered against some interpretive approaches to behaviour within the classroom. In studies which adopt a labelling perspective, the labelling process is described as occurring in the context of an ongoing relationship between teacher and pupils. Thus teachers and pupils have sufficient knowledge of each other to make reasonably informed assessments of the other – which teachers are strict, which pupils are bright and so on. Thus Hargreaves, Hestor and Mellor (1975) comment:

> Although deviant pupils may be classified together under the diffuse label of 'troublemaker' there is nevertheless a uniqueness about every typing when pupils are considered as individuals... *There is a certainty and confidence to the teacher's knowledge of these pupils which, based on multitudinous events few of which are remembered...has been built over time into a coherent and resistant characterisation.* (p.215, my emphasis).

Underlying this perspective is the – not unreasonable – assumption that school pupils attend the same school for the majority of their educational careers. There is little, if any, sociological analysis of less stable school careers. Children looked after, and other transient populations of school pupils, are therefore not easily incorporated into such analyses. The numbers are undeniably small, and such pupils – whether truants, children living in temporary accommodation or traveller children – will invariably represent a tiny minority of a school's population. Some research has also suggested that teachers do not perceive children looked after as a discrete group within the school, but tend to view them as part of a wider subsection of the school population, including children with emotional and behavioural difficulties and children with family problems (Berridge et al. 1997). They are not considered to be necessarily problematic, and in turn need not be part of an 'anti-school' group of pupils.

Yet for the young people in this group, there was no 'honeymoon period' on entry to the school, and it would be difficult to understand their experiences without reference to the context in which they occurred. The immediate setting of the children's home is important; for the children resident in homes run by the private agency in Local Authority 3, they arrived at schools with little information about their educational background. Nicki's case highlights these problems. Aged 13, he had been looked after since the age of eight in a variety of residential placements. Information about his educational background appeared to be non-existent; the last known school he had attended to any significant extent was a primary school prior to entering care. Nicki had been placed at Home G as an emergency placement, and at the same time began attending the education unit linked to the home. The head of home described his behaviour during this period as 'very chaotic' and said that this had led to Nicki being restrained in the education unit. However, just before the summer holidays the education department in Local Authority 2 intervened and said that Nicki should be moved to a mainstream school. During this period Nicki had no social worker, and residential staff assumed responsibility for finding a new school. This proved difficult and at the start of the new term a review was held to discuss Nicki's lack of education. At this meeting the head of home expressed concern at the effect the lack of schooling had on Nicki's behaviour. Social services responded by saying that if the home could not cope with Nicki's behaviour, then he would be moved.

Five months later a place was found at a local Roman Catholic secondary school. Nicki's key worker felt they had been very fortunate in finding a place, but did not think the school had been supportive from the start; 'it was the classic case of a kid in care'. However, the assistant headteacher felt that initially he had not perceived Nicki particularly negatively.

> I interviewed the carer and Nicki, and basically because he was Roman Catholic – though I doubt if he's ever seen the inside of a church – we admitted him. We always try to get hold of the previous secondary school and speak to them at some length, to try to forestall any problems. In Nicki's case, though, we found it impossible to get any previous information.' (Assistant headteacher)

This teacher had consulted with residential staff but claimed there had been no indication that Nicki might be violent '…and so I told him what one would tell any new boy – to settle in, make friends and so on.'

The problems associated with the absence of important information were exacerbated by the fact that private homes in this study lacked links with local schools. Consequently there was no pre-existing relationship on which to base negotiation, which made it less likely that allowances would be made when a pupil presented problems. The local education authority context was also of considerable importance; these schools were under-subscribed and received a steady, sometimes overwhelming stream of 'casual admissions', many of whom had special educational needs and were likely to remain at the school on a temporary basis.

The young people themselves were almost totally disengaged from the school. This group tended to have had little recent experience of full-time education in a large institution, and were therefore unacquainted with the norms of behaviour in this context. They had not, therefore, learned the strategies which would enable adaptation and social survival in relation to teachers or fellow pupils (Woods, 1988); nor were they aware of the roles they should fulfil as 'new' pupils. Paul, for example, did not feel that he had been treated well from the beginning and explained why he had found it difficult to settle in:

> No, I didn't get into trouble – I was new, so I didn't have a timetable. I'd go into one class and I wouldn't like it, so I'd go into another class and they would chuck me out and tell me to go into another class. And I didn't want to go and knock at the office. They all moaned at me and there was nothing I could do to stop them moaning.

Lee, who had moved from the children's home onsite unit to an EBD school, also expressed strong dislike of the change of school: 'I hated it... I used to get bullied. All I had to do was walk across the playground and I got hit.'

It was also notable that young people appeared to have been given little choice in regard to the school they should attend. Nicki, Paul and Lee were quite clear that they had never wanted to change schools and on the fact that they wanted to attend the off-site education unit. While there is no direct evidence, it also seems likely that it is difficult for a young person to exercise choice in a situation where residential carers and social workers were in disagreement over the plans for them (see Chapter 6). Exclusion was, consequently, something of a relief.

This group of cases highlights a recurrent theme in research into young people looked after, namely the importance of planning and preparation in regard to the education of young people who are looked after but have also experienced very troubled educational careers (Grimshaw and Sinclair 1997; Sinclair, Garnett and Berridge 1995). In these circumstances it seems questionable whether the priority should be a school place 'at all costs'. While it is clearly undesirable that children should not be receiving education, the damage that is incurred though ill-planned placements in schools unable or unwilling to take account of the young person's previous schooling, or lack of it, may be greater still. At the same time, if schools are to be able to work with a new pupil, then it is essential that they have access to as much information as possible.

Graduated exclusion

In the third set of cases – Alex, Jack, Michael, Hugh, Graham – exclusion was more firmly linked to the context of the school. All five young people had a school place. Definition of the problem focused firmly on their behaviour, and the fact that unless their behaviour improved, exclusion was likely. The adults involved emphasised that their response to this situation had been to try to prevent such a crisis occurring and the fact that exclusion began to seem inevitable should not be taken to mean that no action was taken to prevent exclusion during the period of build-up. Teachers in these cases talked about how difficult they had found the exclusion, and emphasised that it had not been a decision which had been taken lightly. It was evident that measures had been taken to try to avoid the exclusion, including the involvement of classroom assistants, educational psychologists and in one case a therapist.

In some respects these cases corresponded more closely to other research evidence regarding the reasons for exclusion. However, the outstanding feature of the experiences of these young people was the progressive isolation of the young person from the peer group within the classroom. Thus Hugh, for example, gradually spent less and less time at school in the build-up to his exclusion. A table of his attendance at school in the seven months prior to his exclusion showed that from a possible total of 55 school days, he missed seven through illness, four as a result of unofficial exclusions, three following removal by the staff of his children's home, and nine through fixed-term exclusion, leaving 32 days when he actually reached the school.

What is ironic is the perception held by residential and social workers that support was best offered to the young person by removing them from the classroom situation. Teachers valued this support and in some cases this strategy did appear to extend the young person's career at the school. At the same time, it seemed questionable whether this was realistically a long-term means by which the pupil's situation could be resolved, and at times appeared to beg the question as to whether support was being offered to the school or to the young person.

Several of the group had experienced fixed-term exclusions, which were usually perceived by schools as a sanction to be used as a serious warning. These fixed-term exclusions, as in the cases of Jack and Michael, could therefore in themselves represent a symbolic means of communicating to other actors within the process that the school was prepared to take action. As a consequence of this gradual process of disconnection, the child's experience of schooling became significantly different to that of his peers, and in some respects it could be argued that 'exclusion' had already occurred. Furthermore, the opportunity to develop and sustain a 'working consensus' about behaviour within the school and classroom context became extremely limited (Hargreaves 1975). Understandably, schools and those *in loco parentis* will argue that it is preferable for a child to miss some time at school but to retain a school place. However, in practice it would seem desirable that this takes place on a planned basis and within a specified time limit.

The physical distancing of young people from the environment of the school served to ease the social transition from the young person's membership of the school, no matter how problematic that may have been, to excluded pupil. The decision to exclude was consequently less significant, as the individuals concerned were effectively already excluded from participation in the everyday life of the school. To this extent the exclusion process in these cases closely resembles the model of 'deviancy amplification' described in other studies of offending and difficult behaviour in schools. Traditionally this perspective has been applied to the use of streaming in secondary schools, but it appears equally useful in regard to the exclusions. According to this view, when a pupil's behaviour has been defined as socially deviant, those with formal responsibility for controlling such deviance may come to act towards them in ways which serve to isolate them from their peers. Thus isolated, it is argued, these young people will be integrated into a deviant sub-culture (Willis 1977; Hargreaves 1967). This latter point was not true for the three younger children in this group, though professionals did suggest that in the cases of Alex and Hugh placement in a children's home where several residents did not attend school was unhelpful.

Planned exclusion

Exclusion is usually considered to be a decision made by the school to which others respond. In this final group of cases, which includes those of John, Craig, and Eddie, a rather different approach was taken. While their behaviour was equally problematic, the intervening feature of these cases was the recognition by at least one of the professionals involved that an alternative plan should be prepared in the event of exclusion taking place. Eddie's case illustrates this very well. He had found it difficult to keep up in mainstream education and for a time had been a school refuser. This was noted by an EWO, who in turn arranged a meeting with his social worker and the teacher responsible for pastoral care. Eddie agreed to return to school, where he began attending the special needs department and was encouraged to work at his own pace. Initially a part-time timetable was also worked out. Nevertheless, even with this support the EWO had been doubtful whether the placement would last. She therefore wrote a report recommending that a place be sought at a local tutorial unit. As she had suspected, Eddie's behaviour did deteriorate and he was later excluded. The existence of an alternative plan meant that he was able to move into the tutorial centre almost immediately.

The young people concerned had varying degrees of commitment to these plans, but it seemed that this level of preparation was likely to be helpful in reducing the time children would spend out of school in the event of exclusion taking place. This pattern of interaction depended not only on one individual having a high level of motivation vis-a-vis the young person's education, but also on their having informal links with other key individuals. Perhaps more crucially still, the social workers and EWO who assumed the most active role in these cases were also distinct in their perception of the young person as having the ability to respond positively to education, if this was provided in an appropriate context. The decision to exclude came as no surprise, and was in fact perceived as welcome.

The young people who were interviewed in this category – all adolescents – said that they had wanted to be excluded and even that they had deliberately behaved in such a way that they knew this would happen. These pupils had a much more sophisticated stock of knowledge about school than their peers described above and had already produced a rationalised assessment of their position within the school. Most had been excluded on either a fixed-term or permanent basis in the past, and were aware of the type of behaviour which could trigger exclusion, usually involving rudeness to teachers. At the same time the disruption they had experienced during their school careers meant their investment in any one school was limited. It might therefore be argued that they had learned to cultivate the art of 'role distance', in that they knew but had failed to internalise the norms of behaviour required in the school context (Woods 1979). Also, while some members of this group said they liked being at school because they enjoyed being with friends, the fact that they had access to an alternative peer group in the children's home meant that the prospect of the loss of schoolmates through exclusion had perhaps a lesser impact than might otherwise have been the case.

The decision to exclude: official versus informal procedures

In academic and policy related discussion of exclusion, the question of the extent to which official procedures are followed has aroused considerable concern. However, definition of what is meant by 'informal exclusion' is exceedingly difficult, as the circumstances in and the means by which informal exclusion takes place are exceedingly diverse. In this study it is suggested that the feature of informal exclusion which distinguishes it from other forms of non-attendance is the fact that, like formal exclusion, it is generated by the school.

Obviously, informal exclusion can only take place where there are formal procedures governing the use of exclusion as a sanction. Writing prior to the 1986 Education Act, which introduced a statutory framework for exclusion, Galloway *et al.* (1982) emphasised the importance of informal agreement to the exclusion process. They argue that if exclusion is viewed as resulting from a human interaction, then a legalistic viewpoint is only valid to a limited degree. Similarly, two of the secondary headteachers interviewed felt that greater flexibility was needed in dealing with the issue. They felt that the option of indefinite exclusion offered this, and that 'removal of that option has led to the permanent exclusion of pupils who would otherwise have been excluded on an indefinite basis'.

Closely linked to the issue of informal exclusion is that of trial placements in other schools. It is noticeable that, on a general level, the readmission of pupils excluded from other schools was, in many respects, a more sensitive issue that the actual exclusion process. In Local Authority 1 there was an agreement among headteachers that they would seek to co-operate regarding excluded pupils – a 'quid pro quo arrangement that "I'll take one of yours if you take care of one of mine"'.

Secondary heads in this authority felt that a written policy on readmissions was undesirable and preferred to have a working policy. Two schools which tended to have more available places felt especially 'dumped on'. The headteacher of one of these said that she was willing to consider pupils excluded from other schools, but that it was hard to provide the necessary transitional support due to staff shortages. Heads in this authority also supported the use of trial placements prior to exclusion occurring, with one claiming that 60 per cent of these were successful. The issue of trial placements is a thorny one. Earlier government guidance stated clearly that schools 'may not admit pupils on a trial basis, give pupils a lower priority in admission arrangements or refuse a pupil admission on the grounds that he or she may disrupt the education of other pupils.' (DfE 1994a, para 28). One teacher commented:

> … heads used to co-operate over trial periods at school. Since this became illegal it has meant more children not getting into school. I would like to see a return to this. It only took place in negotiation with other school heads when there had been a confrontation and it would be to the benefit of all if the child was moved. We used to let them do six weeks and it could work… It would allow a more common sense ethos and flexibility between schools. It is another example of government policy working against schools by making them more competitive. (Teacher)

More recently, and since the present study was undertaken, some allowance for such flexibility has explicitly been made: recent guidance suggests that a 'managed move' to another school is a possible response to dealing with a student who is presenting persistently difficult behaviour (DfEE 1999b). Paragraph 5:6 states that a 'fresh start, with the opportunity to develop new relationships, can have a positive impact on a child's progress'. However, the evidence on the outcomes of such moves continues to be at best limited, and further evaluation of the use of such policies is necessary.

Others felt that removal of the indefinite option had been positive. One primary school head acknowledged that it had 'put paid to schools excluding children willy-nilly because the money goes with the child' and considered it positive that schools should try to contain children, but felt that budget constraints worked against this strategy.

Informal exclusion is by its nature difficult to monitor. However, anecdotal evidence attesting to its use is strong. For example, in his 1994/95 annual report the chief inspector of schools notes in regard to primary schools that 'There are examples of informal exclusion in which parents are encouraged to transfer a child to another school before formal procedures are started' (OFSTED 1996b). Stirling (1992) in a paper highlighting the issue of what she terms 'unofficial' exclusions among children looked after in children's homes, describes three different scenarios. First, exclusion may be disguised as a medical problem. She gives the examples of a teenage girl absent for weeks with 'menstruation pains' and a boy whose temporary, authorised absence for flu was extended for a whole term. Second, some pupils are encouraged not to turn up when new rules are introduced, or old rules more strictly enforced, regarding school uniform or hairstyle. These issues may be particularly pertinent for pupils from minority ethnic groups (Bourne, Bridges and Searle 1994). Sewell (1997) records the problems which ensued in the comprehensive he was studying when a new headteacher issued a rule that boys must not have patterns cut into their hair, a style popular amongst some male African-Caribbean pupils. The enforcement of this rule was by no means consistent and resulted in several exclusions taking place. Finally, Stirling states that parents may also persuade parents that their child should remain at home while the school approaches the LEA to make special provision. However, while not disputing the validity of this evidence, Stirling's argument suggests a somewhat conspiratorial approach to this type of exclusion. It is also important to incorporate the views of others involved in the process.

Exclusion from school invariably carries with it serious consequences, but informal exclusion holds particular dangers. The fact that it is difficult to monitor means that little is known about the frequency with which it occurs or, indeed, cases where it is prevented or overturned. Children who are informally excluded are not protected by the law regarding the time limits on exclusion, and have no right to alternative educational provision. Circular 10/94 made clear that exclusion should only take place through official channels (arguably this is also the assumption in the 1999 guidance). The earlier circular also emphasised that permanent exclusion is an inappropriate sanction in relation to such matters as school uniform and truancy. Nor should it be used as a means to speed up special needs assessment procedures. However, informal exclusion clearly has advantages to schools, most obviously that a child who is troublesome is removed from the classroom without an exclusion being recorded for that school. Discord between staff and with governors may also be circumvented, while the fact that the pupil remains on the role means that a place is filled and the school may be able to avoid admitting another pupil, perhaps even more troublesome, as a replacement.

The issue is an extremely complex one, and here it will be argued that it is mistaken to present informal exclusion simply as the clear cut infringement of the law and official guidance. A key factor contributing to this complexity, which is essential to understanding the nature of informal exclusion, is that informal exclusion is likely to be presented as being essentially benign. Teachers, social workers and others may argue, for example, that an informal, co-operative agreement regarding a child's education is infinitely preferable to the stigma of an official exclusion. Galloway *et al.* (1982) support this, pointing out that the problems which result in a child's removal from school are likely to arouse strong feelings in parents, teachers and pupils; consequently the imposition of too rigid a legal framework might reduce the chances of a mutually acceptable compromise being worked out (p.12). Certainly, in those cases studied where informal exclusion had occurred, there was a high degree of consensus as to the need to remove the pupil from the school. The question of whether this took place on a formal or informal basis was not considered to be relevant. As the discussion of post-exclusion experiences demonstrates, the way in which the decision to exclude was made bore no direct relationship to the provision which was subsequently available to the child. However, as the following cases demonstrate, perceptions of the child's behaviour, perceptions of the school's decision and cognisance of the exclusion on the part of carers played a major part in making it possible for informal exclusion to take place.

Alex's exclusion conforms in many respects to the most commonly cited type of informal exclusion. According to the head of year, Alex had been transferred to another school on a 'trial' placement. Formal exclusion, she explained, was inappropriate as this would have resulted in Alex being out of school altogether and receiving only a few hours home tuition each week. While the school's reasons for not officially excluding Alex are understandable, this process was less benevolent than it might first appear. He was transferred to another school on a trial placement, but no other changes were made to his education. On moving school Alex did not settle down, and his behaviour continued to be erratic. The trial placement failed and in time Alex was officially excluded. However, it is important to stress that this exclusion took place with the knowledge and co-operation of all those working with Alex. Informal exclusion may therefore take place via the same patterns of interaction between professionals as those leading to official exclusions (see Chapter 6).

It might be argued that the key issue to preventing informal exclusion, or minimising the potential dangers, is that those responsible for the young person concerned are aware of what is happening and are able to respond effectively. Paul's case provides an excellent example of a situation where this was patently not the case, and corresponds more closely to the situation described by Stirling, where the school could be said to initiate exclusion by stealth.

As explained above, Paul's brief career at Hilltop school was ended by a letter, from a senior teacher to the head of Home G. In this letter, concern was expressed at Paul's failure to settle and his frequent absences. Paul had failed to make friends and had not developed positive relationships with staff, who found him 'quiet and withdrawn' in lessons. Overall, however, Paul was said to accept classroom discipline. At no point is it suggested that Paul is to be excluded, but the final paragraph indicates that he is not expected to return. The grounds for this were that Paul was clearly finding it difficult to cope with a large group situation and the school was not equipped to provide him with smaller classes. It was stated that if he should decide to try again and return to school, support would be offered. In the short term, however, the school felt that the children's home should seek to resolve Paul's social problems.

In many respects this letter is a masterpiece in evasion; yet the point is made clear. The head of home, however, did not view the situation as problematic, in that she felt the school had been 'very good about it all'. Nevertheless, Paul was not receiving any education in the interim and generally it seemed unlikely, at the age of 15, that he would ever return to any form of mainstream education. The exclusion is also very difficult to justify. It could not be said that Paul's behaviour provided any grounds for a formal exclusion. Little account was taken, it would seem, of the fact that Paul had been out of school for approximately a year and had also experienced a difficult time at Home F before moving to Home G. It is also striking that in this case no suggestion was made that another school be sought, and the implication is that the children's home was an acceptable alternative to full-time education.

If anything, Paul's experience demonstrates how easy informal exclusion can be. Both the school and children's home appeared to have given up on his education, and remarkably little was done to enable him to remain in school. The case is marked more by passivity than by any activity on the part of the adults involved. It might well be argued, therefore, that while it would be far from easy to claim that official exclusion necessarily represents better practice, there is still greater protection in following official procedures. However, the intervening factor determining perceptions of the outcome would appear to be the nature and extent of the involvement of other professionals. Where social workers and others were closely monitoring a case, and where the education department was also aware of the situation, the potential dangers of informal exclusion were much reduced or non-existent. Where they were uninformed, on the other hand, young people like Paul could slip through the net of provision.

Conclusion

Increasingly, it seems, investigation of 'exclusion' needs to be replaced by the more generic issue of 'children out of school'. This is already happening in policy discussions – for example through the linking of exclusion and truancy (DfEE 1999b; Social Exclusion Unit 1998). Certainly the evidence presented in this study suggests that an adequate theoretical formulation of exclusion must somehow incorporate unofficial, as well as official, exclusions. This is possible if exclusion is conceptualised as a process which begins some time prior to the decision to exclude, and continues until the young person is placed in a new school. Attention is therefore shifted from the fact that these young people are excluded – which in turn leads to an emphasis on individual or institutional failure – to the specific nature of the educational problem which needs to be addressed. In all the categories outlined above, this concerned the young person's relationship to the educational system generally or to a specific school. Only through an accurate assessment of this situation could professionals respond in a way which enabled the young person to continue in some form of education. Importantly, this sometimes involved removing the individual from a mainstream setting. As Cooper (in Lloyd-Smith and Davies 1995) points out, this should not be seen as necessarily unhelpful and may be welcomed by the young person. Chapter 8 will develop discussion regarding the professional response to these questions by examining in greater detail the role of the care system in the exclusion process, and the experiences of the sample group following their departure from school.

8

Exclusion
The Social Work Response

Introduction

Research into exclusion has tended to focus on the characteristics of pupils who experience exclusion or the policy and practice of the schools which they attend. Thus we are well aware that boys, children with special educational needs and pupils from some minority ethnic groups are at greater risk of exclusion than others. There are, however, a number of problems with this kind of analysis of the issue. An emphasis on pupil characteristics confuses ascribed characteristics, such as age, ethnicity and gender, with characteristics which result from other socially constructed processes, such as being assessed as having special educational needs or being looked after in residential or foster care. Nor does this account for the overlap between these different groups. Equally, research and policy debate on exclusion which focuses entirely on school processes seems one-sided and fails to provide an accurate representation of the exclusion process as a whole. Other research has shown that the majority of excluded pupils and their families are in contact with a range of welfare agencies (Hayden 1997; OFSTED 1996a; Parsons *et al.* 1994), but while social disadvantage is recognised as a risk factor in relation to a child's education, the actions and decisions of other professionals have not always been incorporated into explanations of why exclusions occur.

Increasingly, however, attempts have been made to contextualise the issue. Osler (1997) is right to comment, in a report on exclusions in Birmingham schools, that it is important to look at characteristics of low excluding schools in order to understand some of the characteristics which help prevent exclusion. Such an approach helps overcome the problem posed by research findings showing that rates of exclusion vary greatly between schools and between local authorities (OFSTED 1996a; Imich 1994; Galloway *et al.* 1982). Research into the schooling experiences of black pupils has also emphasised the importance of classroom interaction in understanding the way in which disciplinary sanctions are applied (Sewell 1997; Gillborn 1990). However, while it is widely recognised that children looked after are at risk of exclusion, the relevance of the context of residential and foster care has not been explored in detail.

This chapter will examine in greater detail the significance of the residential care context. The discussion will begin by describing, more generally, the consequences of exclusion, by whatever means, for residential staff. The chapter will then go on to focus on the roles taken by social workers and residential carers in regard to the education of the 17 young people studied. It is important to emphasise that, in accordance with the interactionist approach outlined in Chapter 3, these are the roles as perceived by the individuals concerned. To some extent, this means that, following the arguments of Chapters 6 and 7, emphasis is shifted from exclusion *per se* to the educational welfare of the group. Thus it is recognised that social work professionals are engaged in responding to processes of 'exclusion' which go beyond statutory definitions of that term. The negotiations in which social work professionals engage are also made more complex by such issues as the timing of the young person's entry to care and the relationship of this to educational problems and the availability of expert advice.

In addition to drawing on evidence from previous chapters, data will also be presented relating to the post-exclusion experiences of the young people. This is especially relevant to the chapter for two reasons. First of all, some of the young people were already, or almost, excluded on entry to the children's home and this was therefore the situation with which residential social workers had to deal from the outset, for example the 'exclusion by non-admission' group described in Chapter 7. Second, it is striking that social services usually appeared to take sole responsibility for the young person's future education following exclusion, and the role of social work professionals was thus highlighted. For the 17 young people studied, exclusion – in whatever form – had varying consequences. Other research has demonstrated that exclusion is frequently followed by a lengthy period out of school (Hayden 1997; Parsons *et al.* 1994) and that reintegration into mainstream education is problematic (Parsons 2000; DfE 1995). In the present study, research into the young person's exclusion took place anything up to a year after the exclusion had actually occurred. Therefore, while no systematic attempts were made to follow-up the cases, sufficient information is available to make consideration of the post-exclusion experience worthwhile.

The consequences of exclusion

In all the cases studied, a major constraint on what happened was the availability of alternative educational provision. This has repeatedly been raised as a major problem and deserves some separate consideration.

In discussing this dimension of the exclusion process, it is helpful to briefly consider the type of provision available in each local authority. In Local Authority 1 interviewees generally felt that the amount of alternative provision available for young people out of school was inadequate. Head teachers and staff in the two PRUs and one EBD school agreed that demand was very high, but one commented that increasing the number of places was not necessarily the answer. He argued that the money spent on segregated schooling would be better spent on improving support within schools. This demand was explained in a similar way to the rise in exclusions – namely the pressure on schools arising from increased competition, limited resources and an inflexible curriculum. However, it was also pointed out that the embargo against out-of-county placements must necessarily have affected the flow of pupils into special provision within the local authority.

> A further problem is that when cuts were made in EBD provision, out-of-county placements were cut. This clogged up in-county EBD provision with more severe cases, which means we get young people with more serious problems – what happens to the young people we used to get? They are still failing in school. (Headteacher)

Local Authority 1 had two PRUs, but these had quite different roles. One provided for pupils in Years 6 to 9 who were experiencing behavioural problems, and might be on the verge of exclusion, but still had a school place. The second had only just been designated a PRU, and catered specifically for secondary school pupils who had been excluded or were school refusers. Pupils were referred by EWOs or educational psychologists, and cases were then processed through a Young People's Admissions Panel. Those refused entry to the PRU were transferred to the home tuition service. Interviewees favoured entry to this PRU against home tuition, on the grounds that young people had access to a peer group and a more 'school-like' atmosphere. The amount of teaching was also greater; young people came to the unit for 12½ hours each week compared to 5 hours home tuition. In Local Authority 1 younger pupils and children with special needs were particularly disadvantaged in finding alternative provision. The head of the PRU in Local Authority 1 had noted an increase in the number of children being referred from special schools, and commented '…we can't take them – we don't feel able to meet that level of need and we don't have the facilities to deal with non-readers. They have to go back into the home tuition service.'

The situation in Local Authority 2 was more complex, and illustrates well the way in which the history of education in an area affects the provision available. Like all London boroughs, Local Authority 2 was still experiencing the effects of the demise of the Inner London Education Authority (ILEA). Under ILEA, this Authority had provided a rich variety of schooling for children with a range of special needs, including three EBD boarding schools, two day EBD schools, three schools for 'delicate' children in addition to provision for children with visual impairments and moderate/severe learning disabilities. Most of these had either already closed or were in the process of doing so. However, excluded children had a range of options. In contrast with Local Authority 1, the borough had separate provision for primary and secondary pupils who had been excluded. There were also four projects operated by external agencies which offered educational support for young people out of school, most of which were targeted at pupils aged 15–16. This corresponded with the borough's overall policy of contracting out.

Children living in private homes in Local Authority 3 had access to home tuition, but the authority unsurprisingly prioritised children who belonged to the area in regard to places in PRUs. The private agency included in the sample did not perceive such provision to be an option, preferring that as many children as possible attended their own education unit when they did not have a mainstream place. The ambivalence of Local Authority 2 towards this arrangement therefore continued to cause difficulties following exclusion.

Clearly, then, there was considerable variation in the range of local provision offered. However, it seemed that regardless of local authority, in the event of exclusion, responsibility for the young person's education was placed with social services. Education, in whatever guise, became a non-player in the process. Social workers and residential staff took the initiative in finding another placement and, in some cases, in seeking extra funding. While the young people themselves most obviously suffered from the exclusion, the fact that they were out of school also had direct consequences for residential staff. As the above discussion indicates, there were considerable delays in finding alternative placements and most young people received home tuition for only a few hours each week. This was usually provided within the home and, aside from this, children were supervised by the residential staff on duty. This was viewed with some resentment; it was acknowledged that children who were excluded 'get on the nerves of staff' and that it was 'very difficult to engage them in anything educational'. One commented

> Why should we supplement the incompetencies of the educational system? …the home has to organise activities, which has a knock-on effect as other young people want to join in these and get themselves expelled. (RSW)

Another remarked

> You've got them 24 hours a day. I know we're here for that, but the housework still has to be done. They all need constant supervision. They want one-to-one attention. It's not good for them. Like Lee – he used to see the others go off to school. He couldn't really understand why. Then they expect you to pay attention to them. (RSW)

Home tuition was consistently dismissed as wholly inadequate. Where tuition took place within the home, residential staff might also be called upon to help. Jack remained out of school for more than a year. His key worker remarked

> Education was out the window. He had home tuition on his own for an hour a day, but that didn't give staff here any respite – they were constantly going back and forwards to see if it was all OK.

...on a one-to-one basis he could be entertained. He would watch a video or do some colouring. If he completed anything he would instantly destroy it. He was bloody hard work. He was violent to staff and other children and resented by other children because he had to have one-to-one. He could swing from being loving and caring to taking chunks out of you. The ferocity of his punches was amazing. (RSW)

In Local Authority 1 efforts had been made to address the problem. A working party, organised jointly by Education and Social Services, had suggested that money was needed to provide an organised day for young people out of school, and that someone be employed to do this. The lack of resources made it somewhat doubtful whether this would actually happen; however, the fact that the issue was being discussed is important in itself. In the two homes for younger children, guidelines had also been drawn up for residential staff outlining good practice in regard to children both in and out of school. These suggested that where a child was out of school, staff should ensure that the day should be as structured as possible. Children should adhere to a school routine and should, for example, wear school uniform. The education co-ordinator felt that while staff were still resistant to the idea of supervising excluded pupils, attitudes were gradually changing. However, in the other homes in the sample the development of policy and practice in relation to this issue remained at best limited, and the constraints were particularly great in private homes where links with local authority services were minimal.

Group perspectives and the exclusion process

Chapter 7 has suggested that within the sample it is possible to distinguish four ways in which exclusion – in its broadest sense – occurred in the 17 cases. These were: exclusion by non-admission; exclusion on admission; graduated exclusion and planned exclusion. These situations elicited quite different professionals responses, and were conceptualised as 'group perspectives' (Becker *et al.* 1961). Group perspectives are 'modes of thought and action' developed and held collectively by a group of individuals encountering a problematic situation. The choice of a particular combination of thought and action becomes established through custom, to the extent that they appear to group members as the 'natural and legitimate' way to think and act in that situation; at the same time other possibilities will exist. The previous experiences of group members and the constraints which bear upon the situation will be important in influencing the set of ideas that is adopted.

This concept is useful in that it first of all requires definition of the problem to which individuals are trying to respond. In regard to excluded pupils, this problem is not, initially at least, exclusion itself or even the behaviour of the young person. As Chapter 7 has pointed out, in distinguishing different experiences of exclusion it is essential to clarify the nature of the problem which must be addressed. There is not, however, a direct relationship between the problem defined and the response elicited. Other, contextual difficulties will also be present. For headteachers, for example, the attitudes of other parents could be a major constraint when considering whether or not a child should be excluded. The views of the families of the young people themselves were also sometimes perceived as problematic. For social workers, a change in care placement may need to be negotiated alongside the young person's educational arrangements. Knowledge of the consequences of the decision to exclude is also influential. For example, it is clear that residential staff perceived exclusion as carrying with it heavy responsibilities for day-time care, though this did not necessarily mean that they were able to take action to prevent exclusion occurring. While professionals may be denigrated for the decisions they have made, it is only by understanding the constellation of issues which individuals are trying to resolve that alternative practice can be identified.

It is also worth remembering the findings outlined in Chapter 5. The majority of social workers and residential staff were unaware of any local authority policy regarding the education of looked after children. This question was, in fact, usually met with some embarrassment. One social worker suggested that guidance on inter-agency working in child protection might be relevant (DoH 1991a), but most stated they did not know of any guidance. The roles which social workers and residential staff performed in relation to the education of young people seemed therefore to be fashioned by individuals, or through the culture of the individual children's homes. It was striking that a small minority of interviewees, who saw themselves as being highly committed to the educational welfare of children looked after, also perceived this to be a highly individualised role – one social worker, for example, commented that cases where education was especially problematic tended to be passed to her because 'they know it's my thing'. There was, therefore, an absence of a sense of 'corporate parenting' as envisaged in the Children Act 1989 (DoH 1989).

Analysis of interviews with residential social workers and their fieldwork colleagues revealed four perspectives which were used to explain professional responses to exclusion – quiescence, advocacy, collaborative support and expertise. Table 9.1 shows how these perspectives were distributed across the 17 cases.

Table 9.1 Responses of social work professionals to exclusion

Case	Social workers	Residential social workers
Alex	Quiescence	Quiescence
Brian	Quiescence	Collaborative support
Carl	Advocacy	Quiescence
David	Collaborative support	Quiescence
Eddie	Advocacy	Quiescence
Fred	Advocacy	Collaborative support
Graham	Advocacy	Advocacy
Hugh	Salvage	Quiescence
Ian	Advocacy	Advocacy/collaborative support
Jack	Salvage	Collaborative support
Kris	Salvage	Advocacy
Lee	No social worker interviewed	Advocacy
Michael	Collaborative support	Quiescence
Nicki	Salvage	Advocacy
Paul	No social worker interviewed	Quiescence
Omar	Advocacy	Expert
Roland	No social worker allocated	Advocacy

This table shows that the perspectives taken by residential staff and field social workers were not always the same. Sometimes the roles were considered to be complementary; in others, and as Chapter 7 has examined in detail, more conflictual. However, definition and description of how these roles were performed is now required.

Advocacy

Residential social workers who assumed an advocacy perspective considered themselves to have a central role in ensuring the educational welfare of the relevant young people. It is encouraging to find that at least one social work professional assumed this perspective in 12 of the 17 cases. However, it is notable that this perspective featured more often in the cases of younger children than adolescents.

The common strand in these cases was also the way in which the young people were perceived by the adults involved in the case. Rather than being defined as essentially problematic, they tended to be perceived as victims of circumstances beyond their control. There was a strong sense on the part of carers that the decisions taken in regard to the education of these young people had been more in the interests of schools or the local authority than the children themselves. This raises the possibility that these children were in fact viewed as more 'deserving' than those whose behaviour was considered serious enough to warrant exclusion.

Advocacy before, during or after exclusion tended to involve exploration of a range of options for the young person. Perhaps surprisingly, given the apparent predictability of exclusion, the knowledge that the young person's situation was precarious only occasionally led to individuals making alternative plans in the event of an exclusion taking place. Residential staff and social workers took the initiative in finding an alternative school place, which often proved difficult and sometimes impossible. However, successful outcomes were very rewarding – for example in the case of Kris, who move to an Intermediate Treatment (IT) Centre in the borough. He was due to sit a Maths GCSE and hoped to go to college to do a range of NVQs. Given the disruption which Kris had experienced in his school career, this was a remarkable achievement.

However, it is important to stress that taking an advocacy perspective did not smooth the paths of social workers and carers, who often found themselves fighting other, structural constraints. Funding, for example, was a major barrier to obtaining specialised provision, and to those involved the system appeared almost deliberately obstructive. Jack was excluded a month prior to entering Home B. Even before the exclusion, however, it had been argued by his school that a therapeutic placement was desirable. His new social worker agreed.

> About funding, my argument was that there was no choice – if there was no provision for him here, you can't leave him with home tutors for the rest of his life… The process of joint funding is a very confusing one for social workers. My understanding is that education and social services have made a block funding agreement and have already put aside money. When you go there they agree on the need, but say 'you've got the money already' – which is a clever move. He [Jack] has a statement which says education and social services are to give joint funding, but my manager is saying, 'where is the £10,000 to come from?' … There has been a protocol set up between health, social services and education. I wrote a report and took it to the joint funding panel. They agreed on the need but we never heard anything more about it. (Social worker)

Eventually the social worker felt that he had to take the initiative and 'I just placed him.'

After spending a year out of school, Jack was placed with an independent fostering agency in the south-east of England, with an educational placement attached. He was attending school full-time, supported by a classroom assistant, and in the view of his social worker he was beginning to progress both socially and educationally.

In the light of such difficulties, other social workers tried to avoid following the special provision/EBD route and aimed for reintegration into mainstream. Following his formal exclusion, Ian was placed in home tuition for two months. Again, various options were considered.

> ...when I got involved in the case decisions were being made about sending him to a boarding school. I was opposed to such a move and they hadn't explored other schools. There are lots of other problems with his family and his only stability is the children's home. It would have been disastrous to move him.'

A place was then found for Ian at another primary school, which he initially attended on a part-time basis. Two months later this was working well and it was hoped that he would soon be able to attend there full-time.

> ...His behaviour at school is quite reasonable and the head said you wouldn't single him out from any others. So far he is maintaining the placement. As his family situation becomes more stable, so Ian becomes more stable... If he can't function in mainstream, I'm going to worry if he ends up in [EBD school] or something, not because of what they do there but because of the kind of child Ian is – easily led.' (Social worker)

The initiative taken by individual children's homes also proved remarkably successful in the case of one young person receiving support at Home D. In Roland's case, the efforts of his key worker led to his being accepted by a further education college which had been very reluctant to admit him. Although it was felt that staff there were still doubtful about the placement, so far it had been maintained.

It is important to recognise, however, that a change in schooling arrangements was also accompanied by other changes, such as a change in care placement, and social workers and carers considered these to be key to what they perceived to be successful outcomes. However, the cases outlined above are also intended to give some indication of the lengthy and sometimes conflict ridden processes which could accompany the search for alternative education. Constraints relating to the young person's age, perceived needs and the provision available within an authority could all affect the nature of this.

Graham's case illustrates these problems well. As described earlier, Graham had been informally excluded from his primary school, but had lost an earlier opportunity to be placed on the waiting list for the primary department of the local EBD school. At a planning meeting it was agreed that Graham should be referred back to the county panel which would consider whether Graham could be placed on a list for EBD resources. Meanwhile Graham received home tuition. This was not without difficulties, as after five weeks Graham refused to work with his first tutor and another had to be found. Academically he continued to struggle, and a report on his progress recorded that his concentration span was very limited and he was still unable to read age-appropriate material. The report concluded that it must be an 'urgent priority' to establish a full-time/appropriate educational placement.

Seven months later Graham was still in home tuition. His social worker was angry with the education department, and stated unequivocally 'It is totally unacceptable that a child of nine should be out of school for over a year.'

The children's home and social worker tried to negotiate for more home tuition for Graham, but 'after a two and a half hour fight' only managed to persuade the head of special education to provide one extra hour each week. Other options were also explored, such as whether Graham could be diagnosed as having ADD. Meanwhile worries were emerging about the care placement, specifically that without an education placement it would be impossible to find a foster placement. Eventually, a month or so later, Graham was offered a place in the primary department of the EBD school, and began joining in some activities there. However, by the time he started there on a full-time basis, he had been out of school for some 14 months.

Lee was out of school and receiving home tuition for six months following exclusion. He was more fortunate than others in the sample, and received 15 hours tuition each week. Lee, who had been glad to be excluded, found this period boring but commented that 'it was a lot better than going to that school'.

Meanwhile, both the children's home and his tutor were trying to persuade the education department that Lee should return to the education unit attached to the home. Letters sped to and fro. The tutoring service wrote to the education department, suggesting 'most strongly' that a return to the unit was desirable. The education department then wrote to the consultant psychiatrist used by the private home, explaining that they had been 'attempting to clarify' why Lee was not in school. In the end, Lee did return to the private unit.

Initially it was very awkward but by the end we were all okay. They [LA2 education department] were adamant that they were not sending Lee back. The liaison officer then wrote a very lengthy report saying that the provision wasn't really suitable, but then in the last part that although the unit wasn't fully adequate and they wouldn't generally send children there, there would be occasions when a child would be placed at the centre. Some of his criticisms were fair comment – for example that children wouldn't have a sense of moving up from one stage to another – but there was nothing major. It made us laugh, but it made me angry.' (Head of the education unit)

Notwithstanding these problems, what is striking in these cases are the efforts made by social workers and carers to enhance the educational prospects of the child and the strong belief that what was happening to the young person was intrinsically wrong.

Experts

In the majority of cases studied, residential staff felt strongly that a children's home was not an educational establishment and that provision of education was not part of their role. One case, however, was an exception to this, in that the children's home was being used as an educational resource itself. Omar lived in Home D, which provided care for disabled children, usually through short-breaks but also looking after a small group of children on a more permanent basis. The social worker had decided, after one unsuccessful attempt to place Omar in a mainstream school, that Home D could act as a useful interim experience for Omar, and would help teach him the social and behavioural skills he would need at a school. Omar's development had been seriously impeded by physical abuse and neglect, and needed a stimulating environment which would help him to reach an appropriate level for his age. His social worker commented that the staff at Home D were very patient and able to tolerate very difficult behaviour. The home had a list of activities which were designed to help Omar with his concentration, language and self-help skills. In addition to daily visits there, he also spent two weeks at the home while his father was in hospital, and during this time was able to develop relationships with other children. Omar was subsequently placed in a PRU for primary school children. His social worker felt that without the support of Home D, Omar would have been unable to cope with the demands of the PRU.

This contrasts strongly with the perceptions of other social workers interviewed in this study; as Chapter 5 has already shown, many saw placement in a children's home as extremely detrimental to a young person's education. Equally, children's homes are rarely renowned for their stimulating educational environments. This case was exceptional in many respects, but other research has also highlighted differences in the approach taken in care for disabled children, and has suggested that this is characterised by a more integrated approach towards education and welfare (Berridge and Brodie 1998).

Collaborative support

This perspective was assumed in five cases by residential staff – interestingly those who felt they had access to another professional whom, they felt, had the expertise which would enable them to act more effectively. Thus, in Homes B and C (both for younger children), where there was an education co-ordinator, the heads of home spoke of the benefits of the informal knowledge this individual possessed about schools and also her ability to talk to teachers 'on the same level'. One commented

> I dread to think what we would do if she wasn't here. She knows about the education process and speaks their jargon and holds schools to account, so it's not easy for them to exclude. (Head of home)

The support of a psychologist employed by social services in Local Authority 1 was also valued. Similarly, in Brian's case, the EWO was considered to be acting in the young person's interests and residential staff were willing to support this where possible – ironically in contrast to the social worker, who felt there was little hope of a positive outcome.

This was the approach which seemed most likely to be acceptable to residential staff, in the sense that the majority felt they should not be expected to take the place of teachers and a full-time education. However, development of this position clearly demanded another individual who was prepared to take the lead in regard to schooling. Those individuals who were taking the lead role also felt they should be able to expect support from residential social workers, and thought it important that their role should be clearly defined.

Quiescence

Quiescence refers to professionals who saw their role vis-a-vis the young person's education as subordinate to that of the school or another professional. This perspective was assumed by at least one professional in seven of the cases studied. Individuals who assumed this position were not necessarily unconcerned about education, but felt that the young person's attitude or behaviour made any positive action difficult or impossible. Staff thus perceived themselves to be powerless in relation to the young people, whom, interviewees felt, would use their knowledge of their 'rights' against them. As one RSW commented 'you can be as persistent as you like, but ultimately if they don't want to go you can't do anything about it'.

It is noticeable that, in this group, quiescence was most evident in cases involving adolescents. It was also more likely to be a perspective assumed by children's homes staff than by field social workers. In the majority of these cases, the residential placement was perceived negatively, or as a stop-gap, by the field-worker; a view that did not enhance a sense of partnership in relation to education.

The constraints arising from the local authority context and residential setting were also significant. Staff working in the local authority homes – in both local authorities – appeared to have greater autonomy in finding a school for the young person and were able to use their resources more creatively than RSWs in private homes. There was a closer partnership between social workers and residential staff and suggestions made by RSWs were taken seriously and followed through – for example in regard to the involvement of other experts to support their case. Residential staff and social workers also worked hard with schools and were sometimes able to negotiate gradual re-integration or part-time attendance at school. While the situation continued to be somewhat precarious in at least two of these cases, a considerable investment was made by the children's homes concerned in maintaining the young person at school.

In contrast, staff based in the private homes in LA3 were bound by the decisions of local authority officials and the social worker. At the same time, social workers were not available and in any case lacked the necessary local knowledge to provide support in finding the new school place. Residential staff were therefore closely involved in finding the young people a school place, but from the start were pessimistic of success in the placement and sometimes appeared to feel that the school was generous in accepting the child at all. The alternative was that no alternative education could be found, at least in the short-term. In the months following his exclusion, Nicki was allocated a new social worker who started work to find him a boarding school placement. In the meantime, however, there was a long delay and considerable tension between Home G, the social worker and Local Authority 2. The head of home described the situation as having gone from bad to worse.

> …Nicki is the one coming off the worst. He has become deviant; he followed one of our older lads around and imitated him. He has been arrested a couple of times and reported as a missing person ten times in the last two weeks. He has developed a taste for deviance but it is constantly fighting with the good kid in him. (Head of home)

Paul also remained out of school, and thought it unlikely he would ever return to mainstream provision. Like Nicki, he said he would like to go to the onsite unit, but did not believe the local authority would permit this. The prospects for both young men seemed poor. Similarly Hugh, who had been excluded from an EBD school, was considered to have reached 'the end of the road'.

Where this position was taken by both the social worker and residential staff, it was possible that another professional might intervene. David was the only young person in the sample to gain entry to a PRU in Local Authority 1. Thanks to the foresight of his EWO, he had been recommended for a place prior to his exclusion and was able to transfer there almost immediately. This was agreed by all those involved to be the best solution available. David himself stated that he definitely preferred the unit to his secondary school, especially the smaller classes and the fact that he did not have to attend on a full-time basis. Six months later, the unit head commented that he was 'one of our brightest lads'. By this time, David had been placed with foster carers. He had continued to attend the PRU and was perceived to be quiet and well behaved. He still wanted to join the Marines and the head of the PRU felt this was a realistic possibility. Although John continued to find academic work difficult, he was expected to sit some exams later in the year. However, the appearance of such an individual was by no means guaranteed, and cases characterised by a quiescent response were therefore most prone to drift.

Salvage

This position was assumed by field social workers rather than residential staff, and was perceived to exist in four of the cases. This perspective concerned those who felt that, despite the prior educational difficulties experienced by the young person, a positive outcome was still possible. Their ability to accomplish this appeared to depend greatly on personal motivation and, occasionally, their willingness to break some rules. However, they also perceived the options to be limited due to the young person's previous experiences of the care system. Social workers who perceived themselves to be carrying out a salvage operation identified several issues which had contributed to the situation with which they were now dealing. These included the lack of social work input prior to their assuming responsibility for the case, the inappropriateness of the current placement, and disagreements with residential staff.

Lack of social work input was especially evident in Local Authority 2, where all the cases were characterised by frequent changes of social worker and sometimes the total absence of any social worker for several months at a time. In Kris's case a long-running battle had emerged regarding the lack of continuity in social work input to his case. His mother felt this had an adverse effect on his education and had considered taking the local authority to court. At the time of his exclusion Kris had no social worker, and, indeed, had not had one for five months. She was not replaced until two months later. At the meeting between school representatives and children's homes' staff, no representative from social services was present. Kris himself remarked that: 'I've had so many social workers and key workers it's unbelievable.'

His (new) social worker felt that the overall neglect of Kris's education resulted from the low priority given to his case within the social work system.

> He is a very low priority case. He is accommodated and not under a care order. If he came to social services now, he would not be accommodated. But at that time, when his mother said she couldn't handle him, he was just taken into care. And because he is a low priority case, he has had lots of student social workers who are always moving on. (Social worker)

Similarly his key worker thought that the inconsistency of social work input had meant that care plans had not usually been followed through. The same issues are evident in Nicki's case. His social worker explained:

> Basically he went without a social worker for a long time. He had a social worker called Graham, but [LA2] kept on changing the catchment areas for children and the area offices... The case went to [another social worker], who took it on the basis that it was short-term. She then went on long-term sickness leave. This has happened to Nicki before – he really went without a social worker for a whole year. Sue only visited once before going off sick, so there were no plans or anything. He just drifted round the system. (Social worker)

The difference in social work role in Local Authority 2 was exacerbated by the use of private homes in other local authorities, which meant that social workers were effectively out of reach. This caused considerable frustration among all the parties involved, including teachers, residential staff and young people.

Residential care, social work and exclusion

Encouragingly, several positive messages emerge from examination of the roles of social workers and carers in the cases studied. From this sample at least, it seems that children's homes can act to promote the educational welfare of young people, even when children present very serious difficulties. It would be a mistake to see the perspectives outlined in this chapter as corresponding directly to good and bad practice; it is important to remember that these cases were being examined in retrospect and individuals therefore had the opportunity to reflect on the positive and negative aspects of their experience. It is also evident that all the cases studied presented extremely complex problems at entry to residential care, and that while placement in a children's home was often negatively interpreted by other professionals, it could by no means be considered the main cause of the young person's exclusion.

One could not assume that the ways of thinking and acting which individuals adopted when working with a young person were necessarily those which they had adopted in the past or would use again in the future. It is important to remember that exclusion was, by all accounts, a rare experience for many of the adults involved – indeed, young people themselves might have had greater experience of the process. Even where exclusion was carried out according to official procedure, it is relatively recent in this particular form. Michael's head teacher, who had not excluded any child in 15 years, is a case in point.

The rarity and also the extreme nature of exclusion as a sanction could mean that individuals made conscious efforts to take a different course of action than on a previous occasion. Thus Jack's teacher, in consultation with other professionals and with the backing of the school, was prepared to exclude in an attempt to force the hand of the LEA and so avoid some of the delays which had been experienced during another, similar, case. Exclusion is therefore a process which is subject to some experimentation in thought and action, and the perspectives held by the groups involved were yet to evolve to a stage where they could be considered customary. In dramaturgical terms it could be said that different roles were being attempted and partnerships being tried out. This suggests that current guidance regarding exclusion – both nationally and as formulated by individual local authorities – does not provide professionals other than headteachers with procedures to be followed in the event of exclusion, and bears out protests by researchers and others that young people and parents have insufficient power within the exclusion process (Castle and Parsons 1997; Parsons 1996). Some individuals do manage to develop strategies through which to manage potential exclusions – for example, Eddie's social worker who had identified a sympathetic educational psychologist and used this contact to help find alternative educational provision. These strategies did not, however, usually appear to have become embedded in the practices of institutions or agencies. As the cases above show, social workers and residential carers did not always find managers or even colleagues to be supportive when they did try to act in what they felt to be the best interests of the young person's education.

Changes in the residential context

It would also be mistaken to ignore the wider policy context. The structural arrangements which exist for the care and education of troublesome young people may be an important dynamic in understanding the ways in which the exclusion process unfolds. The last 20 years have seen a steady decrease in the number of institutions of all kinds in which children can be placed. The number of children living in children's homes on any one day in England has declined from some 22,000 in 1980 to just over 6000 in 1997 (DoH 1999; Berridge 1985). Perhaps most pertinent to the present study, social work institutions combining care and education have almost entirely disappeared, at least from the local authority sector – as earlier chapters have shown, there has been something of a resurgence in this kind of provision in the private sector. Children's homes continue to exist, but their profile has changed greatly. The majority of homes are small, open facilities catering for on average six children. Young people are usually placed close to their home communities and will not stay in the same home for a lengthy period: the majority will return home within a few months.

It has been observed that the history of child welfare has, at least since the introduction of the Poor Law, been characterised by the segregation and institutionalisation of the children of the poor (Cunningham 1992; Frost and Stein 1989). This philosophy has undergone a major shift with the introduction of the Children Act 1989 and the principle that children in public care should remain at home or should be cared for within their own communities. As Gooch (1996) remarks, the decline in confidence among professionals in making residential placements has 'set in motion an exodus of the marginal, leaving a core whose problems are much more intractable' (p.23). The 17 children studied are, in most respects, fairly representative of this core, and it is clear that problems at school constitute a significant element in their difficulties.

In many ways a problem of supply and demand emerges as a result of these developments. The number of children presenting extreme behavioural problems, albeit a very small minority of the school population, does not match the alternative educational provision available. This has important implications for our understanding of the exclusion process. Instinctively, it would seem, professionals responsible for managing this process incline towards segregation and institutionalisation. Thus for many children in this study education became the responsibility of residential staff in terms of finding a new school, and in several the method of managing the possibility of exclusion focused on the retreat of the pupil into the children's home.

Yet children's homes are no longer the 'total institutions' which once accepted responsibility for every aspect of a child's life, and children's homes are, in consequence, structurally incapable of fulfilling the role which the exclusion process demands. There are no teachers onsite and residential staff, who do not live in, are unwilling and unable to assume day-time responsibility for young people. The model being established in many private children's homes, with an educational unit attached to the home or even serving a number of private homes in the local area, does present a viable alternative – it is worth considering that several of the exclusions in this sample might not have occurred if the local authority had not decided that the combined care and education package originally intended for these children was inappropriate. There are, however, some significant issues regarding how the quality of education offered in such contexts is to be assessed and monitored.

There is, therefore, a tension between the policies which have governed education in the late 1980s and early 1990s and those which have led to the demise of the traditional model of residential care. Neither set of policies, it would seem, leave room for children whose behaviour is considered to be such that they are excluded from the educational system. Therefore in Chapter 6 a remarkable degree of consensus was described in evaluations of the behaviour of the young people whose cases were studied, but a lack of clarity over what should happen next. For the young people concerned, the result of this is a tendency to occupy a no man's land where they are the responsibility of neither side and lack the consistent advocacy of any one adult (DoH 1996; Triseliotis *et al.* 1995).

9

Conclusion

Exclusion is an issue which can be examined at several different levels, and this has been reflected in the present study. This thesis began by examining the evidence about exclusion which has made it a matter of such concern to politicians, educationalists, the media and a range of welfare professionals, as well as the individual families and young people concerned. Consideration was given to different ways in which the behaviour leading to exclusion, and also the increase in the number of exclusions taking place, might be explained. Many of these theories, whether relating to family background, the emotional problems of the individual child, or changes in education policy, also enter into the explanations provided by individuals interviewed as part of the research.

Additionally, this study has taken the view that it would be naive to suggest that there is any single explanation for why exclusion occurs. As other researchers have convincingly demonstrated, such explanation must be multi-layered, making reference to different aspects of the social world (Hayden 1997; Blyth and Milner 1996). Thus, in the course of the study, various dimensions of exclusion as a social phenomenon have been considered. It has been suggested that exclusion has been symbolically constructed in the public realm as evidence of an increase in the disruptive and violent behaviour being exhibited by young people and, directly related to this, as evidence of a breakdown in 'traditional' values and recognition of parental responsibilities. This discourse, it has been argued, may be viewed as part of a recurring moral panic about the relationships between young and old in modern societies. Exclusion has become symbolic in this way at the same time that it has been redefined in legislation, and concern about the procedures associated with this, for example the reinstatement to schools by local authorities of pupils already permanently excluded, has fuelled the debate. The apparent increase in the number of exclusions taking place has, in turn, been explained through the juxtaposition of exclusion legislation with other major changes in education policy, most notably the introduction of a 'quasi-market' to schools.

This study has, if anything, added to that complexity. It has focused on the experiences of a very small group of children and young people excluded from school and looked after by local authorities in residential accommodation.

Crucially, it has sought to contextualise exclusion in terms of the care setting and the involvement of other professionals in the process. Consequently, it does not pretend to capture to the same extent other, equally important, facets of exclusion as a phenomenon, for example the relationship between school and family during the young person's educational career.

At the same time the intensive, qualitative approach taken in this study has shown the value of applying a sociological theoretical perspective to the problem of exclusion. This has, perhaps, particular benefits when examining an issue which is cross-disciplinary in both the academic and professional spheres. In this study it has enabled a greater differentiation of 'exclusion', and, in turn, specification of some of the ways in which young people looked after become excluded from the educational system.

Four different routes through which young people looked after in residential accommodation have been identified: exclusion by non-admission, exclusion on admission, graduated exclusion and planned exclusion. This model is not exhaustive; it does not perhaps deal sufficiently with exclusion which occurs within the school, or 'self-exclusion' by the young person. At the same time there is scope to develop this model, and it is especially useful in taking account of different residential contexts. Potentially it also offers a framework for intervention at different levels of policy and practice. If, for example, a number of young people in a residential unit/local authority were identified as experiencing exclusion on admission to schools, there would be scope for work to be targeted at preparation for entry to new schools, while schools might be alerted to the need for improved induction procedures. It may also, of course, have value beyond the specific group of young people studied here. Some progress has also been made in teasing out those aspects of professional relationships which contribute to, or help overcome, such exclusion. It appears that these processes are often more important in explaining why the decision to exclude is reached than the behaviour of the child himself. Exclusion, or the threat of this, is also used to signal either the seriousness of the situation to other professionals, or as an indication to parents of the school's attitude to difficult behaviour.

Having discussed in detail the cases of the 17 young people, this chapter will now look to the wider social context. One of the difficulties in researching and writing about an area of social policy currently subject to rapid change is the nagging possibility that the conclusions will become outdated at the same time they are ready to be offered for public scrutiny. This has certainly been true of research into exclusion: in the four and a half years since beginning work on this study one has moved from a situation where there were few publications and only the early tremors of an impending debate on the issue, through 1996 when exclusion was rarely absent from news reports, to the policy initiatives of a different government. During recent years it seems that few organisations have not produced a report on disaffected pupils and/or exclusion (see, for example, Donovan 1998; NACRO 1998; Pearce and Hillman 1998). Select Committee reports from the House of Commons have also examined the education of children looked after (House of Commons Health Committee 1998) and disaffection (House of Commons Education and Employment Committee 1998). Policy developments include the publication of a Green Paper on SEN, the implementation of the Education Act 1997 and the School Standards and Framework Act 1998, which contains a number of provisions relating to exclusion, the publication of the Social Exclusion Unit's (1998) report on exclusion and truancy and, most recently, the publication of draft guidance on the education of children looked after. The Government's 'Quality Protects' initiative also seeks to establish educational objectives for children looked after by local authorities, while other elements of this programme – for example those concerning placement choice and consultation with young people – will also have important implications for policy and practice relating to education.

Crucially, then, this study is part of an ongoing discussion not only about exclusion but disaffection among young people more generally. This is a modest piece of research and caution must be exercised in generalising from its findings. However, it is important that some attempt is made to consider the implications of some of these findings in relation to proposed changes in policy, as well as to the possibilities for future research in this area. This chapter will therefore begin by examining the issue of 'preventing' exclusion. It will then go on to look specifically at policy proposals relating to children looked after. Following from this, it will examine the roles of other professionals in relation to exclusion.

Preventing exclusion

The thrust of much recent debate regarding exclusion has been on the ways in which it can best be prevented. The Social Exclusion Unit report (1998) proposed two targets relating to exclusion: firstly, that by the year 2002 the number of permanent and fixed-term exclusions should be reduced by one third from 1998 levels; secondly, all pupils excluded for three weeks or more should receive alternative full-time and appropriate education. At the time of writing some progress has been made towards the first of these objectives; the most recent research evidence (Parsons 2000) and professional anecdote suggests there is some way to go if the second is to be met.

There is a growing body of literature which seeks to outline what constitutes 'good practice' in avoiding the use of exclusion as a sanction. Much of this focuses on the importance of the broader ethos of the school, for example behaviour and discipline policies which promote inclusion. Numerous case studies of imaginative and, apparently, effective schemes operated by schools and local authorities which seek to support children who show signs of being disaffected (see, for example, DfEE 1999b; DfEE/DoH 1999; Osler 1997; DfE1995; Kinder *et al.* 1995; Knight 1995). Considerable emphasis has also been given to the view that a high quality of teaching, including interesting lessons which are at the appropriate level for the target group, will in itself reduce behavioural problems. There has also been a growing interest in the wider community regarding new methods, such as mentoring, for working with troublesome young people and supporting their families.

The Social Exclusion Unit report suggested a range of measures which can assist in achieving these targets, including improvements in LEA procedures for gathering data on exclusions and making high levels of exclusion a priority in bids for Education Action Zone status. It stated that official guidance should focus more on prevention and should include the requirement that all reasonable steps have been taken by the school to avoid excluding the child. Measures to be taken could include preventative action, meetings with the parents and the child, discussions with other agencies and cooling-off periods to allow the parents and the LEA to put forward their cases. These proposals have been reflected in the School Inclusion: Pupil Support guidance, which outlines a range of ways in which difficult behaviour might be managed, including the use of learning support units, work with parents and modification of the National Curriculum. Where young people do not respond to such strategies, a Pastoral Support Programme (PSP) should be developed in co-operation with parents and external services. The Green Paper issued by the Education Minister in October 1997 also emphasised the importance of 'inclusive' education and the integration of pupils with special needs in mainstream schools wherever this is possible. This principle, it is suggested, should be supported by a raft of measures, including the strengthening of SEN provision in mainstream schools, closer co-operation between mainstream and special schools and with other services such as health and social services, and earlier identification of and intervention in respect of a child's needs. The procedures for assessing pupils' special educational needs are also to be streamlined. More specifically regarding pupils with EBD, teachers are to receive extra training on working with pupils with behavioural problems.

It could also be argued that, welcome though such measures are, that they must still be implemented in a context where schools are still in competition with each other to attract pupils, where parents may still choose to remove children if another pupil is especially disruptive, and where schools are, if anything, under even greater pressure to achieve high academic standards. Schools have continued to express concerns at the difficulty of achieving a balance between meeting the needs of the challenging minority and achieving optimum levels of achievement for the school as a whole. More specifically, it has been argued that the pressure to prevent exclusion and to retain difficult pupils had resulted in mounting levels of disruption within the classroom. While there are a growing number of incentives to encourage schools to avoid exclusion, including increased resources, national school performance tables continue to focus on indicators of academic achievement.

This study has examined a group of young people who might, in many respects, be described as part of the 'hard core', even among excludees. As has been shown, a high proportion had experienced very stressful experiences, including different kinds of abuse, within their family lives. At school, the majority presented emotional and behavioural problems, as well as various learning difficulties. Some had attended several schools, and in a surprisingly high number of cases changes of school had been interspersed with a fragmented care career. More than half of the group had been excluded on a fixed-term or permanent basis on more than one occasion.

'Prevention' clearly has different meanings in these circumstances; specifically, there are long- and short-term objectives to be achieved. In treating exclusion as a social process, this study has highlighted the difficulties associated with treating exclusion as a single event, and problems often developed cumulatively. Prevention of further problems, once an initial exclusion has taken place, appears to become more difficult as the options become fewer. To this extent it seems helpful if problems are identified at as early a point as possible in the young person's career, and the intention to encourage early intervention is therefore encouraging. That said, this sample included cases where significant amounts of intervention had occurred even at the pre-school stage. Several had developmental problems in babyhood; others, like Graham, had been excluded shortly after entry to primary school. There are some children who will always require a disproportionate amount of intervention and support in their school lives. The issue of prevention must then focus on the effectiveness of the intervention which did take place. At the same time, it is important that intervention does not focus entirely on the individual child, but that attention should also be given to support for other family members. Furthermore, there is some evidence to suggest that some children who do not succeed during the years of compulsory schooling, may return to education and training in their late teens and early twenties (Berridge et al. 1997; see also DoH 1996). This is encouraging, but those individuals – especially if they have been looked after – will require both financial and social support if this is to be possible. The Care Leavers Bill acknowledges this, and includes proposals to tighten up planning for care leavers through 'Pathway Plans' which will run until the age of 21, providing help with education and training up to the age of 24, and placing a duty on local authorities to keep in touch will all its care leavers until they are 21 or 24 if they are receiving support with education or training.

The teachers interviewed in this study did not view exclusion lightly and in the majority of cases some preventative measures had been taken. Almost half of the group had been assessed as having special educational needs; the children of primary school age and those attending special schools had also had the benefit of classroom assistants. However, there was evidence in a small number of cases that the school had little commitment to the young person and did not want to have them in the school. This was especially noticeable in the cases of young people living in private homes in Local Authority 3, but was also true for a minority of adolescents. In these circumstances it sometimes seemed that a policy of 'admission at all costs' was questionable. Residential staff highlighted the difficulties of obtaining admission and this issue, which this study has argued to be another form of exclusion, deserves further examination. A recent research report highlighted the problems of admission in relation to 'mobile' pupils who transfer schools outside the normal admissions round, and identified children looked after as a group for whom this is a significant issue (Dobson and Henthorne 1999). This problem is, of course, especially acute if young people have been excluded on more than one occasion. Admitting children who are looked after, however, may depend on existing relationships with other professionals. Fred's school, while initially reluctant to admit him, did so after discussions with the children's home which provided them with evidence that residential staff would offer support. The headteacher also went to visit the children's home to talk to Fred himself. In other cases, where face-to-face contact had been minimal or non-existent, subsequent exclusion was made easier.

The exclusion from school of children looked after by local authorities

The benefits of an overall reduction in exclusions would, of course, apply to children looked after as to other pupils. However, targets have also been set for the educational attainment of children looked after. Under the National Priorities Guidance for Modernising Health and Social Services, there is an expectation that 50 per cent of all children looked after should achieve an educational qualification by 2001, and 75 per cent by 2003. Under the Quality Protects programme, broader objectives are to ensure that children in need and children looked after gain maximum life chance benefits from educational opportunities, health care and social care.

It is very encouraging that the educational needs of children looked after are sufficiently high on the political agenda that specific consideration should have been given to them. However, there are a number of problems with the setting of targets for the educational attainment of children looked after which are worth considering. The House of Commons Select Committee on Health, while welcoming in principle the setting of targets, note that current research information indicates that between 50 per cent and 75 per cent of care leavers have no qualifications. If these statistics are accurate, then the Committee points out that the lower of the government's targets is already being met.

A more fundamental problem with the setting of targets is that this fails to take account of the current context of residential care. Too often, it seems, the 'education of children in care' has been treated as a problem affecting a homogenous group of young people. Such an approach fails to identify the areas where problems are shared and those where there are important differences. There is also variation in the attention – including that from researchers – which has been given to different groups of looked after children. Too little is known about the educational experiences of children living in foster care, those in permanent or adoptive placements, and children who experience support through short-breaks (Borland *et al.* 1998; Berridge 1996).

This means that there are significant problems of definition which policy-makers engaged in the setting of targets must address. The question of what is 'value added', or the relative amount of progress which a child makes, is likely to prove vexing.

Another major difficulty in setting targets is the limited amount of empirical information available on the educational attainments and status of the looked after group. As Smith (1998) has shown, the majority of local authorities do not gather such data. This is necessarily being addressed through the establishment of new national and local monitoring systems, but represents a major challenge. Given the mobile nature of the lives of the children concerned the difficulties which local authorities encounter in obtaining such data should not be underestimated. However, it is unlikely that policy can be developed in the absence of this information. Additionally, while various projects have sought to support the education of children looked after, there is little independent information about the outcomes and effectiveness of such work. There is clearly scope for further research in all those areas. It is also important that researchers in this area recognise the importance of viewing children looked after as part of the wider group of 'children in need' (Sinclair, Grimshaw and Garnett 1994) and investigate the links between the different educational and welfare systems with which young people and their families have contact. There is considerable scope, for example, in linking research into the assessment of EBD to the problems of children who are offered support by social services.

Fletcher-Campbell (1998) states unequivocally that the poor achievement of children looked after 'is a product of the system; the problem, though awesome, is solvable'. Consequently, she argues, if education is sufficiently prioritised through planning and the provision of appropriate support, and if those working with young people have a clear understanding of their responsibilities in this respect, then 'there can be achievement in the normal range' (p.4). Evidence from this study supports this statement to the extent that the social work professionals working with young people assumed different perspectives towards education, some of which were more favourable to the promotion of individual educational welfare. However, even those who saw themselves as advocating for young people, or tried to work collaboratively with others, faced formidable constraints. These arose not only from the very serious difficulties which young people had already experienced in their lives, but also in the form of structural barriers, such as the absence of alternative educational provision for some groups of children and difficulties in obtaining funding.

Encouragingly, some evidence regarding the potential for residential care to act positively in relation to a young person's education has also emerged. In almost two-thirds of the cases studied, the residential social workers saw themselves as advocating on behalf of the young person at school. Unfortunately, however, social workers and residential staff found themselves involved too late, or engaged in patching up a situation which had reached crisis point. It also seemed that greater input was made to cases of younger children, who also received support from a wider range of professionals. Other research has shown that adolescents, although the majority, continue to be neglected in welfare services.

This study has shown that the experiences of children living in residential accommodation are extremely varied and also very complex. Different types of residential care do pose different educational problems. Issues specific to children living in private homes are perhaps especially worthy of note. Private homes offer residential places to some 1500 children in England and on the whole the educational arrangements made for these young people have received too little attention. This study has shown that the greater distance children were living from their homes, and consequently the local authorities responsible for their care, could cause particular difficulties in regard to professional relationships. The need for clarity regarding the educational arrangement for young people seemed especially important in these cases. A worrying feature of these cases was also the disparity between the actions of the local authority, represented by the social worker, and the views of residential staff and young people. This seemed to relate largely to the status of the educational establishments operated by private homes, an issue on which some social workers seemed to lack important information.

While it seems that, overall, young people spend a shorter period of time in any one placement, care careers may still be characterised by a series of moves between home, foster and residential care (Berridge and Brodie 1997; Triseliotis *et al.* 1995). The fact that several changes of placement may occur within a shorter period of time can mean that the level of disruption is even greater. It seems essential that this context is not only recognised but acted upon. If children's homes are admitting young people likely to be resident for only a short period of time, then procedures for dealing with educational issues need to be highly streamlined. While adaptation must be made to the individual child, it is important that the structures and processes are already in existence that the time spent in residence may be optimal for the young person.

Planning and transition have relevance to all the types of exclusion identified in this study. These are, of course, old messages. Once in the care system, as other research has emphasised all too frequently, monitoring of educational progress is essential, a process in which tools such as the Department of Health's (1995) Assessment and Action records should be helpful. In some of the cases in this sample, the absence of adequate monitoring by key professionals, usually social workers, was perceived by others to be a critical factor in the later escalation of problems. In this respect there are clearly advantages in the model proposed in recent research that a mentor or 'champion' be appointed to support children in need on an ongoing basis (DoH 1996; Triseliotis *et al.* 1995). In this study it did not seem to matter who took this role; the worrying fact was that there was no guarantee that any professional would do so. The draft guidance is encouraging in this respect, in that it is clearly stated that carers should actively participate in care and education planning, and that schools should appoint a designated teacher with responsibility for looked after children. Such proposals may not guarantee good practice, but go some way to increasing the likelihood that the education of looked after children will be recognised as, in some degree, the responsibility of all those involved. This study has shown that the children who entered schools hurriedly and with little preparation for either young person or school were at heightened risk of being excluded. This supports the joint SSI/OFSTED (1995) report which commented that when transfer took place at unusual points in the school year, that is, outside the normal arrangements for admission and induction, were problematic and disadvantaged the children concerned. Moves which were insufficiently planned also created difficulties for schools, which reported that children 'turned up' without any information or preparation and that the schools had not been routinely briefed by a social worker on the admission of the child.

Another aspect of the residential context, namely the young person's return home, must also be considered. This study has highlighted occasions in a young person's experience where residential staff offered extremely positive support which helped stabilise schooling. However, when the child returned home problems emerged once again. This was particularly evident in Graham's case, where intensive support had been provided which his mother was quite unable to duplicate. It is therefore important that social work support for education is built into the child's return home. Similarly, if a move to another residential placement has to take place, then it is desirable that the level of support for education is comparable. In Hugh's case, it is noticeable that his exclusion – after a long holding period – occurred after his move from a home for younger children where there was an individual responsible for education, to one where there was no such resource.

The issue of continuity in care and education has frequently been highlighted (Social Services Inspectorate/OFSTED 1995; Jackson 1987). In relation to the cases studied, it seems that concern about frequent changes in care and education may have important implications for the child's risk of exclusion. Specifically, the fact that children looked after may be perceived as pupils likely to leave after a short time, or who are relatively disposable, is a matter of concern. In order for any stable relationship between teachers and pupils to develop it is obviously necessary for the child to be in school. It is unlikely that problems can be resolved in the long-term unless some kind of consensus can be established within the classroom. This is not to say that at moments of crisis a child should never be removed from the classroom. However, the extent to which this occurred in the build-up to exclusion in several cases studied suggests that residential staff should be aware of the weakening of links which can result from support offered in this way.

Inter-agency co-operation

More effective working relationships with other professionals is frequently cited as one measure which can help prevent exclusions. Osler (1997) makes some practical suggestions for the achievement of this, for example that schools should have lists of relevant local agencies so that they can refer parents to the appropriate individual or organisation. The need for consultation with other agencies prior to an exclusion taking place has also been stressed (DfEE 1999b; DfEE/DoH 1999; Munn et al 1998; Social Exclusion Unit 1998; Osler 1997) and may be included in the revised guidance due to be issued by the government (Social Exclusion Unit 1997). Pleas for better relationships between professionals can easily become platitudinous, and little has been said about what should be required from the other agencies involved.

An important finding from this study is that good relationships and consultation do not necessarily help prevent exclusion. If a co-ordinated approach is to be meaningful, it is essential that professionals outside the school are well-informed, firstly about the prior educational experience and current difficulties of the young person, and secondly about exclusion and what this means. Carers and social workers need to be clear about what powers they have in relation to a young person's education and the exclusion process. Unless they have access to this information, it is unlikely they will be able to advocate effectively for the young person. In some of the cases examined in this study, it seemed that good relationships were maintained more through the deference of carers and social workers to the decision of the school than otherwise.

Given that educational problems are a significant reason for children becoming looked after, it is also important that increasing attention is given to the interaction between social services and education in supporting young people and their families to limit the escalation of school-related problems. As research has frequently shown, a child being out of school places immense stress on parents and even other siblings (Parsons 1997; Parsons *et al.* 1994). Several models have been proposed whereby such prevention might take place: for example, the use of schools as a base for family support and other welfare services (Ball 1998). Outreach by children's homes staff and the increased use of mentoring, while not necessarily a panacea, also represent ways in which services can respond flexibly to the needs of young people and their families (Brodie *et al.* 1998).

As other research has emphasised, it is also important that relationships which facilitate educational support of children exist at all levels of the local authority hierarchy. In Local Authority 1, for example, joint work between education and social services on behavioural problems and the education of children looked after was taking place. A continuing problem, however, is the unevenness in practice which continues to exist between schools and local authorities and which was highlighted by the experiences of the young people in this study. The development of Children's Services Plans and Behaviour Support Plans should be helpful at the planning level, though the co-ordination of the different planning processes is potentially problematic.

Young people and the exclusion process

In addition to more effective relationships between professionals, it is also important that adults engage with the young people who are involved in the exclusion. This study has highlighted once more the very different views which young people will hold regarding their education generally and exclusion in particular. The adults interviewed made little, if any, reference to consultation with children or about any opinions they might have expressed. Some children had been unhappy with the changes of school that had been made; others openly declared their dislike for school and their desire to be excluded; others felt they were victims of an unfair system. Unfortunately the views of children looked after often continue to be overlooked in regard to their education, and more work in this area would be very welcome (Goddard 2000).

It has been argued that children have generally little say in the running of schools and that one way in which they can register their protests is through difficult behaviour (see Hill and Tisdall 1997, for a good summary of this position). A strict adherent to a children's rights perspective might take the view that through such behaviour, pupils make themselves justifiably 'ineducable' (Irving and Parker-Jenkins 1995, quoted in Hill and Tisdall 1997). This position does not, perhaps, take adequate account of how the views of the adolescents in this study intensified the problem as it was perceived by relevant adults. No matter how persuasive social workers and other professionals were, the young person's situation within the school could ultimately only be resolved if the child displayed consistent adherence to the norms of the school as an institution. Repeated failure to play by the rules made exclusion increasingly inevitable.

Implicit in some of the current proposals is the view that schools hold too much power in the management of exclusions. Thus the 1997 Education Act gave LEAs the right to be represented and heard at the governors' meeting which should take place to ratify the decision to exclude. However, as Castle and Parsons (1997) point out, the Act did nothing to enhance the rights of parents and young people, and may even have diminished these.

Significantly, however, some recent cases of exclusion which have been subject to judicial review have highlighted the need for schools to give due attention to the young person's point of view. For example, in R v Cardinal Newman's School, Birmingham, ex p S (1997) (*The Times* 26 December QBD), where a classroom assistant identified S as the perpetrator of an attack on another pupil, even though she did not know S by name. The judge stated that the overriding principle was that a pupil accused or suspected of an act of indiscipline must be given a fair opportunity to give an account of the incident so that s/he might establish his/her innocence. The responsibilities for ensuring that this happens clearly lie with the school.

It is disturbing that such principles are not already established as good practice within schools. Unlike social work, there is still no requirement within education legislation that young people should be involved or consulted in the decision-making process. Exclusion therefore continues to carry with it a sense that a quasi-legal judgement has been made, but without the alleged offender having access to proper defence.

Conclusion

This study has sought to highlight the nature of exclusion as a complex and multi-dimensional social phenomenon. The theoretical basis of the study has, however, permitted detailed consideration of the way in which individuals actively negotiate the exclusion process, often little constrained by wider structures. This approach has been especially helpful in highlighting the problematic nature of any debate focused on 'exclusion' per se. Examination of the experiences of the 17 young people has shown that exclusion frequently begins long before the decision to exclude is made, and can continue for even longer after the child's departure. A growing emphasis on the need to assess children's difficulties early in their career, and on seeking new means of 'inclusion' is therefore to be welcomed. A focus on 'children out of school', rather than on exclusion, is also positive.

At the same time, this study has highlighted the ways in which a child being 'out of school' can be related to their experience of being looked after. The absence of effective assessment and planning, together with the sometimes negative perceptions of the schools concerned towards the young person, contributed to an 'exclusion' from school, whether or not this took place on an official or unofficial basis. Those individuals who sought to act in the best interests of the young person's schooling often faced considerable institutional barriers to doing so. These problems do not diminish the other difficulties in the lives of the children concerned, such as the experience of abuse, which affected their school careers. It is likely that a small number of children, including some looked after, will always be excluded. The problems of the young people studied were considerable; it was not, however, always clear that exclusion was the best solution to these difficulties or, indeed, that the presenting behaviour warranted this. However, this study suggests that the kind of educational disadvantage experienced by children looked after can increase their vulnerability to exclusion.

Inevitably, but also regrettably, some of the issues of concern highlighted in this final chapter reiterate long-standing anxieties about the education of children looked after in residential accommodation. These expressions of concern have become ever more audible in recent years and months. This study has shown that residential care can support children who have experienced immense problems in their personal and school careers. It is essential that the growing body of knowledge regarding good practice in this area is evenly applied, thus ensuring that children's access to education is not a matter of chance.

Notes

1 Section 166 of the Education Act 1993 states that social services departments, subject to a qualification similar to that in Section 27 of the Children Act 1989, and district health authorities, depending on the reasonableness of the request in the light of available resources, must comply with a request for help from a LEA in connection with children with special educational needs, unless they consider that the help is not necessary for the exercise of the LEA's functions.

2 Note that Children's Services Plans and Behaviour Plans were not in existence at the time fieldwork for this study was carried out.

3 Section 27 states: 'District health authorities, LEAs, grant maintained schools and City Technology Colleges must comply with a request from a social services department for assistance in providing services for children in need, so long as the request is compatible with their duties and does not unduly prejudice the discharge of any of their functions'.

4 This method is an increasingly popular part of personal and social development programmes, especially in primary schools (Mosley 1995). Children and adults sit in a circle – symbolic of equal status – and issues relevant to the life of the class are shared. Problems are discussed and solutions sought, but emphasis is also given to praise and reward. See Lloyd and Munn (1997) for examples of the technique in practice.

5 In fact, the perception that exclusions did not occur frequently within schools was borne out by local authority data on the number of exclusions taking place each year.

References

Advisory Centre on Education (ACE) (1992) 'Exclusions.' *ACE Bulletin 45*, 9–10.

Advisory Centre on Education (ACE) (1993) *Findings from ACE Investigations into Exclusion.* London: ACE.

Alderson, P. (1995) *Listening to Children: Children, Ethics and Social Research.* Barkingside: Barnardo's.

Aldgate, J., Heath, A., Colton, M. and Simm, M. (1993) 'Social work and the education of children in foster care.' *Adoption and Fostering 17*, 3, 25–35.

Allen, T. (1994) 'The exclusion of pupils from school: the need for reform.' *Journal of Social Welfare and Family Law 2*, 145–162.

Aries, P. (1996) *Centuries of Childhood.* London: Pimlico.

Association of Metropolitan Authorities (1995) *Reviewing Special Educational Needs.* London: Association of Metropolitan Authorities.

Audit Commission (1994) *Seen But Not Heard: Co-Ordinating Community Child Health and Social Services for Children in Need.* London: HMSO.

Audit Commission (1996) *Misspent Youth...Young People and Crime.* London: Audit Commission.

Ball, M. (1998) *School Inclusion: The School, the Family and the Community.* York: Joseph Rowntree Foundation.

Ball, S. (1990) *Politics and Policy Making in Education.* London: Routledge.

Bebbington, A. and Miles, J. (1989) 'The background of children who enter local authority care.' *British Journal of Social Work 19*, 5, 349–368.

Becker, H., Geer, B., Hughes, E. and Strauss, A. (1961) *Boys in White.* Chicago: University of Chicago.

Bennathan, M. (1993) 'The care and education of troubled children.' *Therapeutic Care and Education 1*, 1, 37–49.

Berridge, D. (1985) *Children's Homes.* Oxford: Blackwell.

Berridge, D. (1996) *Foster Care: A Research Review.* London: HMSO.

Berridge, D. and Brodie, I. (1998) *Children's Homes Revisited.* London: Jessica Kingsley Publishers.

Berridge, D., Brodie, I., Ayre, P., Barrett, D., Henderson, B. and Wenman, H. (1997) *Is Anybody Listening? The Education of Young People in Residential Care.* Warwick: University of Warwick/Social Care Association.

Berridge, D., Brodie, I., Pitts, J., Porteous, D. and Tarling, R. (forthcoming 2001) *The Independent Effects of Permanent Exclusion from School on the Offending Careers of Young People.* Luton: University of Luton.

Biehal, N., Clayden, J., Stein, M. and Wade, J. (1992) *Prepared for Living? A Survey of Young People Leaving the Care of Three Local Authorities.* London: National Children's Bureau.

Birchall, E. and Hallett, C. (1995) *Working Together in Child Protection.* London: HMSO.

Bird, C., Chessum, R., Furlong, J. and Johnson, D. (1981) *Disaffected Pupils.* London: Brunel University Educational Studies Unit.

Bloor, M. (1997) 'Addressing social problems through qualitative research.' In D. Silverman (ed) *Qualitative Research: Theory, Method and Practice.* London: Sage.

Blumer, H. (1969) *Symbolic Interactionism.* Englewood Cliffs: Prentice Hall.

Blyth, E. and Milner, J. (1993) 'Exclusion from school: a first step in exclusion from society?' *Children and Society 7*, 3, 255–268.

Blyth, E. and Milner, J. (1994) 'Exclusion from school and victim blaming.' *Oxford Review of Education 20*, 3, 293–306.

Blyth, E. and Milner, J. (eds) (1996) *Exclusion From School: Inter-Professional Issues For Policy and Practice.* London: Routledge.

Booth, T. A. (1981) 'Collaboration between the health and social services: Part 1, a case study of joint care planning.' *Policy and Politics 9*, 1, 23–49.

Booth, T. (1996) 'Stories of exclusion: natural and unnatural selection.' in E. Blyth and J. Milner (eds) *Exclusion From School: Inter-Professional Issues for Policy and Practice.* London: Routledge.

Borland, M., Pearson, C., Hill, M., Tisdall, K. and Bloomfield, I. (1998) *Education and Care Away From Home.* Edinburgh: Scottish Council for Research in Education.

Bourne, J., Bridges, L. and Searle, C. (1994) *Outcast England: How Schools Exclude Black Children.* London: Institute of Race Relations.

Bradshaw, J. (2000) 'Prospects for poverty in Britain in the first twenty-five years of the next century.' *Sociology 34*, 1, 53–70.

Brannen, J. (ed) (1988) *Mixing Methods: Qualitative and Quantitative Research.* Aldershot: Avebury.

Brindle, D. (1995) 'Education failing children in care, inspectors say.' *The Guardian* 5 April, 5.

Broad, B. (1998) *Young People Leaving Care: Life after the Children Act 1989.* London: Jessica Kingsley Publishers.

Brodie, I. (1997) 'School exclusion, risk and community safety.' in A. Marlow and J. Pitts (eds) *Planning Safer Communities.* Hemel Hempstead: Russell House, 121–129.

Brodie, I. and Berridge, D. (1996) *School Exclusion: Research Themes and Issues.* Luton: Luton University Press.

Brodie, I., Berridge, D., Ayre, P., Barrett, D., Burroughs, L., Porteous, D. and Wenman, H. (1998) *Family Support for Adolescents: An Evaluation of the Adolescent Community Support Team.* Luton: University of Luton.

Bryman, A. (1988a) *Quantity and Quality in Social Research.* London: Unwin Hyman.

Bryman, A. (1988b) *Doing Research in Organisations.* London: Routledge.

Bullock, R., Little, M. and Millham, S. (1993) *Going Home.* Aldershot: Dartmouth.

Bulmer, M. (1984) *Sociological Research Methods: An Introduction (2nd Edition).* London: Macmillan.

Buston, K. (1997) 'NUDIST in action: its use and its usefulness in a study of chronic illness in young people.' *Sociological Research Online 2*, 3.

Carlen, P., Gleeson, D. and Wardhaugh, J. (1992) *Truancy: The Politics of Compulsory Schooling.* Buckingham: Open University Press.

Castle, F. and Parsons, C. (1997) 'Disruptive behaviour and exclusions from schools: redefining and responding to the problem.' *Emotional and Behavioural Difficulties 2*, 3, 4–11.

Challis, L., Day, P., Klein, R. and Scrivens, E. (1994) 'Managing quasi-markets: institutions of regulation', in W. Bartlett, C. Propper, D. Wilson, and J. Le Grand (eds) *Quasi-Markets in the Welfare State.* Bristol: University of Bristol School for Advanced Urban Studies.

Charter, D. (1996) 'Teachers vote to strike in row over "violent" boy of 10.' *The Times* 28 August, 2.

Charter, D. (1996) 'Parents withdraw pupils over cost of disruptive boy.' *The Times* 10 September, p.5.

Chazan, M. (1994) 'The attitudes of mainstream teachers towards pupils with emotional and behavioural difficulties.' *British Journal of Special Needs Education 9*, 3, 261–275.

Clark, A. (1996) 'Policy and provision for the schooling of children living in temporary accommodation: exploring the difficulties.' *Children and Society 10*, 293–304.

Cleaver, H. (1991) *Vulnerable Children in Schools*. Vermont: Dartmouth Publishing Company.

Cleaver, H. and Freeman, P. (1995) *Parental Perspectives in Cases of Suspected Child Abuse*. London: HMSO.

Cohen, R., Hughes, M. with Ashworth, L. and Blair, M. (1994) *School's Out*. Ilford: Family Service Units/Barnardo's.

Cohen, S. (1972) *Folk Devils and Moral Panics*. Oxford: Martin Robertson.

Colton, M., Drury, C. and Williams, M. (1995) 'Children in need: definition, identification and support.' *British Journal of Social Work 25*, 711–728.

Commission for Racial Equality (1996) *Exclusion From School: The Public Cost*. London: Commission for Racial Equality.

Cooper, P. (1993) *Effective Schools for Disaffected Students: Integration and Segregation*. London: Routledge.

Cooper, P. (1996) 'Giving it a name: the value of descriptive categories in educational approaches to emotional and behavioural difficulties.' *Support for Learning 11*, 4, 146–150.

Cooper, P. and Ideus, K. (1995) 'Is attention deficit hyperactivity disorder a Trojan Horse?' *Support for Learning 10*, 1, 29–34.

Crawford, A. and Jones, M. (1995) 'Inter-agency co-operation and community-based crime prevention: some reflections on the work of Pearson and colleagues.' *British Journal of Criminology 35*, 1, 17-33.

Cullingford, C. and Morrison, J. (1996) 'Who excludes whom? The personal experience of exclusion.' In E. Blyth and J. Milner (eds) *Exclusion From School: Inter-Professional Issues for Policy and Practice*. London: Routledge.

Cunningham, H. (1992) *The Children of the Poor: Representations of Childhood Since the Seventeenth Century*. Oxford: Blackwell.

Cunningham-Burley, S. and McKeganey, N. (eds) (1990) *Readings in Medical Sociology*. London: Routledge.

D'Ancona, M. (1992) 'Injured teacher sues council for negligence.' *The Times* 15 August, p.2.

David, M., West, J. and Ribbens, J. (1994) *Mother's Intuition? Choosing Secondary Schools*. London: The Falmer Press.

Dean, H. (ed) (1996) *Ethics and Social Policy Research*. Luton: University of Luton Press.

Dean, H. (1997) 'Underclassed or undermined? Young people and social citizenship.' In R. Macdonald (ed) *Youth, the 'Underclass' and Social Exclusion*. London: Routledge.

Delamont, S. (1976) *Interaction in the Classroom*. London: Methuen.

Delamont, S. (2000) 'The anomalous beasts: hooligans and the sociology of education.' *Sociology 34*, 95–111.

Dennington, J. and Pitts, J. (1991) *Developing Services for Young People in Crisis*. London: Longman.

Dennis, N. and Erdos, G. (1992) *Families Without Fatherhood*. London: Institute for Economic Affairs.

Denzin, N. (1976) *The Reasearch Act*. Chicago: Aldine.

Denzin, N. (1992) *Symbolic Interactionism and Cultural Studies*. Oxford: Blackwell.

Department for Education (1995) *National Survey of Local Education Authorities' Policies and Procedures for the Identification of, and Provision for, Children Who Are Out of School by Reason of Exclusion or Otherwise*. London: DfE.

Department for Education (1994a) *Pupils with Problems (Department for Education Circulars 8-13/94)*. London: DfE.

Department for Education (1994b) *Code of Practice on the Identification and Assessment of Special Educational Needs*. London: DfE.

Department for Education (1993) *Exclusions: A Discussion Paper*. London: DfE.

Department for Education and Employment (1997) *Permanent Exclusions From Schools in England 1995-96, Press Release 342/97*. London: DfEE.

Department for Education and Employment (1998) *Morris reveals ambitious new plans to cut truancy and exclusion from school, Press Release 386/98*. London: DfEE.

Department for Education and Employment (1999a) *Schools in England 1998*. London: The Stationery Office.

Department for Education and Employment (1999b) *Social Inclusion: Pupil Support*. London: DfEE.

Department for Education and Employment/Department of Health (1999) *Draft Guidance on the Education of Children Looked After By Local Authorities*. London: DfE.

Department for Education and Employment (2000) 'Jacqui Smith welcomes reduction in exclusions.' *Press release 102/00*. London: DfEE.

Department of Education and Science (1978) *Special Educational Needs: Report of the Enquiry into the Education of Handicapped Children and Young People (The Warnock Report)*. London: HMSO.

Department of Education and Science and the Welsh Office (1989) *Discipline in Schools. Report of the Committee of Enquiry Chaired by Lord Elton*. London: HMSO.

Department of Health (1989) *An Introduction to the Children Act*. London: HMSO.

Department of Health (1991) *A Study of Inquiry Reports 1980–1989*. London: HMSO.

Department of Health (1995) *Child Protection: Messages From Research*. London: HMSO.

Department of Health (1996) *Focus on Teenagers*. London: HMSO.

Department of Health (1998a) *Modernising Social Services*. London: DoH.

Department of Health (1998b) *The Quality Protects Programme: Transforming Children's Services*. London: DoH.

Department of Health (1999) *The Children Act Report*. London: The Stationery Office.

de Pear, S. and Garner, P. (1996) 'Tales from the exclusion zone: the views of teachers and pupils.' in E. Blyth and J. Milner (eds) *Exclusion From School: Inter-Professional Issues for Policy and Practice*. London: Routledge.

Devlin, A. (1996) *Criminal Classes: Offenders at School*. Winchester: Waterside Press.

Dimigen, G., Del Priore, C., Butler, S., Evans, S., Ferguson, L. and Swan, M. (1999) 'Psychiatric disorder among children at time of entering local authority care: a questionnaire survey.' *British Medical Journal 319*, 7211.

Dingwall, R. and Lewis, P. (eds) (1983) *The Sociology of the Professions: Lawyers, Doctors and Others*. Basingstoke: Macmillan.

Dobson, J. and Henthorne, K. (1999) *Pupil Mobility in Schools. DfEE Research Report No. 168*. London: Department for Education and Employment.

Donovan, N. (ed) (1998) *Second Chances: Exclusion from School and Equality of Opportunity*. London: New Policy Institute.

Douglas, J. (1964) *The Home and the School*. London: McGibbon and Kee.

Equal Opportunities Commission and OFSTED (1996) *The Gender Divide: Performance Differences Between Boys and Girls at School*. London: HMSO.

Etzioni, A. (1969) *The Semi-Professions and their Organisations: Teachers, Nurses, Social Workers*. Collier-Macmillan.

Express, The (1996) 'A baby for the mother of all school tearaways.' 22 October, p.1.

Farmer, E. and Pollock, S. (1998) *Caring for Sexually Abused and Abusing Children Away From Home.* Chichester: Wiley.

Farrell, P. (ed) (1995) *Children with Emotional and Behavioural Difficulties.* London: Falmer Press.

Filmer, P., Phillipson, M., Silverman, D. and Walsh, D. (1972) *New Directions in Sociological Theory.* London: Collier-Macmillan.

Finch, J. (1984) '"It's great to have someone to talk to": the ethics and politics of interviewing women.' In C. Bell and H. Roberts (eds) *Social Researching - Politics, Problems, Practice.* London: Routledge and Kegan Paul, 70–87.

Fine, G. and Sandstrom, K. (1988) *Knowing Children: Participant Observation with Minors, Qualitative Research Methods Series 15.* Newbury Park: Sage.

Fisher, M., Marsh, P., Phillips, D. and Sainsbury, E. (1986) *In and Out of Care: The Experiences of Children, Parents and Social Workers.* London: Batsford in association with the British Agencies for Adoption and Fostering.

Fletcher, B. (1993) *Not Just A Name: The Views of Young People in Foster and Residential Care.* London: National Consumer Council.

Fletcher-Campbell, F. (1998) 'Progress or procrastination? The education of children who are looked after.' *Children and Society 12,* 3–11.

Fletcher-Campbell, F. and Hall, C. (1990) *Changing Schools? Changing People? The Education of Children in Care.* Slough: National Foundation for Educational Research.

Francis, J. (2000) 'Investing in children's futures: enhancing the educational arrangements of 'looked after' children and young people.' *Child and Family Social Work 5,* 23–33.

Frost, N. and Stein, M. (1989) *The Politics of Child Welfare.* Hemel Hempstead: Harvester Wheatsheaf.

Furlong, V. (1976) 'Interaction sets in the classroom.' In M. Stubbs and S. Delamont (eds) *Explorations in Classroom Observation.* Chichester: Wiley.

Furlong, V. (1985) *The Deviant Pupil: Sociological Perspectives.* Milton Keynes: Open University Press.

Furlong, V. (1991) 'Disaffected pupils: reconstructing the sociology of education.' *British Journal of Sociology of Education 12,* 3, 293–307.

Galloway, D. and Goodwin, C. (1987) *The Education of Disturbing Children.* London: Longman.

Galloway, D., Armstrong, D. and Tomlinson, S. (1994) *The Assessment of Special Educational Needs: Whose Problem?* London: Longman.

Galloway, D., Ball, T., Blomfield, D. and Seyd, R. (1982) *Schools and Disruptive Pupils.* London and New York: Longman.

Gersch, I. and Nolan, A. (1994) 'Exclusions: what the children think.' *Educational Psychology in Practice, 10,* 1, 35–45.

Gewirtz, S., Ball, S. and Bowe, R. (1995) *Markets, Choice and Equity in Education.* Buckingham: Open University Press.

Gibbons, J., Gallagher, B., Bell, C. and Gordon, D. (1995) *Development After Physical Abuse in Early Childhood: A Follow-Up Study of Children on Protection Registers.* London: HMSO.

Giddens, A. (1979) *Central Problems in Social Theory.* London: Macmillan.

Gillborn, D. (1990) *'Race', Ethnicity and Education: Teaching and Learning in Multi-Ethnic Schools.* London: Unwin Hyman/Routledge.

Gillborn, D. and Gipps, C. (1996) *Recent Research on the Achievements of Ethnic Minority Pupils.* London: Office for Standards in Education.

Gilligan, R. (1998) 'The importance of schools and teachers in child welfare.' *Child and Family Social Work 3*, 13–25.

Gittins, D. (1998) *The Child in Question*. Basingstoke and London: Macmillan.

Glaser, B. and Strauss, A. (1965) *Awareness of Dying*. Chicago: Aldine.

Glaser, B. and Strauss, A. (1967) *The Discovery of Grounded Theory*. Chicago: Aldine.

Glatter and Woods (1993) *Competitive Arenas in Education: Studying the impact of enhanced competition and choice on parents and schools*. Buckingham: The Open University Centre for Educational Policy and Management.

Gleeson, D. (1992) 'School attendance and truancy: a socio-historical account.' *Sociological Review 40*, 3, 437–490.

Glennerster, H. (1991) 'Quasi-markets for education.' *The Economic Journal 101*, 408, 1268–1276.

Goddard, J. (2000) 'The education of looked after children.' *Child and Family Social Work 5*, 79–86.

Goffman, E. (1969) *The Presentation of Self in Everyday Life*. Harmondsworth: Penguin.

Goffman, E. (1974) *Frame Analysis*. Harmondsworth: Penguin.

Grey, P. and Panter, S. (2000) *'Exclusion or Inclusion? A Perspective on Policy in England for Pupils with Emotional and Behavioural Difficulties.' Support for Learning, 15*, 1, 4–7.

Gregg, P., Harkness, S. and Machin, S. (1999) *Child Development and Family Income*. York: York Publishing Services for the Joseph Rowntree Foundation.

Grimshaw, R. (1991) *Children of Parents with Parkinson's Disease*. London: National Children's Bureau.

Grimshaw, R. and Sinclair, R. (1997) *Planning to Care: Regulation, Procedure and Practice under the Children Act*. London: National Children's Bureau.

Grunsell, R. (1980) *Beyond Control? Schools and Suspensions*. London: Writers and Readers.

Guardian, The (1996) 'New school option for boy in strike row'. 23 April, Section 2, p.1.

Guardian, The (1996) 'Exclusion row head blames "forked tounge"'. 2 May, p.3.

Hallett, C. (1995) *Inter-agency Co-ordination in Child Protection*. London: HMSO.

Halsey, E. (1988) *Change in British Society*. Oxford: Oxford University Press.

Hansard, HL 547, col 173

Hammersley, M. and Woods, P. (eds) (1976) *The Process of Schooling*. London: Routledge and Kegan Paul.

Hargreaves, D. (1967) *Social Relations in a Secondary School*. London: Routledge and Kegan Paul.

Hargreaves, D. (1975) *Interpersonal Relations and Education*. London: Routledge and Kegan Paul.

Hargreaves, D., Hester, S. and Mellor, F. (1975) *Deviance in Classrooms*. London: Routledge and Kegan Paul.

Harris, N. (1992) 'Youth, citizenship and welfare.' *Journal of Social Welfare and Family Law 3*, 175–192.

Harris, N. (1995) 'Access to justice for parents and children over schooling decisions - the role and reform of education tribunals.' *Child and Family Law Quarterly 7*, 3, 81–94.

Hart, D. (1996) 'The needs of the many and the few – can they be reconciled?' Paper presented at the National Children's Bureau conference 'Exclusion – or inclusion – and the school system'. London 9 July.

Hayden, C. (1994) 'Primary age children excluded from school: a multi-agency focus for concern.' *Children and Society 8*, 3, 257–273.

Hayden, C. (1997) *Children Excluded From Primary School*. Buckingham: Open University Press.

Hayden, C. and Martin, T. (1998) 'Safer Cities and exclusion from school.' *Journal of Youth Studies 1*, 3, 315–331.

Hayden, C. and Ward, D. (1995) 'Faces behind the figures: interviews with children excluded from primary school.' *Children and Society 10*, 4, 255–266.

Hayden, C., Sheppard, C. and Ward, D. (1996) *Primary Age Children Excluded From School. Report No. 33*. Portsmouth: University of Portsmouth.

Hazel, N. (1996) 'Elicitation techniques with young people.' *Social Research 12*. Guildford: University of Surrey.

Heath, A., Colton, M. and Aldgate, J. (1994) 'Failure to escape: a longitudinal study of foster children's educational attainment.' *British Journal of Social Work 24*, 241–260.

Hendrick, H. (1997) 'Constructions and reconstructions of British childhood: an interpretive survey, 1800 to the present.' In A. James and A. Prout (eds) *Constructing and Reconstructing Childhood*. London: Falmer, 34–62

Hill, M. (1997) 'Participatory research with children.' *Child and Family Social Work*, 2, 171-183.

Hill, M. and Tisdall, K. (1998) *Children and Society*. London: Longman.

Hill, M., Laybourn, A. and Borland, M. (1995) 'Engaging with primary-aged children about their emotions and well-being: methodological considerations.' *Children and Society 10*, 129–144.

Hillman, J. (1998) *Wasted Youth*. London: Institute for Public Policy Research.

HMSO (1944) *The Education Act 1944*. London: HMSO.

Holdsworth, N. (1995) 'Excluded children in care "a scandal".' *Times Educational Supplement*, July 7, p.10.

Homan, R. (1991) *The Ethics of Social Research*. London: Longman.

Home Office (1995) *Young People and Crime. Research Study 145*. London: Home Office.

Home Office, Department of Health, Department of Education and Science and Welsh Office (1991) *Working Together Under the Children Act 1989*. London: HMSO.

Houghton, S., Wheldall, K. and Merrett, F. (1988) 'Classroom behaviour problems which secondary school teachers say they find most troublesome.' *British Educational Research Journal 14*, 3, 297–312.

House of Commons Education and Employment Committee (1998) *Disaffected Children. Volume 1: Report and Proceedings of the Committee*. London: The Stationery Office.

House of Commons Health Committee (1998) *Children Looked After By Local Authorities. Volume 1: Report and Proceedings of the Committee*. London: The Stationery Office.

Howarth, C., Kenway, P., Palmer, G. and Miorelli, R. (1999) *Monitoring Poverty and Social Exclusion 1999*. York: Joseph Rowntree Foundation.

Hunt, A. (1997) '"Moral panic" and moral language in the media.' *British Journal of Sociology 48*, 4, 629–648.

Imich, A. (1994) Exclusions from school: current trends and issues. ' *Educational Research 36*, 1, 3–11.

Jackson, S. (1987) *The Education of Children in Care*. University of Bristol: School of Applied Social Studies.

Jackson, S. (1989) 'Residential care and education.' *Children and Society 2*, 4, 335–250.

Jackson, S. (1994) 'Educating children in residential and foster care.' *Oxford Review of Education 20*, 3, 267–279.

Jackson, S. (1998) *High Achievers: A Study of Young People Who Have Been in Residential or Foster Care. Final Report to the Leverhulme Trust*. Swansea: University of Wales, Swansea.

James, A. and Prout, A. (eds) (1997) *Constructing and Reconstructing Childhood*. London: Falmer.

James, H. (1898) *The Turn of the Screw.* Harmondsworth: Penguin.

Jenks, C. (1996) *Childhood.* London: Routledge.

John, M. (1996) 'Monitoring children's rights to education in the south-west of England.' In E. Verhellen (ed) *Monitoring Children's Rights.* Dordrecht: Martinus Nijholt.

Jones, A. and Bilton, K. (1994) *The Future Shape of Children's Services.* London: National Children's Bureau.

Jones, G. (1995) *Family Support for Young People.* London: Family Policy Studies Centre.

Kahan, B. (1989) *Child Care Research, Policy and Practice.* London: Hodder and Stoughton in association with the Open University.

Kahan, B. (1994) *Growing Up In Groups.* London: HMSO.

Kendall-Tackett, K., Williams, L. and Finkelhor, D. (1993) 'Impact of sexual abuse on children: a review and synthesis of recent empirical studies.' *Psychological Bulletin 113,* 1, 164–180.

Kendrick, A. (1995) 'The integration of child care services in Scotland.' *Children and Youth Services Review 17,* 619–635.

Kinder, K., Harland, J., Wilkin, A. and Wakefield, A. (1995) *Three to Remember: Strategies for Disaffected Pupils.* Slough: National Foundation for Educational Research.

Kinder, K., Wilkin, A. and Wakefield, A. (1997) *Exclusion: Who Needs It?* Slough: National Foundation for Educational Research.

Knight, R. (1995) *Educational Provision for Excluded Pupils.* Slough: National Foundation for Educational Research.

Kumar, V. (1993) *Poverty and Inequality in the UK: The Effects on Children.* London: National Children's Bureau.

Law Commission (1996) *Report on the Consolidation of Certain Enactments Relating to Education.* London: HMSO.

Layder, D. (1993) *New Strategies in Social Research.* London: Sage.

Leathard, A. (1993) *Going Inter-Professional: Working Together for Health and Welfare.* London: Routledge.

Lee, R. (1993) *Doing Research on Sensitive Topics.* London: Sage.

Le Grand, J. (1991) 'Quasi-markets and social policy.' *The Economic Journal 101,* 408, 1256–1267.

Le Grand, J. and Bartlett, W. (1993) *Quasi-Markets and Social Policy.* Hampshire: Macmillan Press.

Levacic, R. (1994) 'Evaluating the performance of quasi-markets in education.' In W. Bartlett, C. Propper, D. Wilson, and J. Le Grand (eds) (1994) *Quasi-Markets in the Welfare State.* Bristol: University of Bristol School for Advanced Urban Studies.

Levitas, R. (1999) 'Defining and measuring social exclusion: A critical overview of current proposals.' *Radical Statistics 71,* Summer.

Levy, A. and Kahan, B. (1991) *The Pindown Experience and the Protection of Children: The Report of the Staffordshire Child Care Inquiry 1990.* Stafford: Staffordshire County Council.

Little, M. (1998) 'Whispers in the library: a response to Liz Trinder's article on the state of social work research.' *Child and Family Social Work 3,* 49–56.

Lloyd, G. and Munn, P. (eds) (1997) *Sharing Good Practice.* Edinburgh: Moray House Publications.

Lloyd-Smith, M. and Davies, J. (1995) *On the Margins: The Educational Experiences of 'Problem' Pupils.* Stoke-on-Trent: Trentham Books.

Lovey, J., Docking, J. and Evans, R. (1993) *Exclusion From School: Provision for Disaffection at Key Stage 4.* London: David Fulton.

Macdonald, R. (ed) (1997) *Youth, the 'Underclass' and Social Exclusion.* London: Routledge.

Majors, R., Gillborn, D. and Sewell, T. (1997) 'The exclusion of black children: implications for a racialised perspective.' *Multicultural Teaching 16,* 3, 35–37.

Malek, M. (1993) *Passing the Buck.* London: The Children's Society.

Marks, D. (1995) 'Accounting for exclusion: giving a 'voice' and producing a 'subject'.' *Children and Society 9,* 3, 81–98.

Marsh, P., Rosser, E. and Harre, R. (1978) *The Rules of Disorder.* London: Routledge and Kegan Paul.

Mason, J. (1996) *Qualitative Researching.* London: Sage.

Mauthner, M. (1997) 'Methodological aspects of collecting data from children: lessons from three research projects.' *Children and Society 11,* 16–28.

Mayall, B. (1994) *Children's Childhoods: Observed and Experienced.* London: Falmer.

McAuley, C. (1996) *Long-term Foster Care.* Aldershot: Avebury.

McCann and Jones (1996) *Paper presented to the Association of Child Psychologists and Psychiatrists, Midlands branch,* 10 October 1996.

McFie, B. (1934) 'Behaviour and personality difficulties in school children.' *British Journal of Educational Psychology 3,* 30–36.

McGrath, M. (1991) *Multi-disciplinary Teamwork.* Aldershot: Avebury.

McLean, A. (1987) 'After the belt: school processes in low exclusion schools.' *School Organisation 7,* 3, 303–310.

McManus, M. (1989) 'Suspension and exclusion from high schools: the association with catchment and school variables.' *School Organisation 7,* 3, 261–271.

McRobbie, A. (1994) *Postmodernism and Popular Culture.* London: Routledge.

Meltzer, B., Petras, J. and Reynolds, L. (1975) *Symbolic Interactionism: Genesis, Varieties and Criticism.* London: Routledge and Kegan Paul.

Merrett, F. and Wheldall, D. (1984) 'Classroom behaviour problems which junior school teachers find most troublesome.' *Educational Studies 10,* 87–92.

Miller, J. and Glassner, B. (1997) 'The "inside" and the "outside": finding reality in interviews.' In D. Silverman (ed) *Qualitative Research: Theory, Method and Practice.* London: Sage.

Millham, S., Bullock, R., Hosie, K. and Haak, M. (1986) *Lost in Care.* Aldershot: Gower.

Mongon, D. and Hart, S. with Ace, C. and Rawlings, A. (1989) *Special Needs in Ordinary Schools - Improving Classroom Behaviours.* London: Cassell.

MORI (1993) Survey reported in 'A Class Apart.' *Panorama,* BBC, 19 March 1993.

Morris, S. and Wheatley, H. (1994) *Time to Listen: The Experiences of Young People in Foster and Residential Care.* London: Childline.

Morrow, V. and Richards, M. (1996) 'The ethics of social research with children: an overview.' *Children and Society 10,* 2, 90–105.

Mortimore, P., Sammons, P., Stoll, L., Lewis, D. and Echo, K. (1988) *School Matters: the Junior Years.* Wells: Open Books.

Mosley, J. (1995) *Turn Your School Around.* Cambridge: LDA.

Munn, P., Cullen, M., Johnstone, M. and Lloyd, G. (1998) *Exclusion and In-school Alternatives. Interchange Series 47.* Edinburgh: Scottish Office.

NACRO (1998) *Children, Schools and Crime.* London: NACRO.

NASWE (1998) *Truancy and School Exclusion: Interim Report - Submission to the Social Exclusion Unit.* NASWE/UNISON.

National Association of Head Teachers (1994) *Dramatic Increase in Permanent Exclusion of Pupils.* Press Release 9 December.

National Union of Teachers (1992) *Survey on Pupil Exclusions*. London: National Union of Teachers.

'News' *Special Children* Issue 92, May 1996, p.6.

Norwich, B. (1990) *Reappraising Special Needs Education*. London: Cassell.

OFSTED (1993) *Education for Disaffected Pupils*. London: Office for Standards in Education.

OFSTED (1995a) *Pupil Referral Units: The First Twelve Inspections*. London: Office for Standards in Education.

OFSTED (1995b) *The Challenge for Education Welfare*. London: Office for Standards in Education.

OFSTED (1996a) *Exclusions from Secondary Schools*. London: HMSO.

OFSTED (1996b) *The Annual Report of Her Majesty's Chief Inspector of Schools Standards and Quality in Education 1994–95*. London: Office for Standards in Education.

OFSTED (1996c) *The Education of Traveller Children*. London: Office for Standards in Education.

OFSTED (1998a) *School Evaluation Matters*. London: Office for Standards in Education.

OFSTED (1998b) *Inspection of Manchester Local Education Authority*. London: Office for Standards in Education.

O'Leary, J. (1992) 'Heads fear increase in pupil violence.' *The Times* 27 May, p.2.

O'Leary, J. (1995) 'Public school pupils will be tested for suspected drug use.' *The Times* 13 October, p.6.

O'Leary, J. (1996) 'Mother agrees to move boy from strike-hit school.' *The Times* 9 November, p.7.

Osler, A. (1997) *Exclusion From School and Racial Equality*. London: Commission for Racial Equality.

Packman, J., Randall, J. and Jaques, N. (1986) *Who Needs Care? Social Work Decisions About Children*. Oxford: Blackwell.

Page, R. and Clarke, G. (eds) (1977) *Who Cares? Young People in Care Speak Out*. London: National Children's Bureau.

Parffrey, V. (1994) 'Exclusion: failed children or systems failure?' *School Organisation 14*, 2, 107–120.

Parsons, C. (1996) 'Permanent exclusions from schools in England: trends, causes and responses.' *Children and Society 10*, 177–186.

Parsons, C. (1997a) 'Disqualified for life.' *The Guardian* 1 April, 1.

Parsons, C. (1997b) *Exclusion From School: The Public Cost*. London: Commission for Racial Equality.

Parsons, C. (1999) *Education, Exclusion and Citizenship*. London: Routledge.

Parsons, C. (2000) *Include Press Release 23 February 2000*. Cambridge: Include.

Parsons, C., Benns, L., Hailes, J. and Howlett, K. (1994) *Excluding Primary School Children*. London: Family Policy Studies Centre.

Peagam, E. (1995) 'Emotional and behavioural difficulties: the primary school experience.' In P. Farrell (ed) *Children with Emotional and Behavioural Difficulties*. London: The Falmer Press.

Pearce and Hillman (1998) *Wanted Youth: Raising Achievement and Tackling Social Exclusion* London: Institute for Public Policy Reasearch.

Pearson, G. (1983) *Hooligan: A History of Respectable Fears*. London: Macmillian.

Peterson, C. and McCabe, A. (1983) *Developmental Psycholinguistics: Three Ways of Looking at a Child's Narrative*. New York: Plenum Press.

Pitts, J. (1998) 'Juvenile justice.' *Research Matters*. October 1998 – April 1999, 24–25.

Pitts, J., Berridge, D., Brodie, I., Porteous, D. and Tarling, R. (2001) *Research on the Independent Effects of Permanent Exclusion From School on the Criminal Careers of Young People.* Luton: Department of Applied Social Studies.

Plummer, K. (1983) *Documents of Life: An Introduction to the Problems and Literature of a Humanistic Method. Contemporary Social Research Methods 7.* London: Unwin Hyman.

Pole, C., Mizen, P. and Bolton, A. (1999) 'Realising children's agency in research: partners and participants.' *International Journal of Social Research Methodology* 2, 1, 39–54.

Pomeroy, E. (1999) 'The teacher-student relationship in secondary schools: Insights from excluded pupils.' *British Journal of Sociology in Education 20,* 4, 465–482.

Prout, A. and Jenks, C. (1996) 'Public perceptions of childhood criminality.' *British Journal of Sociology 47,* 2, 315–331.

Quortrup, J. (1997) 'A voice for children in statistical and social accounting: a plea for children's right to be heard.' In A. James and A. Prout (eds) *Constructing and Reconstructing Childhood.* London: Falmer.

Rv Cardinal Newman's School, Birmingham, exp S (1997), *The Times* 26 December QBD.

Reder, P., Duncan, S. and Gray, M. (1993) *Beyond Blame: Child Abuse Tragedies Revisited.* London: Routledge.

Reynolds, D. and Cuttance, P. (1992) *School Effectiveness: Research, Policy and Practice.* London: Cassell.

Reynolds, K. (1993) 'Local management, equal opportunities and inner London – a poisonous brew?' In Wallace, G. (ed) *Local Management, Central Control: Schools in the Marketplace.* Bournemouth: Hyde Publications.

Roaf, C. and Lloyd, C. (1995) *The Welfare Network: How Well Does the Net Work? Occasional Paper 6.* Oxford: Oxford Brookes University.

Rutter, M., Cox, A., Tupling, C., Berger, M. and Yule, W. (1975) 'Attainment and adjustment in two geographical areas. I: the prevalence of psychiatric disorder.' *British Journal of Psychiatry 126,* 493–509.

Rutter, M., Maughan, B., Mortimore, P. and Ouston, J. (1979) *Fifteen Thousand Hours: Secondary Schools and their Effects on Children.* New York: Open Books.

Rutter, M. and Smith, D. (eds) (1995) *Psychosocial Disorders in Young People: Time Trends and their Causes.* London: Wiley.

Sanders, D. and Hendry, L. (1997) *New Perspectives on Disaffection.* London: Cassell.

Secondary Heads Association (1992) *Excluded From School: A Survey of Suspensions from Secondary Schools in 1991–92.* Leicester: Secondary Heads Association.

Sewell, T. (1997) *Black Masculinities and Schooling.* London: Unwin Hyman.

Shaw, C. (1998) *Remember My Messages....* London: Who Cares? Trust.

Silverman, D. (1989) *Qualitative Methodology and Sociology.* Aldershot: Gower.

Silverman, D. (1993) *Interpreting Qualitative Data: Methods for Analysing Talk, Text and Interaction.* London: Sage.

Sinclair, I. and Gibbs, I. (1998a) *Children's Homes: A Study in Diversity.* Chichester: Wiley.

Sinclair, I. and Gibbs, I. (1988b) 'Private and local authority children's homes: a comparison.' *Journal of Adolescence* 21, 5, 17-27.

Sinclair, R. (1998) *The Education of Children in Need.* London: National Children's Bureau.

Sinclair, R., Garnett, L. and Berridge, D. (1995) *Social Work and Assessment with Adolescents.* London: National Children's Bureau.

Sinclair, R., Grimshaw, R. and Garnett, L. (1994) ' the education of children in need: The impact of the Education Reform Act 1988, the Education Act 1993 and the Children Act 1989.' *Oxford Review of Education 20*, 3, 281–292.

Smith, R. (1998) *No Lessons Learnt: A Survey of School Exclusions.* London: The Children's Society.

Social Exclusion Unit (1998) *Truancy and School Exclusion.* London: The Stationery Office.

Social Services Inspectorate (1993) *Corporate Parents: Inspection of Residential Child Care Services in 11 Local Authorities.* London: DoH.

Social Services Inspectorate and OFSTED (1995) *The Education of Children Who Are Looked After By Local Authorities.* London: DoH and Office for Standards in Education.

Stake, R. (1995) *The Art of Case Study Research.* Thousand Oaks: Sage.

Stirling, M. (1991) 'Absent with leave.' *Special Children* November, 9–10.

Stirling, M. (1992) 'How many pupils are being excluded?' *British Journal of Special Education 19*, 4, 128–130.

Strauss, A. and Corbin, J. (1990) *Basics of Qualitative Research.* London: Sage.

Tattum, D. (1985) 'Pupil behaviour: a sociological perspective.' *Maladjustment and Therapeutic Education 3*, 2, 12–18.

The Times (1993) 'Concern over fighting in class' 4 December, p.5.

The Times 24 February 2000, p.24.

The Times Educational Supplement 11 February 2000, p.20.

Train, A. (1996) *ADHD: How To Deal with Very Difficult Children.* London: Souvenir Press.

Trinder, L (1996) 'Social work research: the state of the art (or science).' *Child and Family Social Work 1*, 233–242.

Triseliotis, J., Borland, M., Hill, M. and Lambert, L. (1995) *Teenagers and the Social Work Services.* London: HMSO.

Tyerman, M. (1958) 'Research into truancy.' *British Journal of Educational Psychology 28*, 3, 217–225.

Wade, J., Biehal, N. with Stein, M. and Clayden, J. (1998) *Going Missing.* Chichester: Wiley.

Ward, D. (1996) 'Officials defend Ridings stance.' *The Times* 29 October, p.4.

Ward, L. (1997) *Seen and Heard.* York: Joseph Rowntree Foundation.

Watney, S. (1997) *Policing Desire.* London: Cassell.

West, A. (1994) 'Choosing schools: The consumers' perspective.' In Halstead, J. (ed.) *Parent Choice and Education.* London: Kogan Page

Wheldall, K. and Merrett, F. (1988) 'Which classroom behaviours do primary school teachers say they find most troublesome?' *Educational Review 40*, 1, 13–27.

White, S. and Barber, M. (1997) (eds) *Perspectives on School Effectiveness and School Improvement.* London: University of London Institute of Education.

Willis, P. (1977) *Learning to Labour.* Farnborough: Saxon House.

Woods, P. (1979) *The Divided School.* London: Routledge and Kegan Paul.

Woods, P. (1988) *Pupil Strategies: Explorations in the Sociology of the School.* London: Croom Helm.

Yin, R. (1989) *Case Study Research.* London: Sage.

York, R., Heron, J. and Wolff, S. (1972) 'Exclusion from school.' *Journal of Child Psychology and Psychiatry 13*, 259–266.

Subject Index

Author Index